TM
iCONLOGiC

v051417
pc: 296
ISBN's:
    978-1-944607-06-7 (B&W, CB workbook)
    978-1-944607-07-4 (Color, PB workbook)
    978-1-944607-08-1 (ePub/MOBI)

Adobe RoboHelp 2017: The Essentials

"Skills and Drills" Learning

Kevin Siegel
Willam van Weelden

Rank Your Skills

Before starting this book, complete the skills assessment on the next page.

Skills Assessment

How This Assessment Works

Below you will find 10 course objectives for *Adobe RoboHelp 2017: The Essentials*. **Before starting the book**, review each objective and rank your skills using the scale next to each objective. A rank of ① means **No Confidence** in the skill. A rank of ⑤ means **Total Confidence**. After you've completed this assessment, work through the entire book. **After finishing the book**, review each objective and rank your skills now that you've completed the book. Most people see dramatic improvements in the second assessment after completing the lessons in this book.

Before Starting

1. I can create topics. ① ② ③ ④ ⑤
2. I can create books. ① ② ③ ④ ⑤
3. I can link topics together. ① ② ③ ④ ⑤
4. I can create a Cascading Style Sheet (CSS). ① ② ③ ④ ⑤
5. I can create a Responsive HTML5 Layout. ① ② ③ ④ ⑤
6. I can import Captivate eLearning. ① ② ③ ④ ⑤
7. I can create a Browse Sequence. ① ② ③ ④ ⑤
8. I can create a Custom Window. ① ② ③ ④ ⑤
9. I can add Images to a topic. ① ② ③ ④ ⑤
10. I can Publish a project. ① ② ③ ④ ⑤

Now That I Am Finished

1. I can create topics. ① ② ③ ④ ⑤
2. I can create books. ① ② ③ ④ ⑤
3. I can link topics together. ① ② ③ ④ ⑤
4. I can create a Cascading Style Sheet (CSS). ① ② ③ ④ ⑤
5. I can create a Responsive HTML5 Layout. ① ② ③ ④ ⑤
6. I can import Captivate eLearning. ① ② ③ ④ ⑤
7. I can create a Browse Sequence. ① ② ③ ④ ⑤
8. I can create a Custom Window. ① ② ③ ④ ⑤
9. I can add Images to a topic. ① ② ③ ④ ⑤
10. I can Publish a project. ① ② ③ ④ ⑤

iCONLOGiC
"Skills and Drills" Learning

Contents

iCONLOGiC

"Skills and Drills" Learning

About This Book

This Section Contains Information About:

The Authors

Kevin Siegel is the founder and president of IconLogic, Inc. He has written hundreds of step-by-step computer training books on applications such as *Adobe Captivate, Articulate Storyline, Adobe RoboHelp, Adobe Presenter, Adobe Technical Communication Suite, Adobe Dreamweaver, Adobe InDesign, Microsoft Office, Microsoft PowerPoint, QuarkXPress,* and *TechSmith Camtasia.*

Kevin spent five years in the U.S. Coast Guard as an award-winning photojournalist and has three decades experience as a print publisher, technical writer, instructional designer, and eLearning developer. He is a certified technical trainer, a veteran classroom instructor, and a frequent speaker at trade shows and conventions.

Kevin holds multiple certifications from companies such as Adobe, CompTIA, and the International Council for Certified Online Training Professionals (ICCOTP) as a Certified Online Training Professional (COTP). You can reach Kevin at **ksiegel@iconlogic.com**.

Willam van Weelden is a Certified Online Training Professional (COTP), veteran Help Author, RoboHelp consultant, and technical writer based in the Netherlands. He is an Adobe Community Professional, ranking him among the world's leading experts on RoboHelp. Willam's specialties are HTML5 and RoboHelp automation. Apart from RoboHelp, Willam also has experience with other technical communications applications such as Adobe Captivate and Adobe FrameMaker.

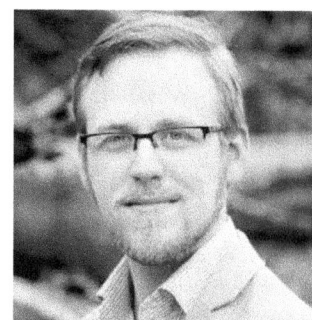

Book Conventions

We believe that learners learn by doing. With that simple concept in mind, IconLogic books are created by trainers/authors with years of experience training adult learners. Before IconLogic books, our instructors rarely found a book that was perfect for a classroom setting. If the book was beautiful, odds were that the text was too small to read and hard to follow. If the text in a book was the right size, the quality of exercises left something to be desired.

Finally tiring of using inadequate materials, our instructors started teaching without any books at all. Years ago we had many students ask if the in-class instruction came from a book. If so, they said they'd buy the book. That sparked an idea. We asked students—just like you—what they wanted in a training manual. You responded, and the methodology is used in this book and every IconLogic training manual.

This book has been divided into several modules. Because each module builds on lessons learned in a previous module, we recommend that you complete each module in succession.

During every module, you will be guided through activities step-by-step. Instructions for you to follow look like this:

❑ choose the **x** command and then and select **y**

When you are asked to press a key on your keyboard, the instructions look like this:

❑   press [**shift**]

We hope you enjoy the book. If you have any comments or questions, please see the end of this section for our contact information.

Confidence Checks

As you move through the lessons in this book, you will come across the little guy at the right. He indicates a Confidence Check. Throughout each module you will be guided through hands-on, step-by-step exercises. But at some point, you'll have to fend for yourself. That is where Confidence Checks come in. Please be sure to complete each of the challenges because some exercises build on completed Confidence Checks.

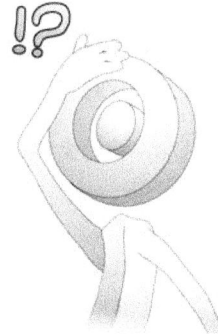

Project Scenarios

During the activities that appear in this book, we're going to ask you to use your imagination and pretend that you are a technical communicator for an awesome, but fictional, company called **Super Simplistic Solutions**. As a technical communicator, it is your job to create all of the documentation for the company's products, services, and internal policies and procedures. During the lessons presented in this book, you will use RoboHelp 2017 to create a Policies and Procedures guide that can be accessed by users on a Windows-based computer, an Apple computer, or a mobile device (such as an iPad, iPhone, Android, or Microsoft Surface). Although the information you create in the policies guide is fictional, the content will likely seem similar to information in most procedure guides. Nevertheless, none of the information in the guide is based on real people, events, or companies. Any similarities are purely coincidental.

Software Requirements For This Book

Prior to starting the lessons in this book, you will need Adobe RoboHelp version 2017 installed on your computer. You can purchase the program (or download the free trial version) via the Adobe website (www.adobe.com/products/robohelp.html). If you want to import or link to Microsoft Word content (see page 78), you will also need a recent version of Word on your computer.

RoboHelp Projects and Other Assets

You're probably chomping at the bit, ready to dive into RoboHelp and begin creating awesome Help Systems. As you'll learn as you work through this book, all you need to create Help Systems on your own is Adobe RoboHelp and some content. Wait, content? You'll need text files, images, videos... the list of supporting assets you'll need to create even a basic Help System could go on and on.

If you have never used RoboHelp before (and this book assumes you have not), you cannot be expected to learn how to use RoboHelp on the fly as you create projects. Learning by discovery isn't necessarily a bad thing, but it will take (and possibly waste) a lot of time. We've got a better idea. You provide RoboHelp (the trial version of the software is fine), and we'll provide all of the project files and supporting

assets (such as images and audio files) you need. During the following activity, you will download those assets (data files) from the IconLogic server.

Note: The data files you are about to download will consist of several RoboHelp projects thousands of assets and support files used to create and/or support those projects. While most of the individual data files are small, you will need approximately 200 MB of disk space available on your computer to install them.

Student Activity: Download Data Files From the IconLogic Website

1. Download the data files necessary to complete the lessons presented in this book.

   ☐ start your web browser and go to the following web address:
   http://www.iconlogic.com/pc.htm
   ☐ click the **RoboHelp 2017: The Essentials** link and **Save** the file to your computer (make a note of exactly where the file goes so you can locate it)

2. After the file has fully downloaded, close the web browser.

3. Extract the data files.

   ☐ find the **RoboHelp2017Data.exe** file you just downloaded to your computer

   The **RoboHelp2017Data.exe** file is **not a program that can harm your computer**. Rather, the EXE is a self-extracting archive of zipped files that consist of RoboHelp project files, images, text files, videos, and other assets that support this book.

   ☐ double-click the file to open it
   ☐ click **Run** or **Yes** if presented with a **Security Warning** dialog box
   ☐ confirm **C:** appears in the **Unzip to folder** area
   ☐ click the **Unzip** button
   ☐ when the extraction is complete, click the **OK** button and then click the **Close** button

Several thousand files were unzipped into a folder called **RoboHelp2017Data**. We know; that's a lot of files. No worries. There are several project folders within RoboHelp2017Data. Although RoboHelp projects can result in a large number of files, the vast majority of those individual files are tiny. As mentioned earlier, the total size of the assets included in the RoboHelp2017Data folder is around 200 MB. As you move through the lessons in this book, you will be opening files from and saving to the RoboHelp2017Data folder. When you have completed the lessons in this book, you can delete both the RoboHelp2017Data folder and the RoboHelp2017Data.exe file you initially downloaded.

How Adobe Software Updates Affect This Book

This book was written specifically to teach you how to use Adobe RoboHelp 2017. At the time this book was written, 2017 is the latest and greatest version of the RoboHelp software available from Adobe.

With each major update of RoboHelp, our intention is to provide a book to support that version and make it available within 30-60 days of the software being released by Adobe. From time to time, Adobe may release patches for RoboHelp to fix bugs or add functionality. For instance, we would expect Adobe to update RoboHelp 2017 with a patch or two every so often. A patched version might be called RoboHelp 2017**.01** or 2017**.1**. Usually these updates are minor (bug fixes) and have little or no impact on the lessons in this book. However, Adobe could make significant changes to the way RoboHelp looks or behaves, even with a minor patch. If something on your screen does not match what we show in this book, please visit the RoboHelp 2017 product page on the IconLogic website for possible book updates or errata information (http://www.iconlogic.com/adobe-robohelp-2017-essentials-workbook.html).

Contacting IconLogic

IconLogic, Inc.
1582 Indian Bluffs Dr., Maineville, OH, 45039 | 410.956.4949
Web: **www.iconlogic.com** | Email: **info@iconlogic.com**

Notes

iCONLOGiC

"Skills and Drills" Learning

Module 1: Introduction to RoboHelp

In This Module You Will Learn About:

- RoboHelp's History, page 2
- Pods, page 4
- Workspaces, page 7
- Topics, page 11
- TOCs and Indexes, page 13
- Microsoft HTML Help, page 14
- WebHelp, page 17
- Responsive HTML5, page 20
- Compliance, page 22

And You Will Learn To:

- Open an Existing Project, page 2
- Explore the Pods, page 4
- Create a Workspace, page 7
- Create and Edit a Topic, page 11
- Delete a Topic, page 12
- Explore a TOC and an Index, page 13
- Generate HTML Help, page 14
- Generate WebHelp, page 17
- Generate Responsive HTML5, page 20
- Generate Compliant HTML5, page 22

RoboHelp's History

What is RoboHelp? Where did it come from? And what can you do with RoboHelp? According to Adobe, "RoboHelp is an easy-to-use authoring and publishing solution." Adobe also says that RoboHelp allows you to "deliver content to the iPad and other tablets, smartphones, and desktops using output formats such as multiscreen HTML5, WebHelp, CHM, Adobe AIR Help, PDF, eBook, and native mobile apps." Everything Adobe says about RoboHelp is true, and you'll see that for yourself as you work with RoboHelp via the lessons in this book.

Kevin started using RoboHelp when it was owned by a company called Blue Sky Software. That company re-branded itself as eHelp Corporation. Later, eHelp was absorbed by Macromedia, which was, in turn, gobbled up by Adobe.

There have been several versions of RoboHelp over the years. RoboHelp versions have included names like RoboHelp 5, 6, 7, 2002, X3, X4, and X5. RoboHelp 6 was Adobe's first RoboHelp version. However, eHelp Corporation also had a RoboHelp version 6. Yes, that's right. There was once eHelp RoboHelp 6, and there was an Adobe RoboHelp 6, creating a bit of confusion early on.

Starting with RoboHelp 2015, Adobe changed the naming convention again, this time using the year that the software version was released. This book focuses exclusively on Adobe RoboHelp 2017.

During the lessons that follow, we're going to have you open a finished RoboHelp project, explore it a bit, and then generate content. As you move through subsequent modules in this book, you will learn how to create the finished project from scratch.

> **Note:** If you have not already downloaded the **RoboHelp2017Data** student data files to your hard drive, see **page x** (in the About This Book section of this book). Also, the RoboHelp 2017 software is not included with this book. If you do not have Adobe RoboHelp 2017 installed on your computer, you can purchase the tool, or download the trial software, from Adobe (www.adobe.com/products/robohelp.html).

Student Activity: Open an Existing Project

1. Start Adobe RoboHelp.

   After starting the RoboHelp application, the first thing you will see is the **Starter** (the word **Starter** appears at the top of the window and in the tab in the upper left). From here, you can open **Recent Projects**, **Create** projects, **Import** assets, and find additional **Resources**.

2. Open an existing project from the RoboHelp2017Data folder.

   ❏ from the **bottom left** of the **Starter**, click **Open Project**

❏ navigate to the **RoboHelp2017Data** folder

The RoboHelp2017Data folder contains all kinds of assets that support the lessons in this book. You will find images, HTML files, Word documents, PDFs, and existing RoboHelp projects. You'll be instructed on how and when to use these assets as you move through the lessons in this book.

❏ open the **RoboHelpProjects** folder
❏ open the **FinishedHelpSystem** folder

There are several subfolders within the FinishedHelpSystem folder. Cumulatively, all of the assets within those folders support the main RoboHelp project file (the project file's name is **finished.xpj**).

❏ open **finished.xpj**

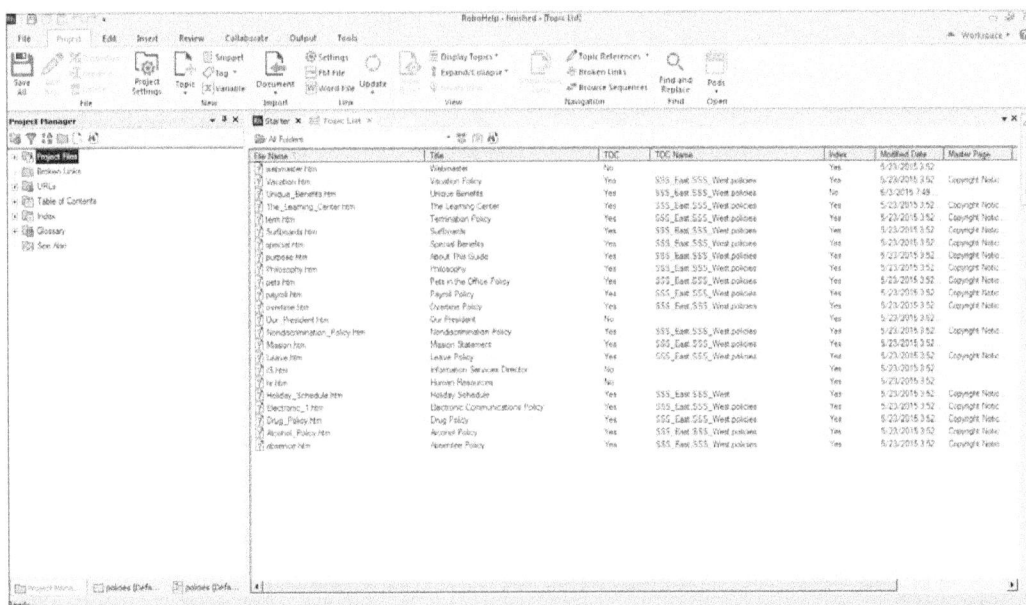

From a scenario standpoint, you now work for a mythical company called **Super Simplistic Solutions**. You have been hired to create, among other things, the corporate policies and procedures guide. Rather than create the guide in a traditional word processor or desktop publishing application, you are going to create the guide using RoboHelp. During the lessons presented throughout this book, you will learn how to re-create this project from scratch.

Before moving forward, we'd like to further explain the RoboHelp project file: the xpj file. The xpj file is usually quite small. Nevertheless, the project file has a massive job. It controls the structure of the entire project (the project's folder structure, the TOCs, the Indexes, etc.). Although the xpj file does not contain the Help System's content, it tracks where the content is stored, manages links, images, and controls a bunch of other behind the scenes functions.

Pods

At first glance, the RoboHelp interface can seem a bit chaotic. To begin, you'll notice that there is a ribbon and several panels, known as pods, all over the place. Because there are so many pods, it makes sense that learning to control them is a great place to start your mastery of the RoboHelp software.

Student Activity: Explore the Pods

1. View a Pod.

   ❐ on the **Ribbon**, select the **Project** tab
   ❐ at the right of the **Project** tab, click **Pods** and then choose **Snippet**

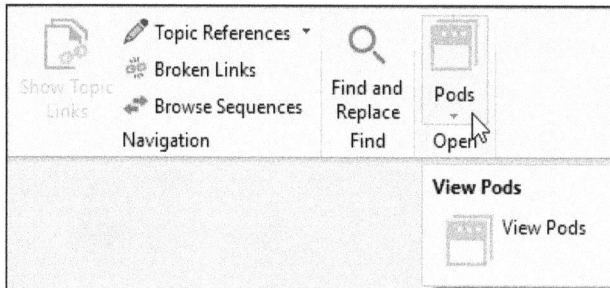

The Snippets pod opens in the right of the RoboHelp window, just below the ribbon. You will learn to create and work with Snippets beginning on page 155.

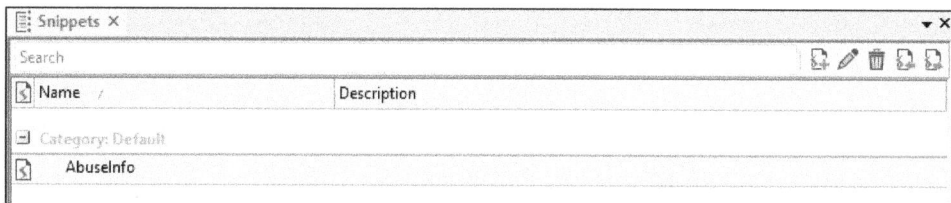

2. Close a Pod.

   ❐ at the top of the **Snippets** pod, right-click the word **Snippets**
   ❐ choose **Close**

The Snippets pod closes, leaving behind the **Starter** and the **Topic List.**

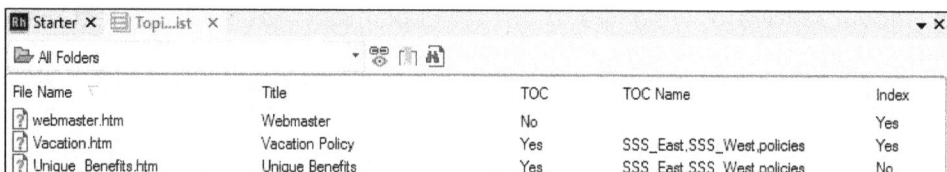

3. Explore the Project Manager pod.

   ❏ click **Pods** and choose **Project Manager**

   By default, the Project Manager pod appears in the upper left of the RoboHelp window. You can use the Project Manager pod to edit, delete, and create topics and folders, as well as manage other project assets.

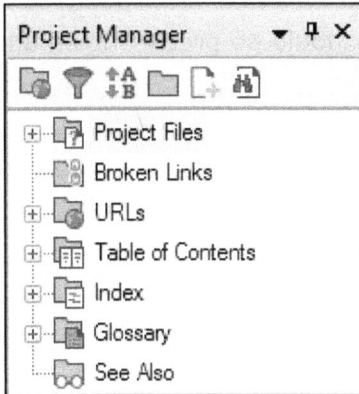

   There are two Project Manager views: **Global** and **Detail** . Unless otherwise instructed to do so in this book, ensure that the Project Manager remains in **Global** view.

4. Toggle the Project Manager Views.

   ❏ from the upper left of the Project Manager pod, click the **Toggle View** tool (it could look like either of the two view tools shown above) to toggle between **Global** and **Detail** view

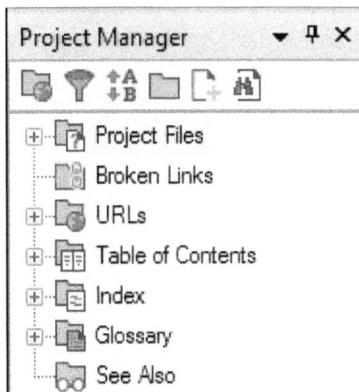

   Detail view is shown at the right.

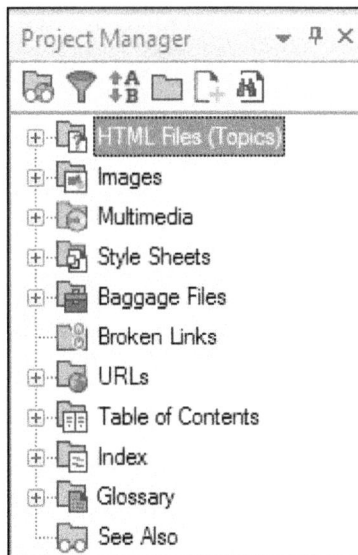

   ❏ ensure that the Project Manager pod is in **Global** View

5. Expand and collapse the folders in the Project Manager pod.

   ❏ click on any of the **plus** icons within the **Project Manager** pod

6. De-clutter the RoboHelp interface.

   ❏ close all of the open pods by clicking the **X** at the top right of each pod (alternatively you can right-click the name of each pod and choose **Close**)

   With all of the pods closed, the RoboHelp window should be pretty barren and look like this:

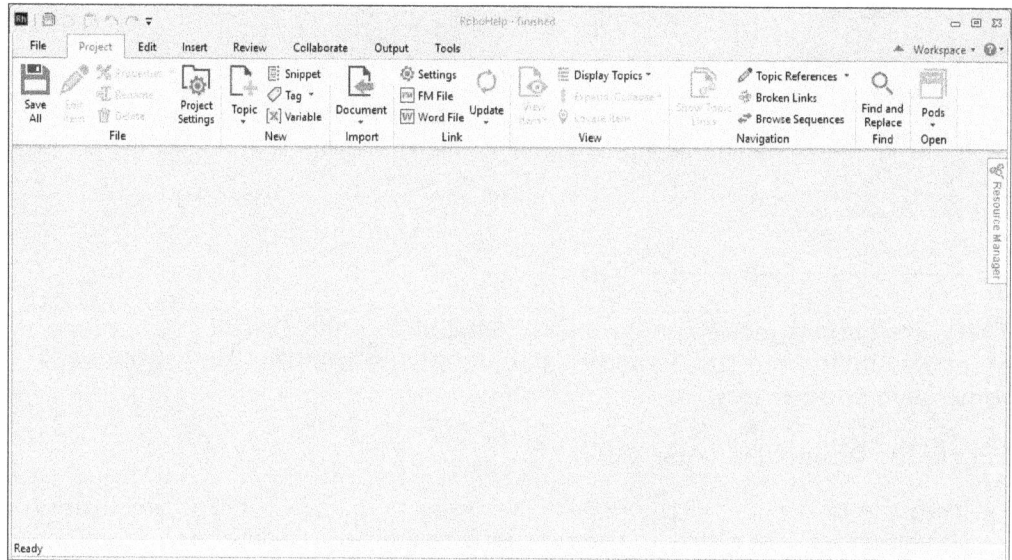

Workspaces

Because there are so many pods available within RoboHelp, you might appreciate the ability to create custom workspaces within RoboHelp. For instance, if you find yourself working on the Snippets pod most of the day, you can create a workspace where the Snippets pod always appears in a specific location on your display, grouped with other pods you use frequently.

Student Activity: Create a Workspace

1. Ensure that all of the pods are closed.

2. View and position the Snippets pod.

   ❐ click **Pods** and choose **Snippet**

   By default, the Snippets pod appears across the top of the RoboHelp window.

   ❐ right-click the word "Snippets" and choose **Dockable** to attach the **Snippets** pod to the top left side of the RoboHelp window
   ❐ drag the Snippets pod to the middle of the RoboHelp window

   As you drag the pod, you'll see arrows appear on your display. Those arrows indicate different dockable areas of the window and will disappear when you stop dragging.

   Note: If the Starter appears after dragging the Snippets pod, go ahead and close it.

3. View and position the Output Setup pod.

   ❐ click **Pods** and choose **Output Setup**
   ❐ drag the **Output Setup** pod just to the left of the Snippets pod
   ❐ position and resize the pods until your RoboHelp window looks similar to the picture below

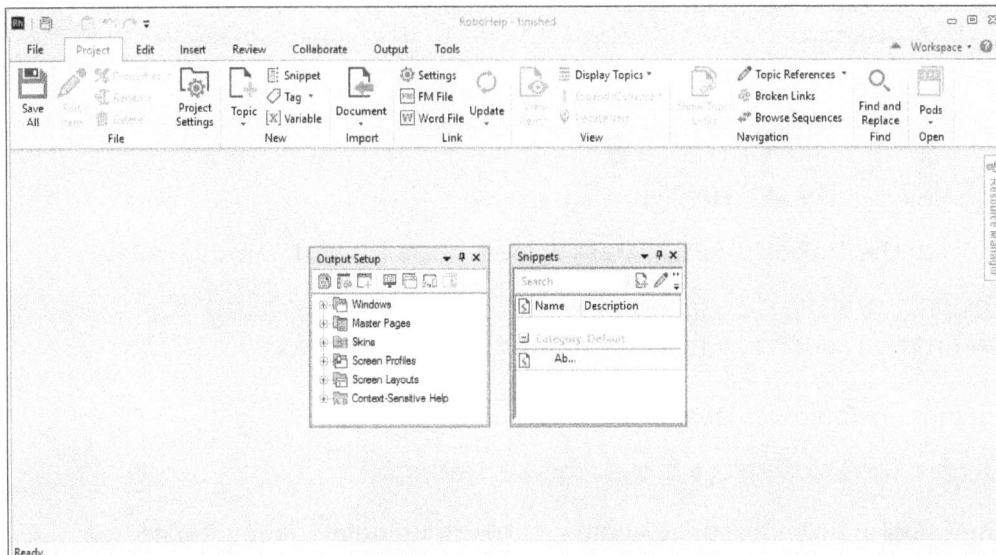

4. Save the workspace.

❒ from the upper-right of the RoboHelp window, click the **Workspace** menu and choose **Save**

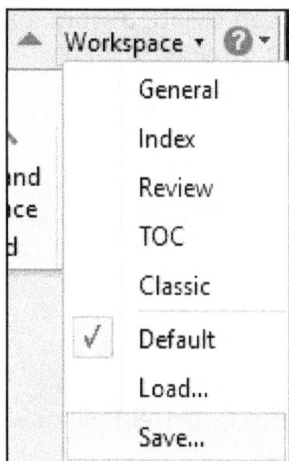

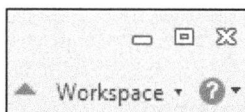

The Save As dialog box opens.

❒ navigate to **C:\RoboHelp2017Data**
❒ name the File name **Output_Snippets**
❒ click the **Save** button

5. Load the default workspace.

❒ from the upper-right of the RoboHelp window, click the **Workspace** menu

❒ from the **Workspace** menu, choose **Default**

The RoboHelp workspace returns to its default appearance.

6. Load a saved workspace.

❒ click the **Workspace** menu and choose **Load**

The Open dialog box opens.

❒ from the **RoboHelp2017Data** folder, open **Output_Snippets.rhs**

All of the pods close, and both the Snippets and Output Setup pods reappear in the location specified when you created the workspace.

7. Load the default workspace.

❒ from the **Workspace** menu, choose **Default**

The RoboHelp window once again returns to its default appearance.

Settings Confidence Check

1. Choose **File > Options**.

   The Options dialog box opens. There are five groups of Settings along the left side of the dialog box.

2. From the **Settings** area at the left, select the **General** category and ensure your options match the picture below.

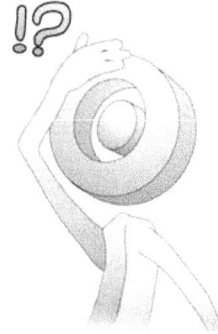

   Default language for new projects: English (US)

   User Interface: Customize...

   Preferences
   ☑ Use underscores in file names
   ☑ Automatically check for updates
   ☑ Allow editing of multiple topics
   ☐ Clear project cache(.cpd file) before opening any project
   ☑ Remember Project State
   ☑ Keep modified files open after applying review comments from Plover

   Review
   Reviewer Name: Willam van Weelden
   ☑ Embed SWF in review PDF

   Generation
   ☐ Auto-compile outdated files
   ☑ Auto-display Output View
   ☐ Convert RoboHelp-edited topics to HTML

   Display confirmation dialog when
   ☐ Auto-generated topics from linked documents are modified
   ☑ A file is saved

   ☐ Do not show notifications   Reset All
   ☑ Show learning resources on Starter page

   The settings in the image above are RoboHelp defaults. You will learn the value of many of these settings as you move through the book. For now, it's enough to ensure the settings here are set to the default.

3. Select the **Recent Projects** category.

   You can remove recent projects that appear in the Starter.

   Recently Opened Projects
   RH C:\RoboHelp2017Data\RoboHelpProjects\content_vars_snipps\content_vars_snipps.
   RH C:\RoboHelp2017Data\RoboHelpProjects\images_multimedia\images_multimedia.xpj
   RH C:\RoboHelp2017Data\RoboHelpProjects\FinishedHelpSystem\finished.xpj

   If you'd like, you can remove any of the recent projects in the list by clicking the **Remove** button. (Removing projects from the list will not affect the lessons in this book or RoboHelp's performance.)

4. Select the **File Association** category.

5. In the **HTML Editors** area, select **Design View** and then click the **Set As Default** button (if necessary).

6. If necessary, select **Use Default Editor** from the bottom of the dialog box.

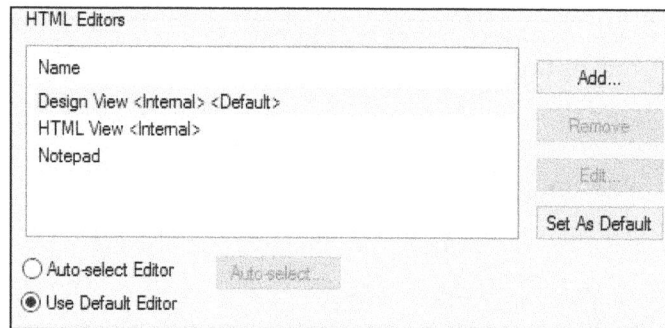

HTML Editors

Name	
Design View <Internal> <Default>	Add...
HTML View <Internal>	Remove
Notepad	
	Edit...
	Set As Default

○ Auto-select Editor   Auto-select...

◉ Use Default Editor

You will soon be importing content into a RoboHelp project from Microsoft Word and other sources (during lessons beginning on page 31). When you select **Use Default Editor**, content that you attempt to edit with RoboHelp always opens in RoboHelp's Design Window instead of in the program used to create the content.

7. Click the **OK** button to close the Options dialog box.

   Note: The changes you have just made while in the Options dialog box will not have an obvious effect in the current RoboHelp project.

8. From the **Workspace** menu, choose **Load** and then, from the **RoboHelp2017Data** folder, open **NoClutter.rhs**.

   We've created the NoClutter workspace for you to ensure that the most commonly used pods are at your fingertips (the lesser-used pods are hidden away). You'll frequently be reminded to load the NoClutter workspace as you move through this book. Ignore that request if you'd prefer to use your own workspace (or any of the workspaces for that matter).

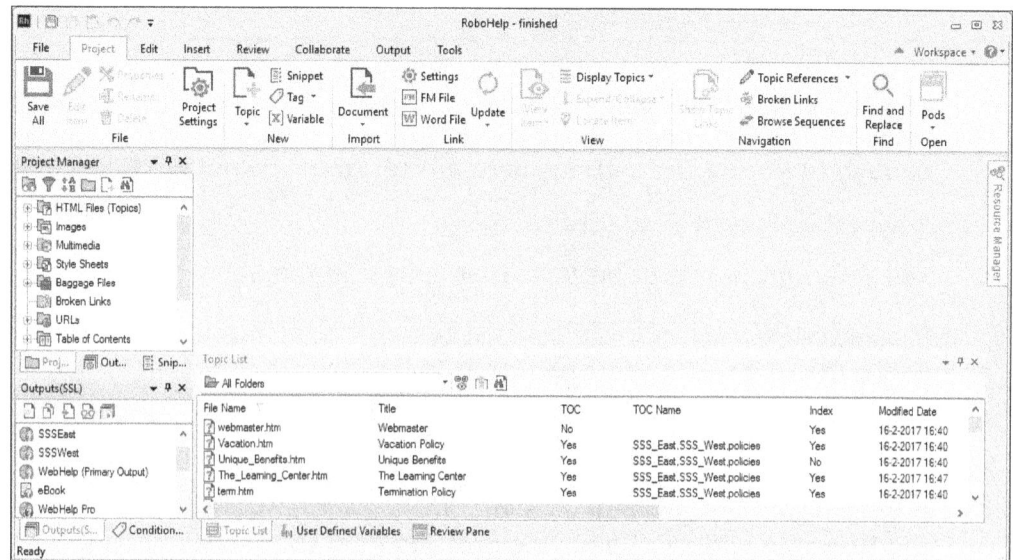

Topics

You've likely heard the saying that "Content is King." It's true. The heart of any Help System is its content. When you create content within RoboHelp, that content is known as a topic. Topics typically consist of text formatted with styles (page 49), images (page 106), hyperlinks (page 83), and more. The project you've opened has all of the topic elements named above. In the next few activities, you'll create a topic, edit it a bit, and then delete it.

Student Activity: Create and Edit a Topic

1. Ensure that the **finished** project is still open. (If you're not sure how to open the RoboHelp project, see page 2.)

2. Create a new topic.

    ❐ on the **Project** tab, **New** group, click **Topic** (click the top part of **Topic**)

    The New Topic dialog box opens.

    ❐ on the **General** tab, change the **Topic Title** to **My First Topic**
    ❐ from the **Master Page** drop-down menu, choose **(None)**

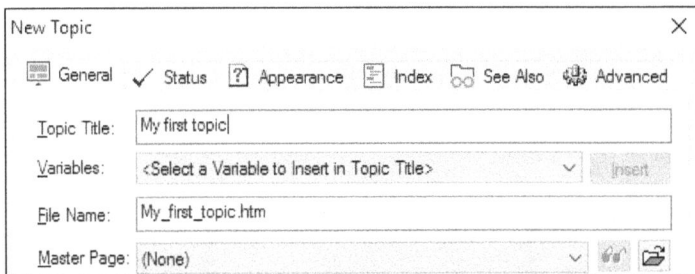

New Topic	×

    General ✓ Status [?] Appearance [=] Index 👓 See Also 🕸 Advanced

Topic Title:	My first topic
Variables:	<Select a Variable to Insert in Topic Title> ∨ Insert
File Name:	My_first_topic.htm
Master Page:	(None) ∨ 👓 📂

    You were asked to choose **(None)** as the Master Page so that no elements from the existing Master Page appear on the topic. You will learn how to create Master Pages and how to use them on page 225.

    ❐ click the **OK** button

    Your new topic opens in Design View.

3. Edit the new topic.

    ❐ replace the words "Type topic text here" with **The best Help topic will contain only enough text to get my point across and no more. One paragraph or two is ideal, supported by an image or two.**

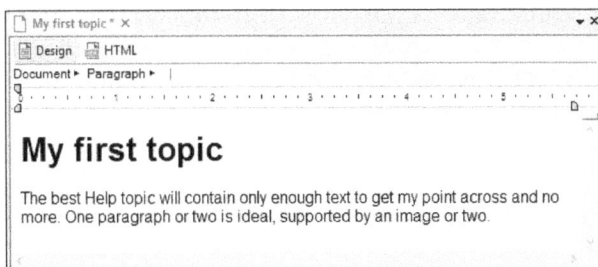

📄 My first topic * ×	▾ ×

    📄 Design 🔲 HTML
    Document ▸ Paragraph ▸ |

    # My first topic

    The best Help topic will contain only enough text to get my point across and no more. One paragraph or two is ideal, supported by an image or two.

Student Activity: Delete a Topic

1. Ensure that the **finished** project is still open.

2. Delete a topic.

   ☐ locate the Topic List pod (if you're using the No Clutter workspace, the Topic List pod is at the bottom of the RoboHelp window)

   ☐ on the **Topic List** pod, scroll down the list until you see the **My First Topic** topic

   ☐ right-click the **My First Topic** topic and choose **Delete**

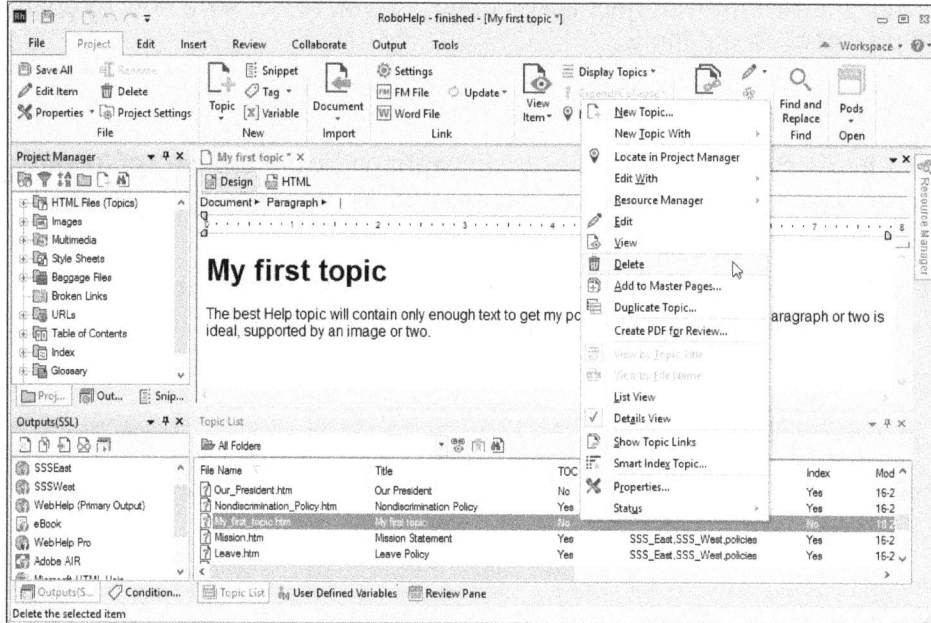

You will be asked to confirm the action.

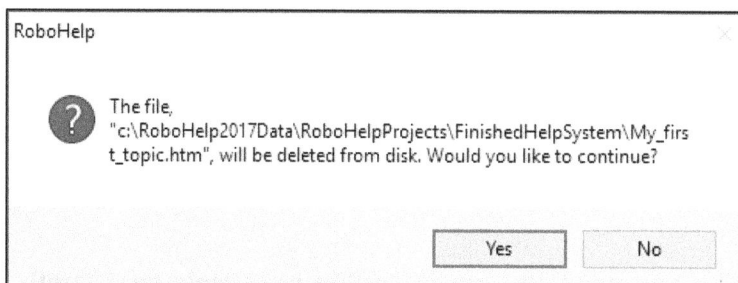

   ☐ click the **Yes** button

The file has been moved to your Windows Recycle Bin. Now that you've deleted the topic file from the project, getting it back isn't as simple as choosing Edit > Undo. Instead, you'd need to first visit the Recycle Bin and Restore the file. Then you'd need to import the file back into the RoboHelp project. You'll learn how to import content in the next module.

TOCs and Indexes

When users access your Help content, they'll typically rely on a Table of Contents (TOC) to understand the structure or logic behind the Help System. Users rely on an Index to quickly find content (just as you might do when reading a reference guide). The finished project you've been exploring already has both a TOC and an Index. You will learn how to create both during lessons presented later in this book.

Student Activity: Explore a TOC and an Index

1. Ensure that the **finished** project is still open.

2. Open an existing TOC.

   ❏ on the Project Manager pod, open the **Table of Contents** folder

   This project contains four TOCs.

   ❏ double-click **SSS_East** to open the TOC

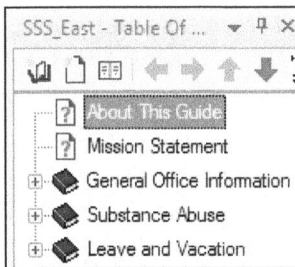

   You will learn how to create this TOC beginning on page 139.

3. Open an existing Index.

   ❏ on the Project Manager pod, open the **Index** folder
   ❏ double-click **policies (Default)** to open the Index

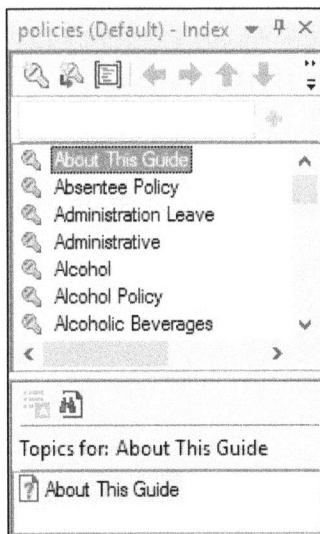

   You will learn how to create this Index beginning on page 188.

Microsoft HTML Help

If you'd like to get a sense of what your users will experience when accessing your Help System, you need to get RoboHelp to output content that your users can access. Those users will NOT have access to RoboHelp. The process of instructing RoboHelp to churn out usable content is known as **Generating**.

The Outputs(SSL) pod, located in the lower left of the RoboHelp window, contains several layouts by default. Arguably, the most commonly used outputs (SSL stands for Single Source Layouts) are **Responsive HTML5**, **WebHelp** and **Microsoft HTML Help**. Most Help authors use either WebHelp or Responsive HTML5. As you move through the remaining lessons in this module, you will generate Microsoft HTML Help, WebHelp, and then Responsive HTML5. (There are other layouts of course, and we'll touch on most of them later.)

Microsoft HTML Help (HTML Help for short) is the oldest of the layouts. When you generate HTML Help, RoboHelp creates a single, compressed CHM file (pronounced "chum"). A CHM file works great if your users are accessing the Help System with a Windows-based PC and if the CHM file has been installed on the user's hard drive. CHM files will not work if your users are accessing the Help System with an Apple computer or a mobile device. CHM files won't work well if users open them via the Internet or an Intranet. Nor do they perform well if accessed from a server. Last, but not least, you are limited by how much you can customize the look and feel of the generated HTML Help window.

Given all the negative stuff we just wrote above, you might think that HTML Help is a layout that is best avoided. Not necessarily. There is much to like about this output. For instance, HTML Help files are self-contained Help Systems (you don't need other programs to use them outside of what is already installed on most Windows-based computers). And CHM files are typically much, much smaller than any of the other layouts. The savings in size alone is one reason that many people rely on CHM files, even given their inherent limitations.

Student Activity: Generate HTML Help

1. Ensure that the **finished** project is still open.

2. Generate the Microsoft HTML Help Layout.

   ❏ on the **Outputs(SSL)** pod, double-click **Microsoft HTML Help**

   The HTML Help Options dialog box opens.

   ❏ from the bottom of the HTML Help Options dialog box, click the **Save and Generate** button

Additional Options

☐ Add Breadcrumbs Links   Format...   Advanced Settings: Edit...

☐ Apply to all Topics   ☑ Optimize CHM File Size

○ Master Page   Copyright Notice in Footer

◉ CSS   default.css

| < Back | Next > | Save and Generate | Save | Cancel |

Because the project is small, generating the layout takes only seconds.

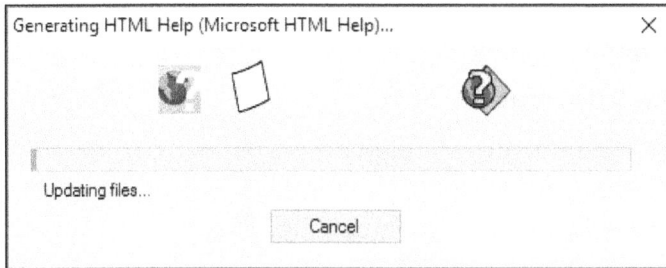

3. View the generated layout.

   ❏ click the **View Result** button

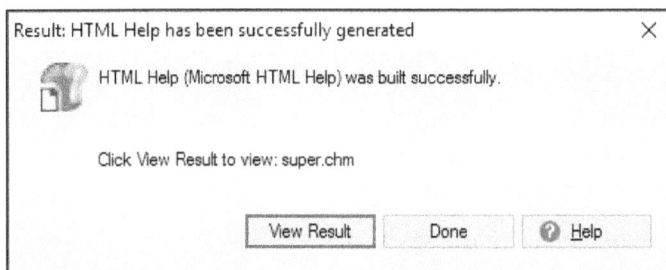

The generated layout opens in the Microsoft Windows Help viewer. The Help Viewer is installed on all PCs running Windows. What you see is exactly what your users will see.

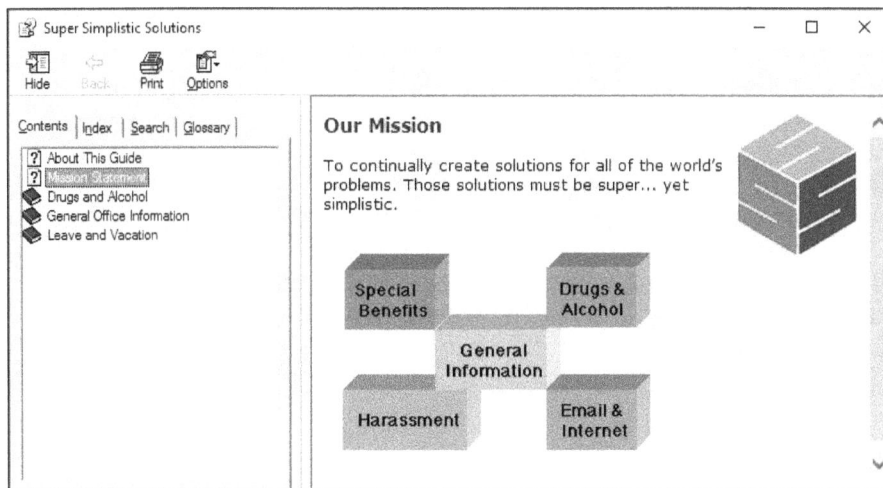

CHM Confidence Check

1. Notice that the TOC in the CHM file is the same TOC you explored a moment ago within RoboHelp.

2. Open the **General Office Information** book.

3. Spend the next few moments selecting the pages you find inside the book.

4. Select the Index tab and notice that this is the same Index that you explored in RoboHelp a moment ago.

5. Close the Help window and minimize RoboHelp.

6. Using Windows Explorer, open the **RoboHelp2017Data** folder.

7. Open the **RoboHelpProjects** folder and then open the **FinishedHelpSystem** folder.

8. Open the **!SSL!** folder and then open the **Microsoft_HTML_Help** folder.

   Within the Microsoft_HTML_Help folder, you'll find the generated HTML Help file. Everything the Help System needs to work on your user's computer is included in this one highly compressed CHM file.

9. Double-click the CHM file to open the generated Help System.

Name	Date modified
super.chm	18-2-2017 12:04

10. Close any open windows and return to the RoboHelp project.

    Note: Keep the following in mind if you elect to go with HTML Help as your layout of choice. First, HTML Help files (the CHM file) run only on PCs that use Microsoft Windows. Consumers who use Macs, Linux, or Unix-based computers cannot open an HTML Help file. Second, HTML Help relies on Internet Explorer. Internet Explorer does not need to be the default browser, and it never needs to run when the user uses the HTML Help file, but it must be on the user's PC. Third, the HTML Help file works reliably only when it is installed locally on each user's hard drive.

WebHelp

You generated Microsoft HTML Help during the last activity. Although Microsoft HTML Help results in the fewest and smallest output files to manage (the single CHM file), CHM files are limited in many ways (see page 14).

As an alternative to HTML Help, WebHelp is a great layout choice for producing cross-browser, cross-platform Help Systems that work on just about any computer. WebHelp works great when posted to a web server, eliminating the need to install a CHM file on every user's computer. And you will learn later in this book that WebHelp is very customizable via a Skin Editor (page 220). One of the downsides of WebHelp is the sheer number of files that are generated. Remember that Microsoft HTML Help results in a single CHM file. When you generate WebHelp, you could potentially be generating thousands of co-dependent files that must always be kept together on a web server to ensure that the Help System works as expected. The other major downside of WebHelp is that it doesn't support mobile devices. For those, use Responsive HTML5 (page 20).

Student Activity: Generate WebHelp

1. Ensure that the **finished** project is still open.

2. Generate WebHelp.

   ☐ on the Outputs(SSL) pod, right-click **WebHelp (Primary Output)** and choose **Generate**

   The WebHelp Settings dialog box opens.

   ☐ in the **Title Bar** area, replace the existing text with **Super Simplistic Solutions**

Title Bar:	Super Simplistic Solutions

   The text you just typed appears in the web browser's Title Bar. Because the Title Bar is the first thing your users see as the Help content loads within the Web browser, you should always spend a moment and add a descriptive phrase to the Title Bar field.

   ☐ click the **Save and Generate** button

   As with HTML Help, once the layout is generated, you will be asked if you would like to view the output.

   ☐ click the **View Result** button

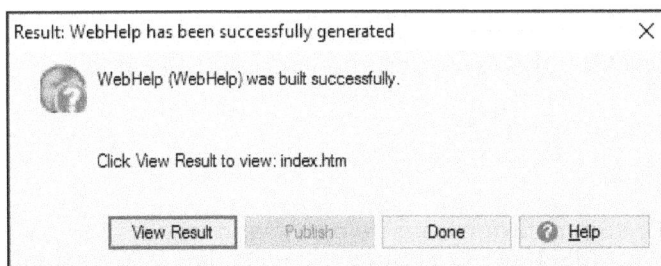

   Result: WebHelp has been successfully generated   ✕

   WebHelp (WebHelp) was built successfully.

   Click View Result to view: index.htm

   [View Result] [Publish] [Done] [⑦ Help]

The Help System opens within your computer's default web browser. On our computer, we routinely use Chrome, Internet Explorer, Edge, FireFox, and Safari. We've tested our Help System using all of the browsers and have been mostly satisfied with the results. We would encourage you to install any web browser your consumer is likely to use and test your Help System in each. Below is the way the Help System looks through Mozilla Firefox.

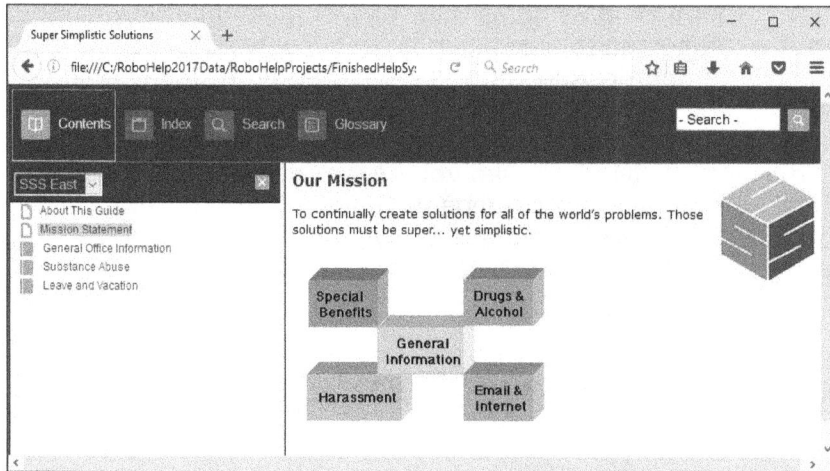

Notice that the Navigation area at the top of the window (Contents, Index, etc.) is graphical. We saw the same thing when we used Google Chrome. However, when we viewed the Help System in Internet Explorer, the results weren't very good. As shown below, the images in the Navigation area are missing, and we received a warning about ActiveX controls. If Internet Explorer is your default web browser, we're betting your Help System looks very much like the picture below.

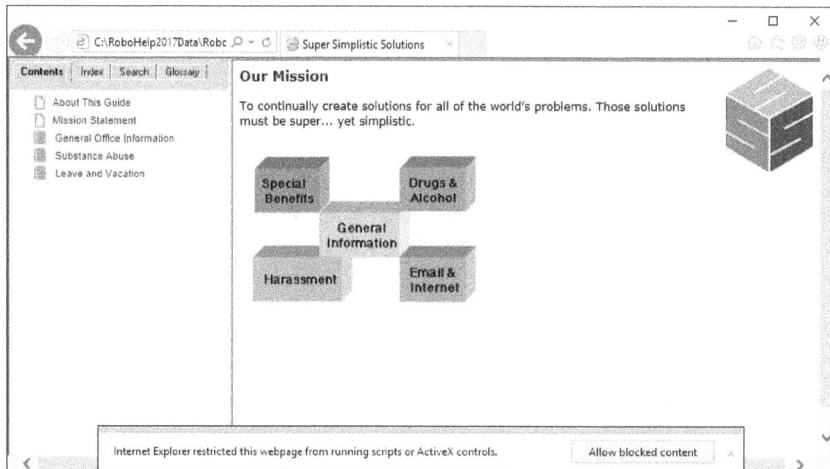

Note: You can view your generated layout in any browser installed on your computer by right-clicking the layout on the Outputs(SSL) pod and choosing **View With**.

3. Close the browser window.

Some web browsers block certain content from being viewed locally. In the image above, Internet Explorer blocked my ActiveX controls, which is preventing parts of the Help System from loading into the browser window. The blocked content would appear just fine if the Help System was opened from within a web server. But because you are working locally, it's likely that you are not viewing a fully functioning version of the Help System. You can allow RoboHelp to bypass the browser blocks by enabling a feature known as **Mark of the Web**. Basically, Mark of the Web allows you, as a Help Author, to bypass the blocked content so you can accurately test your Hep system.

4. Enable Mark of the Web.

❏ close the browser window and return to RoboHelp

❏ on the Outputs(SSL) pod, right-click **WebHelp (Primary Output)** and choose **Properties**

The WebHelp Settings dialog box re-opens.

❏ select **Navigation** from the list of options at the left of the dialog box

❏ select **Add Mark of the Web**

☑ Add Mark of the Web

❏ click the **Save** button

5. View the Help System with a specific web browser.

❏ on the Outputs(SSL) pod, right-click WebHelp (Primary Output) and choose **View With** and then select **Internet Explorer**

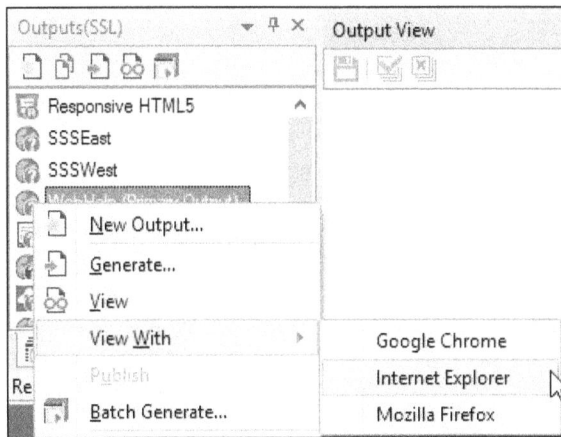

❏ click **Yes** when prompted to compile the layout before running

Thanks to Add Mark of the Web, the images now appear in the Navigation area. (You may still see alerts about ActiveX controls, but those errors can be ignored. You're getting those messages because you are still testing web content locally, which can always lead to blocked content.)

6. Close the browser window and return to RoboHelp.

Responsive HTML5

The sale of smartphones is exceeding the sale of traditional phones; the sale of tablets exceeds those of desktop computers. This trend has led to a need for help authors to create content that can be accessed from both mobile devices and desktop computers. The size of the screen that learners use vary widely. Consider the size of a typical mobile phone compared to the various shapes and sizes of tablets, such as the Apple iPad, Microsoft Surface, and Amazon Kindle Fire. Using RoboHelp, you can generate responsive content that provides optimal viewing across a wide range of devices and screen sizes. Responsive design is an approach to development that allows for flexible outputs and flexible images and assets. Although the word **responsive** was traditionally used for building web pages, with Adobe RoboHelp, responsive design can be used to develop help systems that detect the user's screen size and orientation, and automatically change what the learner sees.

Student Activity: Generate Responsive HTML5

1. Ensure that the **finished** project is still open.

2. Set up Responsive HTML5.

   ❑ on the Outputs(SSL) pod, double-click **Responsive HTML5** to open the Responsive HTLM5 options

   ❑ in the **Title Bar** area, replace the existing text with **Super Simplistic Solutions**

   ❑ click the **Save and Generate** button

3. View Responsive HTML5.

   ❑ click the **View Result** button

   ❑ spend a few moments resizing your browser window

   Note: If, after clicking the View Result button, you only see a series of animated squares instead of the Help System, look for a yellow information bar at the bottom of the screen and click **Allow blocked content** to view the Help System.

Internet Explorer restricted this webpage from running scripts or ActiveX controls.	Allow blocked content	×

Notice that the layout changes (responds) as you resize the browser window.

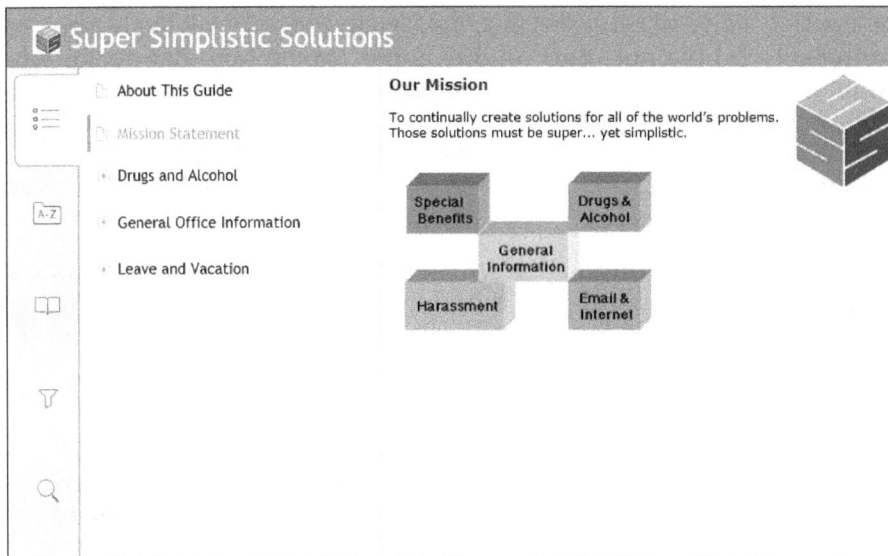

4. Explore the Responsive HTML5 layout.

5. Close the browser window and return to the RoboHelp project.

Compliance

If you work for the U.S. Federal Government, your Help System will likely need to be Section 508 compliant. Simply put, Section 508 is part of the U.S. Rehabilitation Act of 1973 and requires that many things that are accessible to the general public also must be accessible to people with disabilities. You should visit **www.section508.gov** and familiarize yourself with the 508 Compliance rules, see if you are required to generate compliant content, and if so, ensure that all of your Help System output is compliant.

A more general accessibility system is the WAI-ARIA: Web Accessibility Initiative - Accessible Rich Internet Applications. This is an international standard that describes the accessibility features required for web pages and web applications.

Responsive HTML5 is WAI-ARIA and Section 508 compliant. You can use this output in all situations.

> **Note:** At that time that this book was written, only the **Indigo Screen Layout** (skin) is fully compliant. According to Adobe, future patches to RoboHelp will result in Responsive HTML5 layouts being compliant.

Student Activity: Generate Compliant HTML5

1. Choose a compliant Responsive HTML5 layout

   ❑ on the Outputs(SSL) pod, double-click **Responsive HTML5** to open the Responsive HTLM5 options

   ❑ in the **Manage Layout** area, click the **Select** drop-down menu and choose **Indigo**

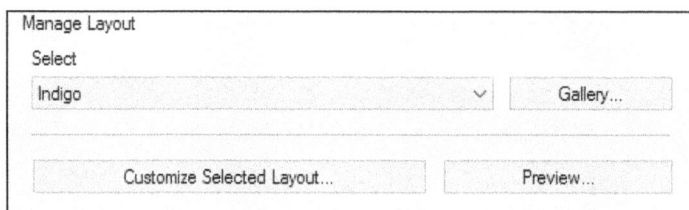

   ```
   Manage Layout
   Select
   [ Indigo                              ⌄ ]   [ Gallery... ]

   [   Customize Selected Layout...   ]    [   Preview...   ]
   ```

   ❑ click the **Save and Generate** button

2. View Responsive HTML5

   ❑ click the **View Result** button
   ❑ click the **OK** button

   Although many parts of this layout would now pass compliance testing, there is much more you would need to do to the topics to make this Help System fully compliant. For instance, you would have to ensure that all hyperlinks and images have ALT text. You'll be working with ALT text later.

iCONLOGiC

"Skills and Drills" Learning

Module 2: New Projects and Adding Content

In This Module You Will Learn About:

And You Will Learn To:

Creating New Projects

During the last module, you opened and explored an existing project. That module was designed to get you comfortable with the RoboHelp interface. Now that you know your way around RoboHelp a bit more, let's create a blank project that will become the policies and procedures guide for your mythical employer, Super Simplistic Solutions. The new project you create will have humble beginnings. It will not have much structure or content. However, as you work through the modules in this book, your project will evolve. In the end, your project will contain plenty of content, graphics, multiple forms of navigation, and many of the same type of high-end features you saw when you explored the project in the last module.

Student Activity: Create a Blank Project

1. Create a Blank Project.

   ☐ choose **File > New Project**

   The New Project dialog box opens.

   ☐ on the **New** tab, select **Blank Project**

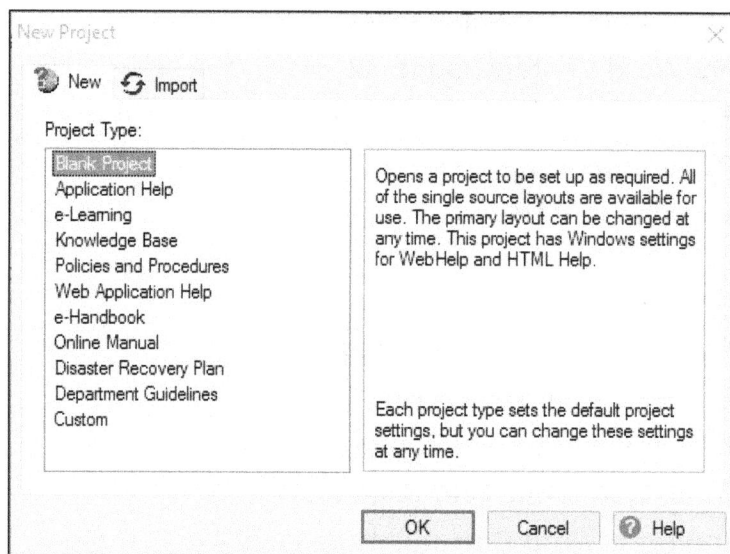

New Project	×

   New   Import

   Project Type:

Blank Project	Opens a project to be set up as required. All of the single source layouts are available for use. The primary layout can be changed at any time. This project has Windows settings for WebHelp and HTML Help.
Application Help	
e-Learning	
Knowledge Base	
Policies and Procedures	
Web Application Help	
e-Handbook	
Online Manual	
Disaster Recovery Plan	
Department Guidelines	
Custom	Each project type sets the default project settings, but you can change these settings at any time.

   OK   Cancel   Help

   ☐ click the **OK** button

   The New Project Wizard dialog box opens.

2. Give the new project a title and file name.

   ☐ change the title of the new project to **Policies & Procedures**
   ☐ change the file name of the project to **policies**

   Enter the title of this project:

   Policies & Procedures

   Enter the file name for the project:

   policies

The project title will be seen by your users when they access the Help System. You can be as descriptive as you like with the title and use spaces between the words. However, a project's file name leads directly to project support files and output files. Because you are essentially dealing with web content, spaces in file names are never a good idea.

3. Select a working location for the project.

   ❑ from the **Enter the location for the project** area, click the yellow folder
   ❑ open the **RoboHelp2017Data** folder

   Note: You should have already downloaded and unzipped the RoboHelp2017Data folder to your hard drive as instructed in the "About This Book" section of this book (see page x).

   ❑ select the **RoboHelpProjects** folder and then click the **Open** button

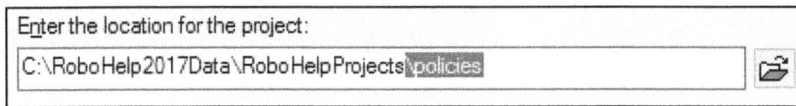

   Enter the location for the project:

   `C:\RoboHelp2017Data\RoboHelpProjects\policies`

4. Specify a title for the first topic and set the project's Language.

   ❑ in the **Enter the title of the first topic** field, type **Mission**
   ❑ ensure the Language is set to **English (US)**

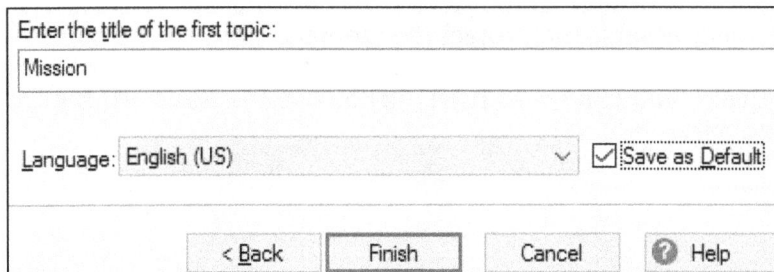

   Enter the title of the first topic:

   Mission

   Language: English (US)   ☑ Save as Default

   < Back   Finish   Cancel   ❓ Help

   ❑ click the **Finish** button

   Your new RoboHelp project opens. The Mission topic is open in the Design window, ready for editing. (If it's not open for some reason, you can easily open it by double-clicking the file on the Topic List pod.)

5. Reload the NoClutter workspace.

   ❑ from the **Workspace** menu, choose **Default**
   ❑ from the **Workspace** menu, choose **NoClutter**

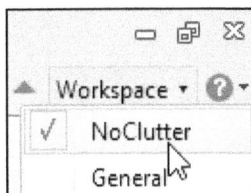

   Workspace ▾ ❓▾
   ✓   NoClutter
        General

   Although we've created the NoClutter workspace to make the RoboHelp interface as clean as possible while you are learning the program, you can work with any

workspace that you like. Moving forward, you won't be prompted to load a specific workspace unless the success of an activity is dependent upon using one workspace over another.

6. Edit the Mission topic.

   ❑ click in front of the "Mission" heading and type **Our** (the heading should now read **Our Mission**)

   ❑ highlight the remaining text in the topic and replace it with:
   To continually create solutions for all of the world's problems. Those solutions must be super... yet simplistic.

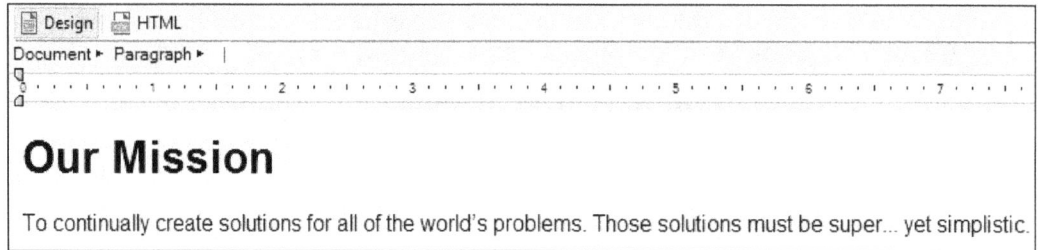

   📄 Design 🖥 HTML

   Document ▸ Paragraph ▸ |

   0 · · · I · · · 1 · · · I · · · 2 · · · I · · · 3 · · · I · · · 4 · · · I · · · 5 · · · I · · · 6 · · · I · · · 7 · · · I · ·

   # Our Mission

   To continually create solutions for all of the world's problems. Those solutions must be super... yet simplistic.

   ---

7. Save the project.

   ❑ on the **Project** tab, click **Save All**

   When you work within RoboHelp, multiple assets might be open at one time. For instance, it's possible to have several topics open, all in an unsaved state. As you make changes to project assets, the project file (project name.xpj) also remains in an unsaved state. For that reason, it's a good idea to use the Save All option frequently. Alternatively, you can press [**ctrl**] [**s**] or use the **Save All** button in the Quick Access toolbar.

   Rh | 📄 ☐ 📋 ↰ ↱ ⤳

   File

   Save All (Ctrl+S)

   💾 💾 Save all components

   Save
   All   🗑 Delete   Settings

Creating Topics

Your new project contains just a single topic (Mission). In the next few activities, you will learn how to create, rename, and delete topics. Each new RoboHelp topic you create is actually an HTML file. As we promised in the first module of this book, you do not need to know HTML to create HTML topics.

Student Activity: Create a New Topic

1. Ensure that the **policies** project is still open.

2. Create a new topic.

   ❏ on the **Project** tab, **New** group, click **Topic** (click the top part of **Topic**)

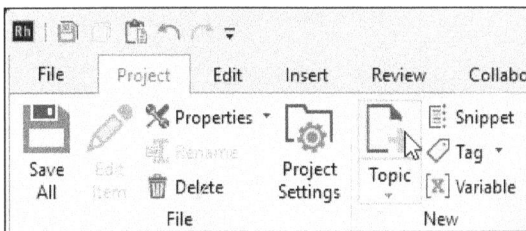

   The New Topic dialog box opens.

   ❏ on the **General** tab, change the Topic Title to **Philosophy**

   The Title is the most important part of a topic. A good title precisely describes what the topic is about: whether it explains a concept or provides instructions on getting something done. Titles are shown in search results and users decide a topic's worth based on the title. Search engines like Google and RoboHelp's own search select pages for a large part on the title. A bad title means that readers are not going to find the topic.

   Notice that a File Name (Philosophy.htm) has been automatically added to the File Name field that mimics the Topic Title you typed. As you create topics, keep in mind that you can give a topic just about any title you want. Because users see titles, we encourage Help authors to be descriptive when creating Topic Titles. You can use one word, multiple words, spaces, and punctuation in Topic Titles. However, File Names are not as flexible. You cannot use spaces or special characters in File Names. If you want to create a topic with multiple words in its title, RoboHelp will automatically replace those spaces with underscores.

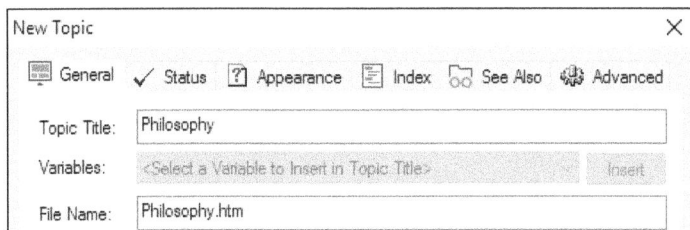

   ❏ click the **OK** button

   The new topic is created and opens in Design view.

3. Add content to the new Philosophy topic.

   ❏ highlight the text **Type topic text here.**

   ❏ type **Super Simple Tactics...**

   ❏ press [**enter**]

   ❏ type **Tactics that focus on motivation, engagement, relevance and usability are standard operating procedures for all of our projects. Working with subject matter experts, we distill and render technical content in logical and easily digestible units. We link concept and application to the real world, with a user-centered perspective.**

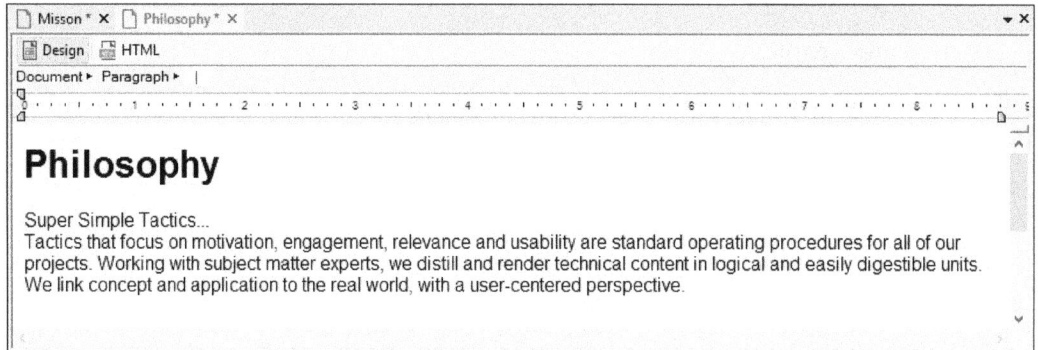

At the top of the Welcome window, notice that there are two tabs for your two open topics: **Mission** and **Philosophy**.

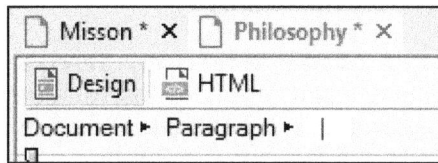

To switch between open topics, you can click the name on the tab across the top of the window, press [**ctrl**] [**tab**], or select the open topic from the Windows menu.

4. Save the project.

   ❏ on the **Project** tab, **File** group, click **Save All**

Student Activity: Rename and Delete Topics

1. Ensure that the **policies** project is still open.

2. Create a new topic using a keyboard shortcut

   ❑ press [**ctrl**] [**t**]

   The New Topic dialog box opens.

   ❑ change the Topic Title to **Ooops**
   ❑ confirm the File Name is **Ooops.htm**

   | General | ✓ Status | ? Appearance | Index | See Also | Advanced |

   Topic Title: Ooops

   Variables: <Select a Variable to Insert in Topic Title>   Insert

   File Name: Ooops.htm

   ❑ click the **OK** button

3. Rename a topic's Title and File Name.

   ❑ on the **Topic List** pod, right-click **Ooops** and choose **Properties**

   The Topic Properties dialog box opens.

   ❑ change the Topic Title to **Delete Me**
   ❑ change the File Name to **Delete_Me**

   | General | ✓ Status | ? Appearance | Index |

   Topic Title: Delete Me

   Variables: <Select a Variable to Insert in Topic Title>   Insert

   File Name: Delete_Me

   ❑ click the **OK** button

   The updated name and title appear in the Topic List pod.

   Topic List

   All Folders

File Name	Title
Philosophy.htm	Philosophy
Misson.htm	Misson
Delete_Me.htm	Delete Me

4. Delete a topic.

    ☐ on the Topic List pod, right-click the **Delete Me** topic and choose **Delete**

    You will be asked to confirm the deletion.

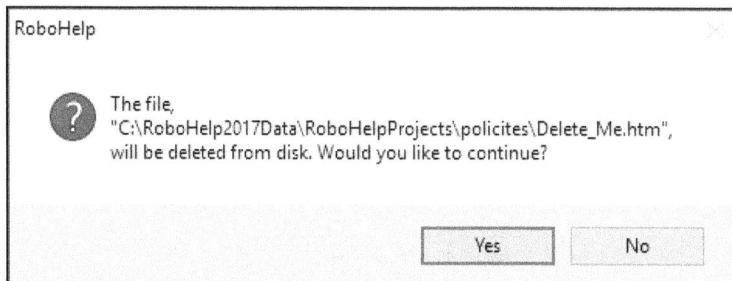

    RoboHelp   ✕

    ❓   The file,
          "C:\RoboHelp2017Data\RoboHelpProjects\policites\Delete_Me.htm",
          will be deleted from disk. Would you like to continue?

                                              [Yes   ]   [No   ]

    ☐ click the **Yes** button

    The file has been removed from the project and moved to the Recycle Bin on your computer. As mentioned previously, if you want the topic back within your project, the recovery process is not as simple as clicking Undo in the Quick Access Toolbar. Instead, you need to move the topic out of the Recycle Bin and then import the topic back into your project. You will learn how to import content into a project next.

Importing HTML Files

You can import several types of documents into a RoboHelp project including HTML files, Microsoft Word documents, Adobe FrameMaker documents, and PDFs. During the import process, new topics can automatically be created based on the formatting used in the content that you are importing. You can also import HTML or XHMTL files created with any of the typical HTML authoring tools. If the HTML files contain links to images or files, those assets will be imported into the RoboHelp project.

Student Activity: Import an HTML File

1. Ensure that the **policies** project is still open.

2. Import an HTML file.

   ❏ on the **Project** tab, **Import** group, click the **bottom half** of **Document**, and choose **HTML**

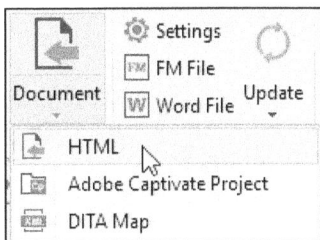

   ❏ from the **RoboHelp2017Data** folder, open the **content** folder

   There are seven HTML files in the content folder.

   ❏ select **absence.htm** and click the **Open** button

   The Output View pod appears (where the Topic List pod was a moment ago) confirming that the absence topic was successfully imported.

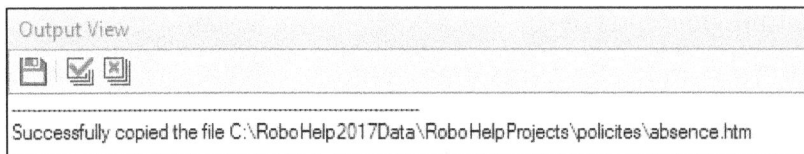

   Successfully copied the file C:\RoboHelp2017Data\RoboHelpProjects\policites\absence.htm

   ❏ select the **Topic List** pod (it is located below and to the left of the Output View pod)

   The newly imported HTML file appears as a topic on the Topic List pod.

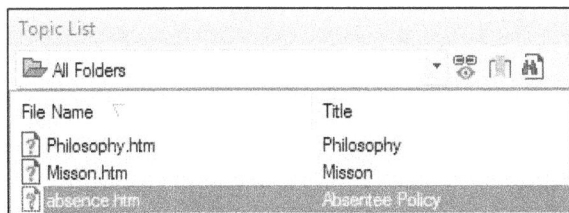

MS Word Content

If Microsoft Word is installed on your computer, you can import Word documents into RoboHelp. During the Word import process, you have a choice of copying the Word document into the RoboHelp project or linking to the Word document. If the Word document is a "moving target" and will be updated by team members, linking to the Word document is ideal. However, if you link to the Word document, you should not edit the topic in RoboHelp. If you intend to make changes to the text from within RoboHelp, a standard import of the Word document is best.

Student Activity: Import a Word Document

1. Ensure that the **policies** project is still open.

2. Import a Word document.

   ❑ on the **Project** tab, **Import** group, click the **bottom half** of **Document**, and choose **Word document**
   ❑ from the **RoboHelp2017Data** folder, **content** folder, open **SubstanceAbuse.doc**

   The Import dialog box opens. This screen contains options that control how the Word document will be formatted as it is imported into RoboHelp.

   ❑ to the right of **Word Document: Edit conversion settings for Word documents**, click the **Edit** button

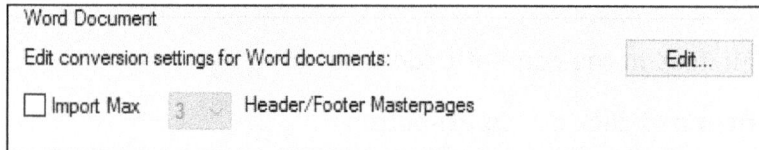

Word Document	
Edit conversion settings for Word documents:	Edit...
☐ Import Max 3 Header/Footer Masterpages	

   The Word document is scanned and the Conversion Settings dialog box opens.

3. Map Word styles to RoboHelp styles.

   ❑ from the **Word Document Settings** area, double-click the word **Paragraph** to open the Paragraph group
   ❑ from the **Paragraph** group, select **Heading 1**
   ❑ from the middle of the dialog box, **RoboHelp Style** drop-down menu, choose **Heading 1**

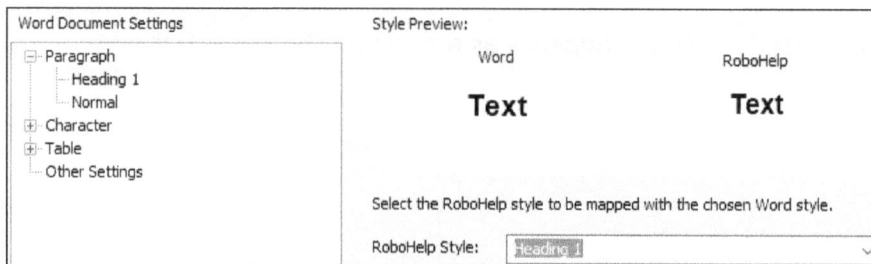

Word Document Settings	Style Preview:	
⊟ Paragraph	Word	RoboHelp
Heading 1		
Normal	**Text**	**Text**
⊞ Character		
⊞ Table		
Other Settings		
	Select the RoboHelp style to be mapped with the chosen Word style.	
	RoboHelp Style: Heading 1 ⌄	

   When the Word document is imported, the Heading 1 style used in Word uses RoboHelp's Heading 1 style.

4. Control how the Word content is split into new topics.

❑ from the Word Document Settings area, ensure that the **Heading 1** Paragraph style is still selected

❑ from the middle of the dialog box, select **Pagination (Split into topics based on this style)**

By selecting Pagination for the Heading 1 style, RoboHelp creates a new topic every time it sees that Heading 1 was used in the Word document.

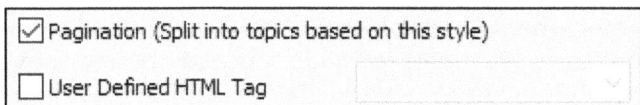

> ☑ Pagination (Split into topics based on this style)
>
> ☐ User Defined HTML Tag

❑ click the **OK** button to close the Conversion Settings dialog box and return to the Import dialog box

❑ click the **Next** button

The Content Settings screen appears. If the Word document contains a Table of Contents and Index, those features will work nicely in the RoboHelp project. For a Glossary, you will have to map styles to Glossary terms and definitions. The document you are importing does not have any of those features, so you will leave all of the check boxes deselected.

❑ click the **Finish** button

On the Output View pod, notice that two topics have been created from the single Word document. In addition, a CSS file has been created (you'll learn about CSS, or Cascading Style Sheets, during the next module).

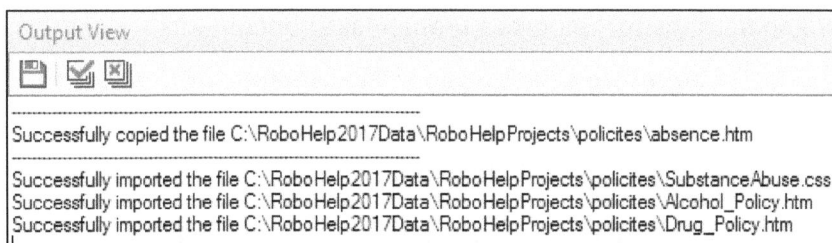

> Output View
>
> ----------
> Successfully copied the file C:\RoboHelp2017Data\RoboHelpProjects\policites\absence.htm
> ----------
> Successfully imported the file C:\RoboHelp2017Data\RoboHelpProjects\policites\SubstanceAbuse.css
> Successfully imported the file C:\RoboHelp2017Data\RoboHelpProjects\policites\Alcohol_Policy.htm
> Successfully imported the file C:\RoboHelp2017Data\RoboHelpProjects\policites\Drug_Policy.htm

On the Topic List pod, you should see two new topics, one for the Drug Policy and another for the Alcohol Policy.

5. Save the project.

FrameMaker Content

If you have Adobe FrameMaker installed on your computer, you can import FrameMaker files into RoboHelp. Once imported, FrameMaker content appears as new topics on the Topic List pod. When you import FrameMaker documents, you can elect to convert the FrameMaker Table of Contents, Index, Glossary, and other settings into RoboHelp counterparts. As with Word documents, you have a choice of copying FrameMaker documents into the RoboHelp project or linking to the FrameMaker asset.

Note: To import FrameMaker documents, Adobe FrameMaker must be installed on your computer. If you do not have FrameMaker, skip this activity and move to the next one. You'll have one less topic than what is shown later in this module, but that's no worry. In fact, during the next module you will be opening a project that has all of the content you need already imported.

Student Activity: Import a FrameMaker Document

1. Ensure that the **policies** project is still open.

2. Import a FrameMaker document.

   ❏ on the **Project** tab, **Import** group, click the **bottom half** of **Document**, and choose **FrameMaker document**
   ❏ from the **RoboHelp2017Data** folder, open the **content** folder
   ❏ open **nondiscrimination.fm**

   The Import dialog box opens.

3. Edit the conversion settings for imported FrameMaker documents.

   ❏ to the right of **Edit conversion settings for FrameMaker documents**, click the **Edit** button

   FrameMaker starts as RoboHelp scans the document.

   ❏ from the **FrameMaker Settings** area, double-click **Paragraph** to open the Paragraph group
   ❏ from the FrameMaker Settings area, select **Heading 1**
   ❏ from the RoboHelp Style drop-down menu, choose **Heading 1**

RoboHelp Style:	Heading 1 ⌄

   ❏ from the middle of the dialog box, select **Pagination (Split into topics based on this style)**

   ☑ Pagination (Split into topics based on this style)

   ❏ click the **OK** button
   ❏ click the **Next** button and then click the **Finish** button

   The Nondiscrimination Policy topic has been added to the project.

PDF Content

A Portable Document Format (PDF) is a file format introduced by Adobe years ago. Because documents in PDF format can easily be seen and printed by users on many computer platforms, they are popular on the Internet. To open a PDF file, you would need a free reader, such as Adobe Reader.

You can import a PDF file into RoboHelp provided the PDF is version 1.4 or newer. During the import process, you can create a single topic or multiple topics.

> **Note:** If the PDF is encrypted (password protected), it will not import into RoboHelp.

Student Activity: Import a PDF

1. Ensure that the **policies** project is still open.

2. Convert a PDF into a RoboHelp topic.

   ❏ on the **Project** tab, **Import** group, click the **bottom half** of **Document**, and choose **PDF document**
   ❏ from the **RoboHelp2017Data** folder, open the **content** folder
   ❏ open **Electronic.pdf**

   The Import PDF Wizard opens. The document you are importing is a simple one-page layout. It was originally created in MS Word and then printed as a PDF.

   ❏ if necessary, select **Create new topic for each PDF page**
   ❏ if necessary, select **Convert as HTML**

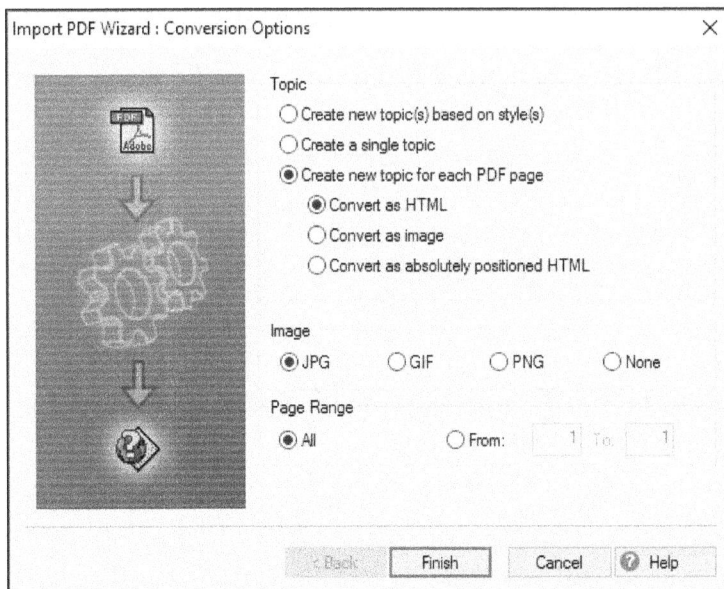

   ❏ click the **Finish** button

   The PDF is converted into a single RoboHelp topic and appears on the Topic List pod.

Topics Confidence Check

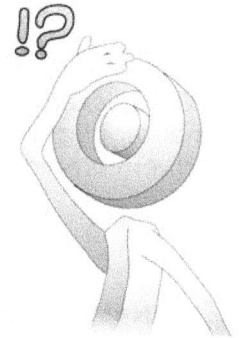

1. Your project should now contain up to seven topics (if you were able to import the FrameMaker document).

File Name ∇	Title
Philosophy.htm	Philosophy
Nondiscrimination_Policy.htm	Nondiscrimination Policy
Misson.htm	Misson
Electronic_1.htm	Microsoft Word - Document2_1
Drug_Policy.htm	Drug Policy
Alcohol_Policy.htm	Alcohol Policy
absence.htm	Absentee Policy

Topic List — All Folders

2. Import the following HTML files into your project. (You can import several files at once by [**shift**]-clicking to select contiguous files or [**ctrl**]-clicking to select noncontiguous files and then clicking **Open**.)

   overtime.htm, **payroll.htm**, **pets.htm**, **purpose.htm**, **special.htm**, and **term.htm**

3. Import the following Word documents into your project.

   Leave.doc and **Vacation.doc**

   While importing the Word documents, edit the Conversion Settings so that Word's **Heading 1** style maps to RoboHelp's **Heading 1** style and ensure that **Pagination** is selected.

   You should now have up to 15 topics in your project.

4. Change the Title of the **Leave** topic from **Administrative Leave** to **Leave Policy**. (You learned how to change a topic's Title on page 29.)

   General   Status   Appearance   Index

   Topic Title: Leave Policy

   Variables: <Select a Variable to Insert in Topic Title>   Insert

   File Name: Leave.htm

   By changing the Topic title, the Title column in the Topic List pod is updated. Note that the File Name was not changed.

Misson.htm	Misson
Leave.htm	Leave Policy
Electronic_1.htm	Microsoft Word - Document2_1

5. Change the Title of Mission.htm topic to **Mission Statement**.

6. Change the Title of overtime.htm to **Overtime Policy**.

7. Change the Title of payroll.htm to **Payroll Policy**.

8. Change the Title of purpose.htm to **About This Guide**.

9. Change the Title of special.htm to **Special Benefits**.

10. Change the Title of term.htm to **Termination Policy**.

11. Change the Title of vacation.htm to **Vacation Policy**.

12. Change the Title of Electronic_1.htm to **Electronic Communications Policy**.

    Do you tend to think of topics first by **Title** or by **File Name**? If by Title, it may be helpful if the Title column on the Topic List pod is the first column on the pod instead of the second.

13. At the top of the Topic List pod, drag the word **Title** left and on top of the words **File Name**. The Title column moves to the left of the File Name column. You can then click the word Title to sort the list of topics alphabetically.

Topic List	
📂 All Folders	▾ 🔘 📄 🔍
Title	**File Name**
About This Guide	[?] purpose.htm
Absentee Policy	[?] absence.htm
Alcohol Policy	[?] Alcohol_Policy.htm

14. Save the project.

Working in HTML View

Although it is not necessary for you to know HTML to work within RoboHelp and create content (as you've already seen, the process of making topics and importing content is very easy), knowing a little HTML can pay off when imported content causes trouble because of misplaced HTML tags. In the Electronic Communications Policy topic, specific HTML tags are not allowing the topic text to wrap within RoboHelp's Design View. The result is text that continues to flow to the right, beyond the topic window. You'll use the HTML View to see the unwanted tags and remove them topic-wide.

Student Activity: Replace an HTML Tag

1. Ensure that the **policies** project is still open.

2. Open the **Electronic Communications Policy** topic.

   This topic was created when you imported the PDF a few moments ago. Notice that the text continues to the right (and out of view) instead of wrapping within the Design View window.

3. Use HTML Code View to identify a tag needing to be replaced.

   ❏ just above the topic content, click the **HTML** button (shown **circled** in the image below)

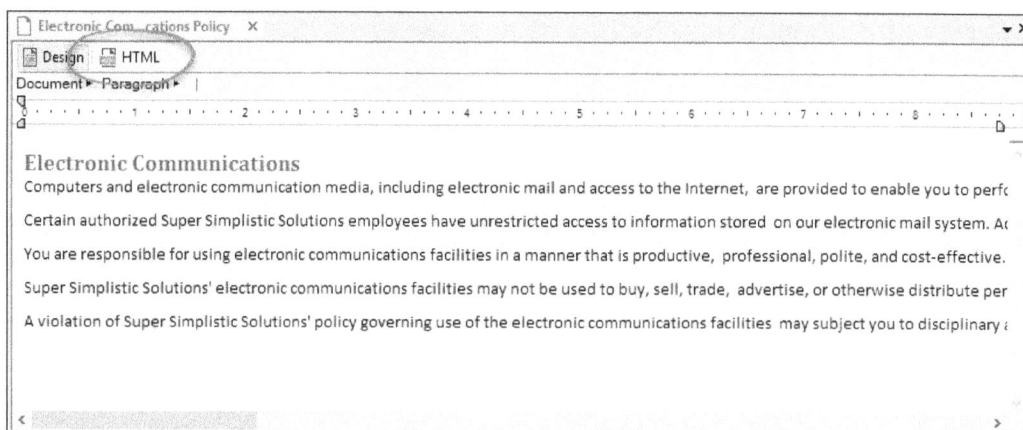

   The Design View is replaced with a view containing HTML tags and topic text. The HTML tags throughout the window can seem like gibberish; however, if you spend a few moments browsing through the content, you'll see words you can understand surrounded by tags and symbols that likely make no sense. Most notably, there is a ** ** tag that is between nearly every word in the topic. This is the tag that is causing the text wrapping issue. You could manually highlight an instance of the tag and replace it with a standard space. However, because there are so many of the troublesome tags, replacing them all could take you a lot of time. It would be more efficient to use RoboHelp's **Replace** feature to take care of the problem.

4. Replace an HTML tag.

   ❏ right click and select **Replace**

The Find and Replace dialog box opens

❏ in the **Find what** field, type ** **
❏ click within the **Replace with** field and press the [**spacebar**]

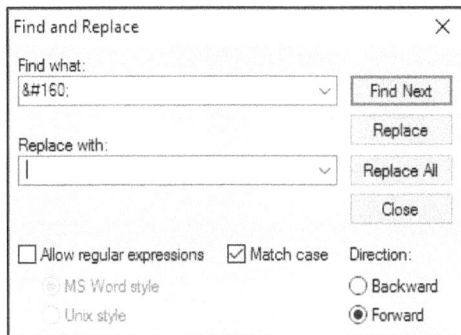

```
Find and Replace                                    ×
Find what:
                           ∨    │ Find Next │
                                     ├───────────┤
                                     │  Replace  │
Replace with:                        ├───────────┤
│                               ∨    │ Replace All │
                                     ├───────────┤
                                     │   Close   │

☐ Allow regular expressions  ☑ Match case   Direction:
  ⦿ MS Word style                            ○ Backward
  ○ Unix style                               ⦿ Forward
```

❏ check your work against the image above (although you will not see anything in the Replace field, ensure that you add a single space to the field)
❏ click the **Find Next** button

The first instance of the ** ** tag is found and selected.

❏ click the **Replace** button

A single instance of the tag is replaced by a space.

❏ click the **Replace All** button

All of the ** ** tags are replaced with spaces.

❏ click the **Close** button to close the Find and Replace dialog box

5. Return to Design View.

❏ select the Electronic Communications Policy tab
❏ click the button **Design** just above the topic content

The text within the topic is now wrapping correctly within the Design window.

> **Electronic Communications**
> Computers and electronic communication media, including electronic mail and access to the Internet, are provided to enable you to perform your duties as a Super Simplistic Solutions employee more efficiently and productively. These are corporate resources which are to be used only for business and business-related purposes. Your use of Super Simplistic Solutions' electronic communications facilities, including computers and network access, constitutes your consent to monitoring and the interception of messages, as permitted by law.
>
> Certain authorized Super Simplistic Solutions employees have unrestricted access to information stored on our electronic mail system. Activities performed by these authorized personnel may include

Admit it, making changes to the topic using the HTML Code window wasn't nearly as scary as you thought it was going to be, right? And now that you've done it, go ahead and call yourself a webmaster! (Okay, maybe not yet, but you're close... real close!)

6. Save your work and then close the project.

Notes

Module 3: Project Structure and CSS

In This Module You Will Learn About:

And You Will Learn To:

Project Structure

Creating folders and subfolders on the Project Manager pod can help you organize your project's topics, images, and other assets. Folders make it easier to access and edit your content as your Help project grows and becomes more sophisticated. As an added bonus, the folder structure you create on the Project Manager pod can be re-purposed and used to automatically create a TOC later (it's a nifty process you'll come to appreciate later in this module).

Student Activity: Create Project Folders

1. Open an existing RoboHelp project.

   ❑ from the **bottom left** of the Starter, click **Open Project**
   ❑ from the **RoboHelp2017Data** folder, open the **RoboHelpProjects** folder
   ❑ open the **css** folder
   ❑ open **css.xpj**

2. Create a folder on the Project Manager pod.

   ❑ click anywhere within the **Project Manager** pod
   ❑ right-click **Project Files** and choose **New > Folder**

   The new folder appears in the Project Files folder. By default, new folders are always named **New_Folder**.

   ❑ change the name to **General Office Information**

   Because folder names cannot contain spaces, the spaces you typed are automatically replaced with underscores: **General_Office_Information**.

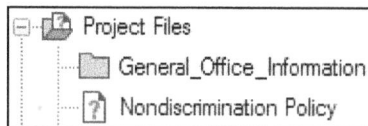

   ```
   ⊟ 📇 Project Files
         📁 General_Office_Information
         ❓ Nondiscrimination Policy
   ```

3. Move a topic into a project folder.

   ❑ on the **Project Manager** pod, drag the **Absentee Policy** topic **up** and **into** the General_Office_Information folder

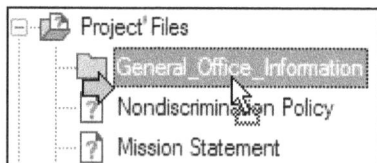

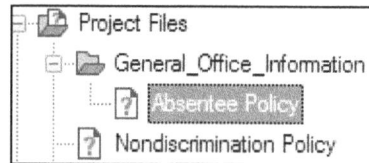

   ```
   ⊟ 📇 Project Files
         📁 General_Office_Information
         ❓ Nondiscrimination Policy
         ❓ Mission Statement
   ```
   ```
   ⊟ 📇 Project Files
      ⊟ 📂 General_Office_Information
            ❓ Absentee Policy
         ❓ Nondiscrimination Policy
   ```

Project Structure Confidence Check

1. Select the **Project Files** folder and create a new folder named **Drugs_and_Alcohol**.

2. Select the **Project Files** folder and create a new folder named **Leave_and_Vacation**.

3. On the Project Manager, click **Sort by Name**.

   Your folders, which are now sorted alphabetically, should look like this:

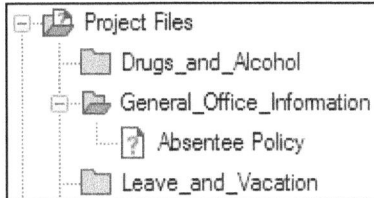

   ```
   Project Files
       Drugs_and_Alcohol
       General_Office_Information
           Absentee Policy
       Leave_and_Vacation
   ```

4. Add topics to the project folders as necessary to make your Project Files folder look like the pictures below.

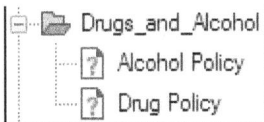

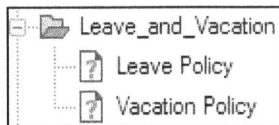

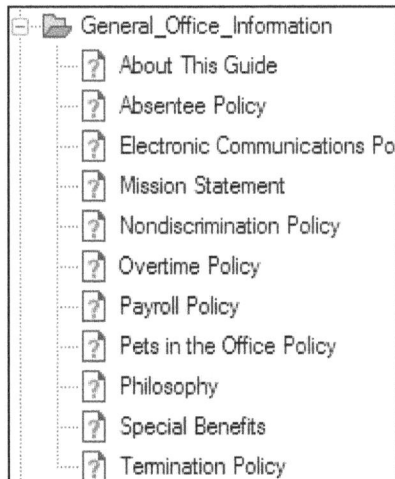

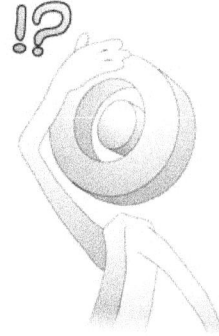

   ```
   Drugs_and_Alcohol
       Alcohol Policy
       Drug Policy

   Leave_and_Vacation
       Leave Policy
       Vacation Policy
   ```

   ```
   General_Office_Information
       About This Guide
       Absentee Policy
       Electronic Communications Po
       Mission Statement
       Nondiscrimination Policy
       Overtime Policy
       Payroll Policy
       Pets in the Office Policy
       Philosophy
       Special Benefits
       Termination Policy
   ```

Table of Contents

A typical Help System has a **Contents** tab which you create in the Table of Contents folder on the Project Manager pod. A typical Contents tab is made up of **books** and **pages**. Books can contain pages or other books. The pages typically point to topics in your project.

Student Activity: Create a TOC Book

1. Ensure that you are still working in the **css** project.

2. Open the Table of Contents folder.

   ☐ on the Project Manager pod, double-click **Table of Contents** to open the folder (or click the plus sign to the left of the folder to open it)

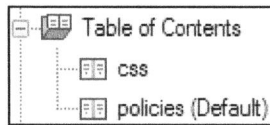

   ```
   ⊟ 📖 Table of Contents
      ├─ 🗏 css
      └─ 🗏 policies (Default)
   ```

   There is a default Table of Contents called **policies** within the Table of Contents folder. You can edit the default or create your own. You will work with new TOCs later in this book. For now, you will edit the default.

3. Add a book to the policies Table of Contents.

   ☐ from within the Table of Contents folder, double-click **polices (Default)**

   The TOC opens in its own pod to the right of the Project Manager pod.

   ☐ from the top of the **policies** pod, click **New TOC Book** 📖

   The New TOC Book dialog box opens.

   ☐ on the **General** tab, type **Book 1** into the Book Title area

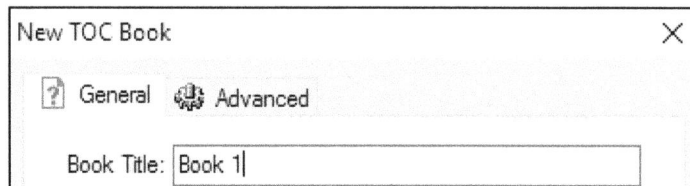

   ```
   New TOC Book                                      ✕
      ?  General   ⚙ Advanced
      Book Title: │Book 1│
   ```

   ☐ click the **OK** button

   The default TOC now contains a single book. The book does not yet contain pages (aliases that point to content within the project), but you will add those soon enough.

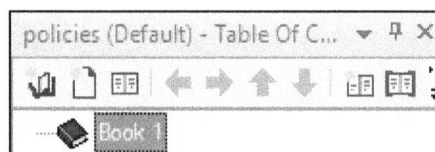

   ```
   policies (Default) - Table Of C...  ▼ 📌 ✕
   📖 🗋 🗏  ⬅ ➡ ⬆ ⬇ │ 🗏 🗏
   ◆ 📕 Book 1
   ```

Books Confidence Check

1. Add three more books to the TOC named **Book 2**, **Book 3**, and **Book 4.**

2. Compare your TOC to this:

3. Select Book 2.

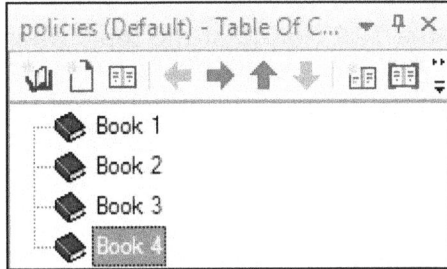

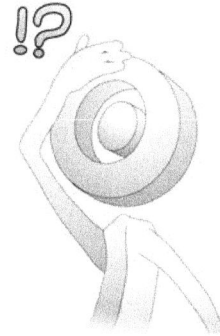

4. From the top of the TOC pod, click the **Move Right** tool.

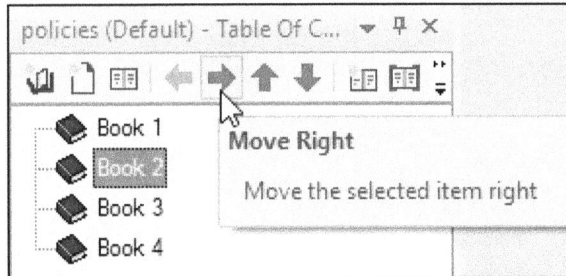

The Book 2 book moves right and is now considered a *nested* book.

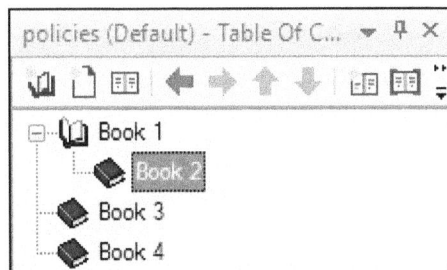

5. With Book 2 selected, click the **Move Left** tool.

Using the remaining Move tools on the TOC, you have the ability to move books Up, Down, Left, or Right.

Student Activity: Add Pages to TOC Books

1. Ensure that you are still working in the **css** project.

2. Use the Topic List pod to add a page to a book.

   ☐ on the Topic List pod, select **any topic**
   ☐ drag the topic to any of the books on the TOC (let go of the topic when the book is highlighted)

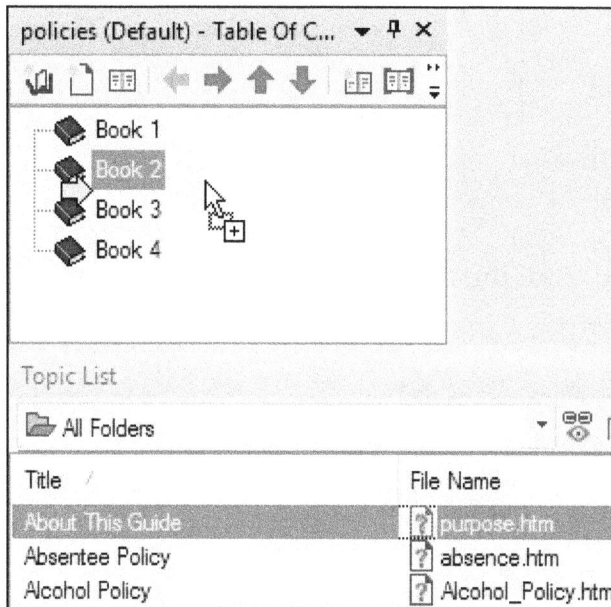

The topic appears in the Book on the TOC. At this point, the topic is known as a **Page** within the book.

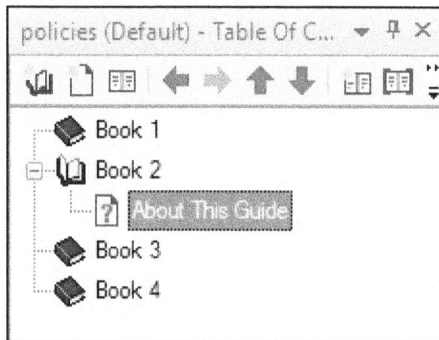

TOC Pages Confidence Check

1. Spend a few minutes adding topics to the TOC books as you see fit. (There is no need to add all of the topics to the TOC because you'll be replacing everything inside the TOC with different books in just a few minutes.)

   As you add the topics to the books, you'll likely discover that you can add topics to books multiple times.

2. When you've had enough practice, save the project.

   Note: You can easily delete books and pages. Right-click the unwanted item and choose [**delete**]. Unlike deleting topics, you are not be asked to confirm your action because you are deleting only pointers to project content, not the content itself.

Automatic TOCs

During the last few activities, you learned how to build a TOC from scratch. However, if you have already spent time creating the structure of the project on the Project Manager Pod (which you did at the beginning of this module when you created the three folders), you can leverage RoboHelp's ability to automatically create a TOC based on that existing structure.

Student Activity: Auto-Create a TOC

1. Ensure that you are still working in the **css** project.

2. Ensure that the policies TOC is still open.

3. Auto-create a TOC based on the topic structure on the Project Manager pod.

   ❐ from the top of the **policies** pod, click **Auto-create TOC** 🔳

   The Auto-create TOC dialog box opens.

   ❐ select **Delete current TOC before creating new**

   Delete current TOC before creating new removes the existing TOC you created. **Create TOC pages for mid-topic links (bookmarks)** is an optional setting. You haven't yet learned how to create bookmarks (you will during the activity on page 87). Because your current project does not contain any bookmarks, it does not matter if you select the option or not.

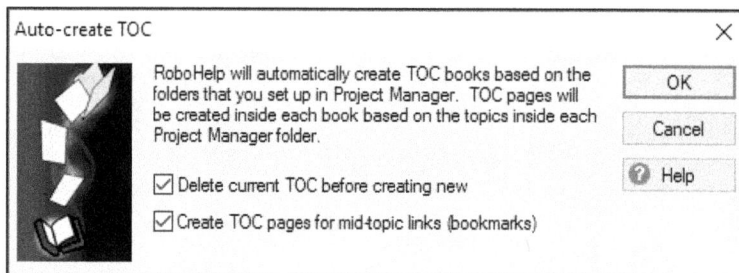

   ❐ click the **OK** button

   The content you originally added to the policies TOC is replaced by books and pages that match the structure you set up on the Project Manager pod.

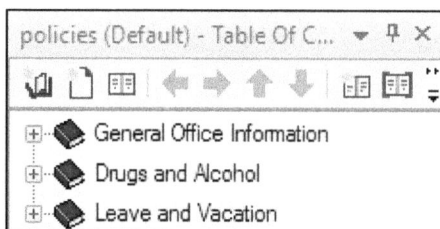

Cascading Style Sheets

A typical project contains hundreds, if not thousands, of topics. For the sake of simplicity, let's assume you have 500 topics. Each of those topics is going to contain one main heading. Several of the topics are likely to contain multiple subheadings. There's going to be normal body copy in every topic. Let's see, 500 main headings, hundreds of subheads, and thousands of normal paragraphs. You will likely want each of those 500 headings to have a consistent look. Perhaps you've decided upon Verdana, Bold, 14 points, and Centered alignment. That's as many as four commands per heading, multiplied by 500. Although Kevin isn't very good at math, even he can figure out that it's going to take 2,000 steps to format all of the headings. Keep in mind that you have not even started formatting any of the remaining text. Tired yet? And don't get me started on how much work it's going to take to update the appearance of the text that you've just spent so much time formatting. We wouldn't want to do all of that work... and we're betting that you wouldn't want to either.

Cascading Style Sheets (CSS) take the drudgery, and the work, out of formatting and updating the look of your topics. CSS files can contain dozens of styles that in turn can contain hundreds upon hundreds of formatting commands that you can assign to any topic. The beauty of a style sheet is that once you have assigned a style sheet to a topic, you can edit the style, which will in turn effect hundreds of changes in your project in minutes.

Student Activity: Apply a Style Sheet to a Topic

1. Ensure that you are still working in the **css** project.

2. Open a topic and display the paragraph markers.

   ❏ on the **Topic List** pod, select the **General_Office_Information** folder from the folder drop-down menu

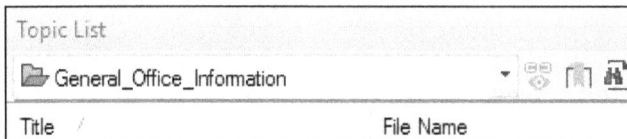

Topic List		
📂 General_Office_Information	▾	⊞ 🗂 🔍
Title ╱	File Name	

   Now that you've selected the General Office Information folder, the topics in the remaining folders are hidden from view on the Topic List pod. Selecting specific folders from the drop-down menu is a great way to segregate your content, especially if your Help System contains multiple folders.

   ❏ from the General_Office_Information folder, double-click the **About This Guide** topic to open the topic for editing

   ❏ on the **Edit** tab, **View** group, click **Show/Hide** and choose **Paragraph Markers**

   You should now be able to see the "hidden" paragraph markers in the topic.

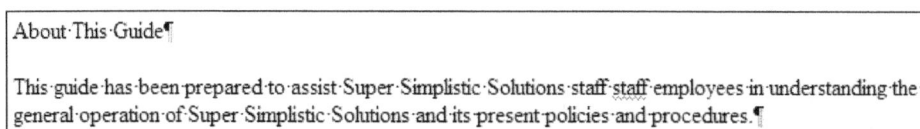

About·This·Guide¶
This·guide·has·been·prepared·to·assist·Super·Simplistic·Solutions·staff·staff·employees·in·understanding·the·general·operation·of·Super·Simplistic·Solutions·and·its·present·policies·and·procedures.¶

Notice the appearance of the topic text. You are about to change the appearance of the text in this topic and then all of your topics in the project.

3. Apply a style to a single topic.

❏ on the **Edit** tab, **CSS** group, click the **Assign Stylesheet** drop-down menu

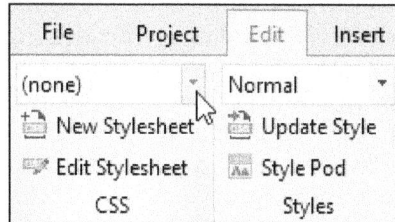

File	Project	Edit	Insert
(none) ▾		Normal ▾	
➕ New Stylesheet		➕ Update Style	
✏ Edit Stylesheet		Aa Style Pod	
CSS		Styles	

❏ select **default.css** from the menu

Notice that the appearance of your topic text changes dramatically to reflect the attributes of the default.css style sheet.

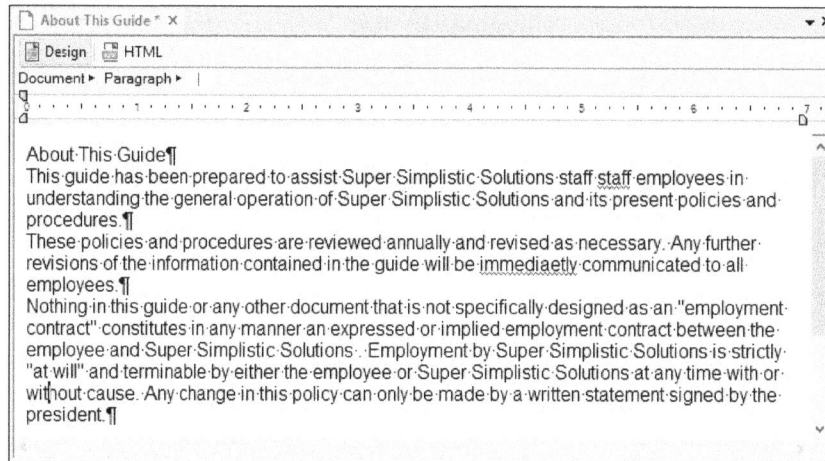

```
About This Guide * ×                                        ▾ ×
📄 Design  📄 HTML
Document ▸ Paragraph ▸  |

  ·  ·  ·  1  ·  ·  ·  2  ·  ·  ·  3  ·  ·  ·  4  ·  ·  ·  5  ·  ·  ·  6  ·  ·  ·  7  ·

About·This·Guide¶
This·guide·has·been·prepared·to·assist·Super·Simplistic·Solutions·staff·staff·employees·in·
understanding·the·general·operation·of·Super·Simplistic·Solutions·and·its·present·policies·and·
procedures.¶
These·policies·and·procedures·are·reviewed·annually·and·revised·as·necessary.·Any·further·
revisions·of·the·information·contained·in·the·guide·will·be·immediaetly·communicated·to·all·
employees.¶
Nothing·in·this·guide·or·any·other·document·that·is·not·specifically·designed·as·an·"employment·
contract"·constitutes·in·any·manner·an·expressed·or·implied·employment·contract·between·the·
employee·and·Super·Simplistic·Solutions·.·Employment·by·Super·Simplistic·Solutions·is·strictly·
"at·will"·and·terminable·by·either·the·employee·or·Super·Simplistic·Solutions·at·any·time·with·or·
without·cause.·Any·change·in·this·policy·can·only·be·made·by·a·written·statement·signed·by·the·
president.¶
```

4. Apply a style to multiple selected topics.

❏ on the **Topic List** pod, select the **Absentee Policy** topic
❏ press [**shift**] and select the **Electronic Communications Policy** topic
❏ release the [**shift**] key

Both the **Absentee Policy** and **Electronic Communications Policy** topics should now be selected.

❏ on the **Project** tab, **File** group, click **Properties**
❏ on the **Appearance** tab, select **default.css** from the list of Style Sheets

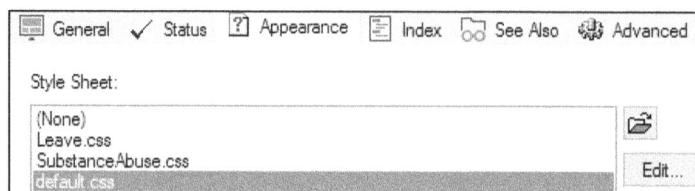

```
🖼 General  ✓ Status  ？ Appearance  ▤ Index  🔗 See Also  ⚙ Advanced

Style Sheet:

(None)                                              📁
Leave.css
SubstanceAbuse.css
default.css                                         Edit...
```

❏ click the **OK** button

Apply CSS Confidence Check

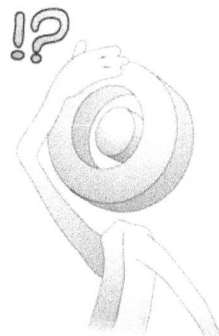

1. On the Topic List pod, change the view to show All Folders.

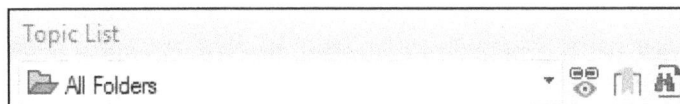

Topic List

All Folders

2. Select all of the topics on the Topic List pod. (One quick way to select all of the topics is to select one and then press [**ctrl**] [**a**])

3. Right-click any of the selected topics and choose Properties. Then, on the Appearance tab, assign the **default.css** style sheet to the topics.

4. Open the **Alcohol Policy** topic.

   Notice that the main heading (Alcohol Policy) and the body text now follow the formatting of the default.css style sheet.

> # Alcohol·Policy¶
>
> Super·Simplistic·Solutions·does·not·permit·or·condone·intoxication·or·drinking·of·alcoholic·beverages·on·the·premises·of·the·company·or·at·an·employee's·assigned·place·of·duty·on·company·time.¶
> Such·action·will·subject·an·employee·to·disciplinary·action·up·to·and·including·dismissal.·It·is·Super·Simplistic·Solutions'·policy·to·offer·assistance·to·an·employee·whose·work·performance·is·adversely·affected·by·repeated·overindulgence·in·the·use·of·alcoholic·beverages.¶

5. Open some of the other topics and notice that some of the headings have not been formatted as headings. You'll fix that next.

> Absentee·Policy¶
> Under·specific·circumstances·Super·Simplistic·Solutions·will·permit·an·employee·to·take·time·off·from·work·without·compensation.·Circumstances·and·internal·work·schedules·will·dictate·where·and·when·this·type·of·leave·will·be·allowed.·Any·request·for·leave·of·this·type·must·be·cleared·in·advance·by·your·division·manager·and·with·the·approval·of·the·division·VP·and·president.·During·such·leave·your·health/life·coverage·may·be·maintained·for·a·period·not·to·exceed·30·days,·but·in·no·case·will·there·be·an·additional·accrual·of·sick·or·vacation·leave.¶

6. Save the project.

7. Close all open topics.

Student Activity: Apply Paragraph Styles

1. Ensure that you are still working in the **css** project.

2. Apply the Heading 1 paragraph style to a paragraph.

   ☐ open the **About This Guide** topic (you can open the topic via the Topic List pod, the General Office Information book on the TOC, or the Project Manager pod)

   ☐ click in the topic's first line of text (**About This Guide**)

   ☐ on the **Edit** tab, locate the **Paragraph Styles** drop-down menu

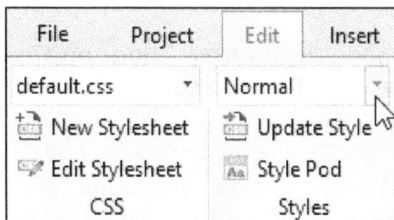

   ☐ select **Heading 1**

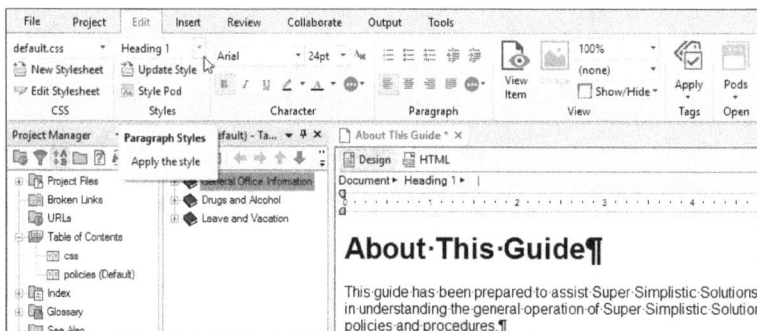

Because every topic in the project is formatted using default.css, every heading is formatted as Arial, Bold, 24 point, and white space has been added below the paragraph. All of the body text is formatted as Arial, 12 point.

3. Apply the Heading 1 style to another paragraph.

   ☐ open the **Overtime Policy** topic and click within the **Overtime Policy** heading at the top of the page

   ☐ use the Apply Style tool to select **Heading 1**

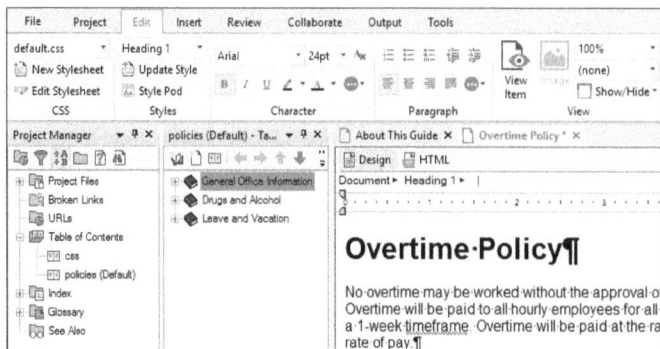

Styles Confidence Check

1. Go through every topic in the project and assign the Heading 1 style to the first line as necessary.

   Note: You can apply styles to selected paragraphs by using keyboard shortcuts: [**ctrl**] [**alt**] [**1**] (to apply the Heading 1 style), [**ctrl**] [**alt**] [**2**] (for Heading 2), [**ctrl**] [**alt**] [**3**] (for Heading 3).

2. Open the **Termination Policy** topic, assign the **Heading 2** style to the following lines:

   Resignation, **Disciplinary Policies and Procedures**, and **Unemployment Insurance**

   Resignation¶

   If you voluntarily terminate your employment with Super Simplistic Solutions, you are required to provide a written statement of resignation. The company requires a minimum of 2 weeks' notice.¶
   You will be required to turn in to the Human Resources Director your Policy and Procedures Manual and your building security cards, keys, credit cards, and any other property belonging to Super Simplistic Solutions. Prior to departure, you will be asked to complete an exit interview.¶

   Disciplinary·Policies·and·Procedures¶

   Super Simplistic Solutions is committed to ensuring the fair, equitable, and consistent

   ---

3. In the **Special Benefits** topic, assign the Heading 2 style to the following lines:

   401(k) Plan, **Workers Compensation Insurance**, and **Employee Assistance Program**

4. Save and close all topics.

Custom Style Sheets

You can create your own style sheets and define your own styles in RoboHelp. Even though you can create the CSS within RoboHelp, the style sheet file you create is an external file. That file can be shared between RoboHelp projects and edited within RoboHelp or any text editor (such as NotePad).

Font Usage

Although there are literally thousands of fonts you can use in your Help System, there are only **two** main font categories: *serif* (fonts with feet) and *sans serif* (fonts without feet). Two popular fonts are Times New Roman (serif) and Arial (sans serif). Below is an example of each.

This is an example of Times New Roman, a serif font.

This is an example of Arial, a sans-serif font.

On paper and in RoboHelp, fonts are measured in points. There are 72 points to an inch. Both of the examples above are set at 14 points. But notice that Arial looks larger. In typical print documents, sans-serif fonts are used for headings and subheadings (because they look better bigger), and serif faces are used on the body-copy fonts (because they are easier to read on hard copy). However, we use Verdana, a sans-serif font, throughout this book—a choice not typically made in the design of print documents. Why did we buck the trend? Verdana is a font that is available on all devices. Because your Help System is usually viewed via a device, it's a good idea to stick with sans-serif fonts (like Verdana), which are easier to read on a screen than serif fonts. Verdana is a particularly good choice as Verdana is installed on all devices and it will show correctly regardless of whether you are reading from a computer, an e-reader or a phone. You will learn more about this on page 59.

No matter your choice when it comes to fonts, consider keeping the number of fonts you use to a minimum. Using more than a few fonts leads to poor design and makes your topics harder to read.

Student Activity: Create a Style Sheet

1. Ensure that the **css** project is still open.

2. Create a style sheet.

   ❑ open the **Special Benefits** topic
   ❑ on the **Edit** tab, click **New Stylesheet**

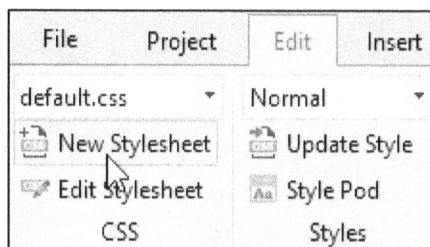

File	Project	Edit	Insert
default.css ▾		Normal ▾	
⊞ New Stylesheet		⊞ Update Style	
⊠ Edit Stylesheet		ᴬᵃ Style Pod	
CSS		Styles	

   ❑ in the **Name** area, type **policies**

❑ from the **Folder** drop-down menu, choose **Top Level Folder**

It isn't a requirement to select a specific folder when creating a style sheet. In fact, you can move a style sheet between folders by simply dragging the file on the Project Manager pod. However, by selecting Top Level Folder, you'll make it a bit easier to find and edit the style sheet in the short term.

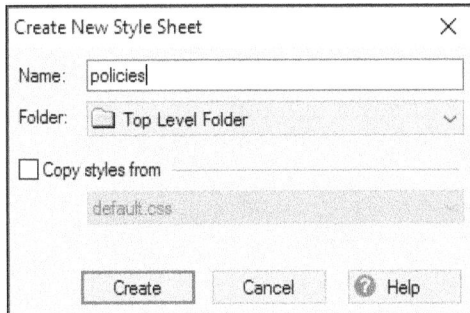

Create New Style Sheet	✕
Name:	policies|
Folder:	☐ Top Level Folder ⌄
☐ Copy styles from	
default.css	⌄
Create	Cancel	❓ Help

❑ click the **Create** button

The Styles dialog box opens.

3. Edit the font and font size used in the Normal paragraph style.

    ❑ at the left of the dialog box, from the list of **Styles**, double-click the word **Paragraph**

Paragraph styles that currently exist in your new style sheet are listed.

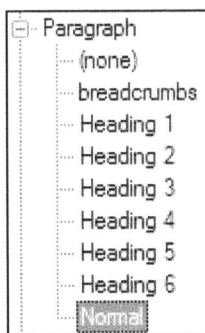

```
⊟ Paragraph
    ┈ (none)
    ┈ breadcrumbs
    ┈ Heading 1
    ┈ Heading 2
    ┈ Heading 3
    ┈ Heading 4
    ┈ Heading 5
    ┈ Heading 6
    ┈ Normal
```

❑ from the list of Paragraph styles, select the **Normal** style
❑ locate the **Formatting** area of the dialog box
❑ from the **Font** drop-down menu, choose **Verdana**
❑ change the Font Size to **10pt**

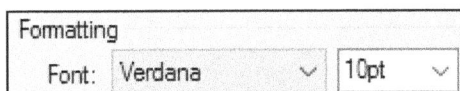

Formatting	
Font:	Verdana ⌄	10pt ⌄

4. Change the paragraph spacing used in the Normal style.

   ☐ with the **Normal** style still selected, from the **Spacing** drop-down menu, choose **After**

   ☐ change the Spacing to **12pt**

Spacing:	After	⌄	12pt

   Note: If you type in the size, make sure to add 'pt' after the number. In RoboHelp you can also use pixels or inches as units of measurement. If you don't specify **10pt**, RoboHelp doesn't know which unit of measurement you want to use.

   ☐ from the **Spacing** drop-down menu, choose **Before**

   ☐ change the Spacing to **0pt**

   ☐ click the **Apply** button

5. Edit the Heading 1 paragraph style.

   ☐ from the list of Paragraph styles, select the **Heading 1** style

   ☐ from the Formatting area, select **Verdana** from the Font drop-down menu

   ☐ change the Font Size to **12pt**

   ☐ change the Spacing Before to **0pt**

   ☐ change the Spacing After to **12pt**

   Formatting
Font:	Verdana	⌄	12pt	⌄
Indents:	Left	⌄	0pt	
Spacing:	After	⌄	12pt	

   ☐ click the **Apply** button

   The Styles dialog box should still be open.

6. Edit the Heading 2 paragraph style.

   ☐ from the list of Paragraph styles, select the **Heading 2** style

   ☐ from the Formatting area, select **Verdana** from the Font drop-down menu

   ☐ change the Font Size to **10pt**

   ☐ change the Spacing Before to **0pt**

   ☐ change the Spacing After to **12pt**

   Formatting
Font:	Verdana	⌄	10pt	⌄
Indents:	Left	⌄	0pt	
Spacing:	After	⌄	12pt	

   ☐ click the **Apply** button and then click the **OK** button

7. Save your work.

Create Paragraph Styles

While RoboHelp style sheets contain several paragraph styles by default, there are going to be occasions when you simply need to create your own. During the activity that follows, you will learn how quick and easy it is to create custom styles.

Student Activity: Create a Paragraph Style

1. Ensure that the **css** project is still open.

2. Assign a style sheet to a topic.

   ❑ open the **Alcohol Policy** topic
   ❑ on the **Edit** tab, **CSS** group, click the **Assign Stylesheet** drop-down menu

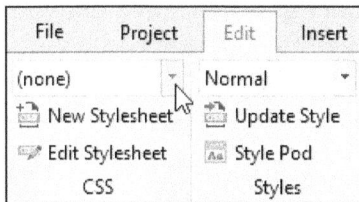

File	Project	Edit	Insert
(none) ▾		Normal ▾	
📄 New Stylesheet		📄 Update Style	
📝 Edit Stylesheet		📄 Style Pod	
CSS		Styles	

   ❑ choose **policies**

3. Create a new paragraph style.

   ❑ on the **Project Manager** pod, open the **Project Files** folder
   ❑ double-click **policies.css** to open the style sheet for editing
   ❑ right-click **Paragraph** and choose **New**

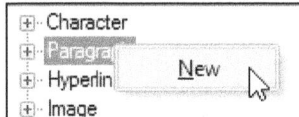

   ⊞ Character
   ⊞ Paragraph   New
   ⊞ Hyperlin
   ⊞ Image

   ❑ type **Severe warning** as the style's name and press [**enter**]

   Because spaces are not permitted in style names, RoboHelp changes the style's name back to **Style1**.

   ❑ right-click **Style1** and choose **Rename**
   ❑ name the style **SevereWarning** and press [**enter**]

4. Edit the SevereWarning paragraph style.

   ❑ if necessary, select the **SevereWarning** style
   ❑ change the Font Color to **Red** and the Font Style to **Bold**

A	✎	**T**	*T*	T̲
≡	≡	≡	≡	☰

   ❑ click the **OK** button

5. Save your work.

6. Assign the style to a paragraph.

   ❏ click within the third paragraph

   ❏ on the **Edit** tab, **Styles** group, choose the **SevereWarning** style

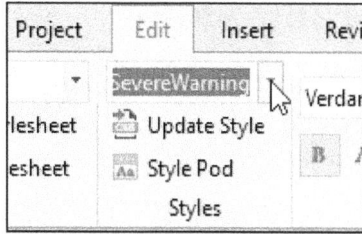

Project	Edit	Insert	Revi

SevereWarning ▾   Verdar

lesheet   Update Style

esheet   Style Pod   B

            Styles

> If·your·work·performance·indicates·you·may·be·having·a·substance·abuse·
> problem,·we·will·request·that·you·seek·treatment.·Refusal·to·seek·help·for·
> your·condition·or·recurrence·of·the·condition·each·constitutes·grounds·to·
> terminate·your·employment.¶

Edit CSS Confidence Check

1. Assign the **policies.css** file to all of the topics in the project (you learned how to do this on page 51).

2. Save the project.

3. On the Project Manager pod, double-click **policies.css** to open the style sheet for editing.

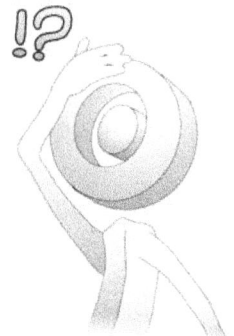

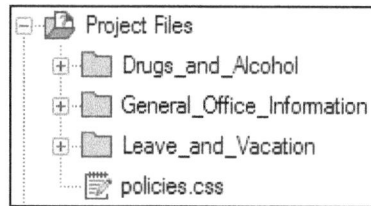

   ⊟ 📂 Project Files
   　⊞ 📁 Drugs_and_Alcohol
   　⊞ 📁 General_Office_Information
   　⊞ 📁 Leave_and_Vacation
   　　📝 policies.css

4. From the Paragraph group, select the Heading 1 style.

5. Use the Change font color tool to change the color to **Maroon**.

   A ✎ T 𝘛 T

   Change font color

6. Click the **OK** button to close the Styles dialog box.

   The color for all of the main headings in your project should now be maroon.

Font Sets

A Font Set tells the computer what font to display for a topic when the topic is opened via a web browser. If the end-user's device does not have a certain font, you can use the font set to show a different font.

For instance, if your topics use a font called "ReallyCoolFont," your users must have that font on their systems. If the font is not available, the user's computer substitutes a different font, possibly ruining your intended page design. Alternatively, if you create a font set, you can instruct the user's system to load a different, but similar, font if "ReallyCoolFont" is not available.

Because you can't control the fonts on the end-user's device, web safe fonts such as Verdana and Arial are recommended in a font set. Web safe fonts are fonts that are available on every device imaginable. You can find out more about web safe fonts at **https://www.w3schools.com/csSref/css_websafe_fonts.asp**

Student Activity: Create a Font Set

1. Ensure that the **css** project is still open.

2. Create a Font Set.

   ❐ open any topic
   ❐ on the **Edit** tab, **Character** group, click the **More** tool, and choose **Font Sets**

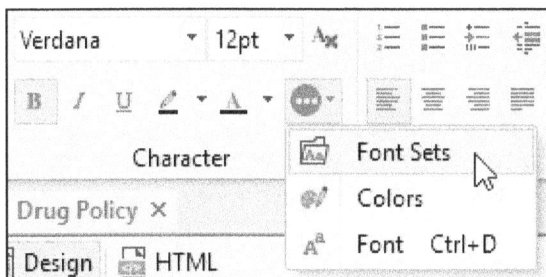

The Font Sets dialog box opens.

   ❐ click the **New** button

The Modify Font Set dialog box opens.

   ❐ in the **Font Set Name** field, type **Policies Font Set**
   ❐ from the **Available Typefaces** list, find and double-click **Verdana**
   ❐ from the **Available Typefaces** list, find and double-click **Arial**

Verdana and Arial are both web safe **sans-serif** fonts.

   ❐ type **Helvetica** into the **Available Typefaces** field

Although Helvetica is probably not installed on your computer, you can still create a Font Set that looks to use it (if the user has Helvetica on his/her computer).

❑ click the **Add** button

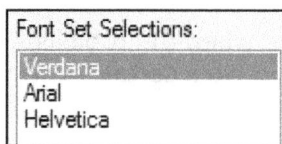

Font Set Selections:

> Verdana
> Arial
> Helvetica

❑ click the **OK** button to close the Modify Font Set dialog box
❑ click the **OK** button to close the Font Sets dialog box

The font set has been created, but it is not being used. Next you will "attach" it to a style.

3. Attach a Font Set to a style.

❑ from the Project Files folder on the Project Manager pod, double-click **policies.css**

The Styles dialog box opens.

❑ from the Paragraph group, select the **Normal** style
❑ from the **Formatting** area, scroll up the Font list and select the **Policies Font Set**

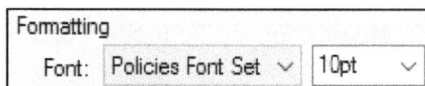

Formatting

Font: | Policies Font Set ∨ | 10pt ∨

❑ click the **OK** button

Because Verdana is most likely on your computer, there aren't any visual changes to your topics. But thanks to the font set, you no longer need to worry about missing fonts fouling up your topics when users view your Help topics.

Font Set Confidence Check

1. Edit the policies.css style again and attach the **Policies Font Set** to the Heading 1 and Heading 2 styles.

2. Open any topic and click within the text.

   On the Formatting toolbar, notice that the font being used by the paragraph is no longer a specific font. Instead, you see the name of the Font Set.

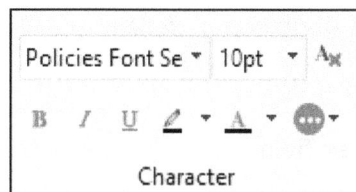

   Policies Font Se ▾ | 10pt ▾ | A✗

   B *I* U ✐ ▾ A ▾ ⬤ ▾

   Character

3. Save the project.

Character Styles

When you format selected text (such as making a word bold and maroon), you are using a technique known as **inline formatting**. Have you ever used the Bold tool on selected text in programs like Microsoft Word or PowerPoint? Ever made text italic? If so, then you've applied an inline format. Using inline formatting is easy, but it can be a bad habit because inline formatting is as stubborn as a mule. If you attach a different style sheet to a topic, the inline formatting does NOT go away.

Imagine having to manually move through a project and changing every occurrence of text that is bold and maroon to italic and navy. That would be a tough task if there were just a few dozen such instances. But a few hundred? Ouch!

Much like Paragraph styles, Character styles allow you to quickly format selected text. Unlike Paragraph styles (such as the Heading styles you used earlier in this module), Character styles can be applied only to selected text. Once applied, Character styles are easy to update (just like Paragraph styles).

Student Activity: Use Inline Formatting

1. Ensure that the **css** project is still open.

2. Format text using inline styles.

   ☐ if necessary, open the **Special Benefits** topic
   ☐ in the first full paragraph, highlight the words **21 years or older**
   ☐ on the **Edit** tab, **Character** group, click the **More** tool, and choose **Font**

   The Font dialog box opens.

   ☐ change the Font style to **Bold** and change the Font color to **Maroon**

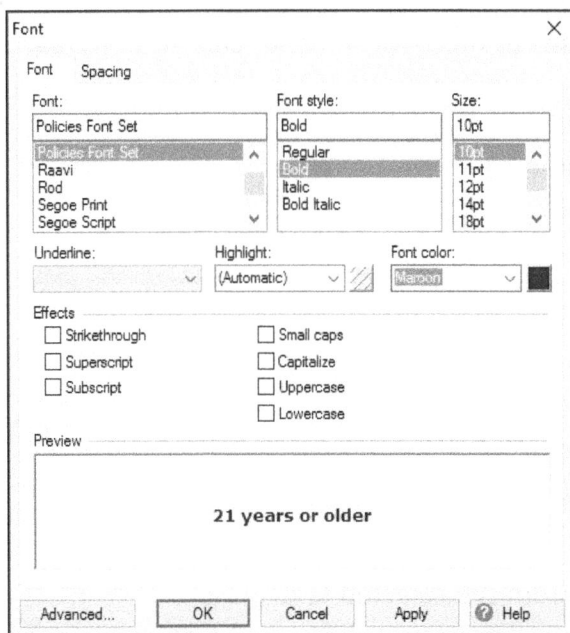

   ☐ click the **OK** button

If you deselect the text, you should notice that it has been formatted as bold and maroon.

> ·you·are·**21·years·or·older**·and·
> ig·with·your·hire·date.·The·plan·

Both of the formatting changes you just made did not use a style from your CSS (like you did when you formatted the heading "Special Benefits" with the Heading 1 style). The manual text formatting you just did is an example of inline formatting.

3. Assign a different style sheet to the topic.

   ❏ with the Special Benefits topic still open, click anywhere in the topic text
   ❏ on the **Edit** tab, **Assign Stylesheet** drop-down menu, choose **default.css**

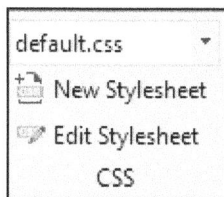

> default.css ▾
> +🗎 New Stylesheet
> 🖉 Edit Stylesheet
> CSS

The appearance of the text in the Special Benefits topic changes to match the specifications of the default style sheet. However, the inline formatting you applied is very stubborn and does not change. Is this a good thing or bad thing? If you need to quickly edit the appearance of inline formatting, it's a bad thing because you'd need to manually make the change every time you applied the specific formats.

4. Assign the policies style sheet to the topic.

   ❏ on the **Edit** tab, **Assign Stylesheet** drop-down menu, choose **policies.css**

5. Clear formatting.

   ❏ select the text **21 years or older**
   ❏ on the **Edit** tab, click **Clear Formatting**

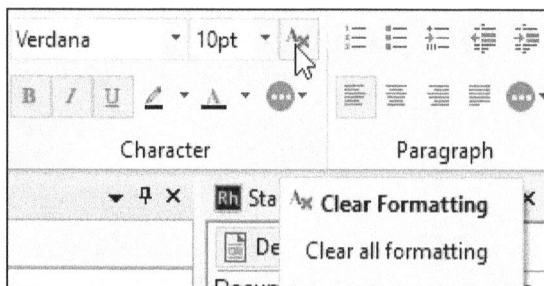

> | Verdana ▾ | 10pt ▾ | ᴬₓ | ≣ ≣ ≣ ≣ ≣ |
> | B I U ✎ ▾ A ▾ ⬤ ▾ | ▦ ▦ ▦ ▦ ⬤ ▾ |
> | Character | Paragraph |
>
> ▾ ⊞ ✕   Rh Sta ᴬₓ **Clear Formatting**   ✕
>   🖾 De   Clear all formatting
>   Docun

RoboHelp has removed all styling from the selected text.

6. Save your work.

Student Activity: Create a Character Style

1. Ensure that the **css** project is still open.

2. Open the Styles pod.

   ❑ on the **Edit** tab, click the **Style pod** tool

   The Styles and Formatting pod appears at the right side of the workspace.

   ❑ from the **Filter Styles** drop-down menu at the top of the Styles panel, choose **Character Styles**

3. Create a New Character Style.

   ❑ click the **Create New Style** tool and then choose **Character Style**

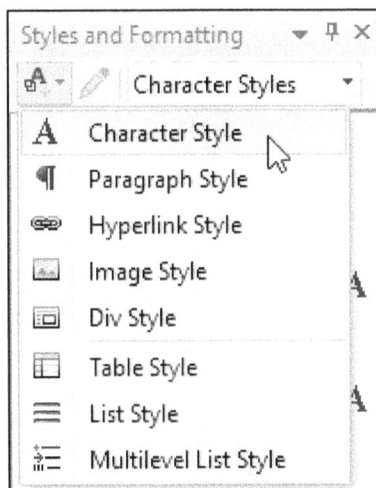

   The New Character Style dialog box opens.

   ❑ change the Style Name to **Emphasis**

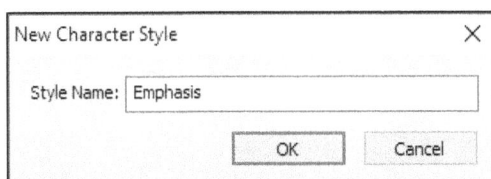

   ❑ click the **OK** button

   The Styles dialog box opens.

❏ change the Font to **Verdana**
❏ change the Font Size to **10 pt**
❏ change the Font Color to **Maroon**
❏ change the Font Style to **Bold**

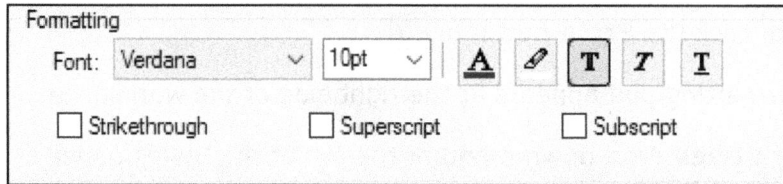

Formatting							
Font:	Verdana ⌄	10pt ⌄	**A**	✎	**T**	*T*	T̲
☐ Strikethrough		☐ Superscript			☐ Subscript		

❏ click the **OK** button

The new style is now listed on the Styles panel.

4. Use the Character Style.

❏ with the Special Benefits topic open, select **pre-tax contributions** from within the first paragraph
❏ from the list of Character Styles at the right, double-click **Emphasis**

The selected text takes on the formatting of the Emphasis style.

❏ from near the bottom of the first paragraph, highlight **$3000**
❏ from the list of Character Styles, double-click **Emphasis**

5. Edit a Character Style.

❏ with the Emphasis style selected, click the **Edit Selected Item** tool

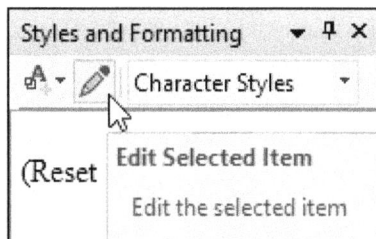

Styles and Formatting	▾ ⏸ ✕
ᵈA ▾ ✎	Character Styles ▾
(Reset	**Edit Selected Item**
	Edit the selected item

The Styles dialog box re-opens.

❏ change the font color to **Navy**
❏ click the **OK** button

Both instances where you applied the Emphasis style have been updated from maroon to navy.

6. Save and then close the project.

iCONLOGiC

"Skills and Drills" Learning

Module 4: Editing Content

In This Module You Will Learn About:

And You Will Learn To:

Spell Check

If you've used the spell check feature in a word processor, you will find RoboHelp's **Spell Check** features easy to use. One of my favorite Spell Check features is the ability to spell check all of the topics in your project at one time. This may not seem like a big deal, but remember that every topic in a project is a different HTML file. Without this feature, you would have to spell check one topic at a time. And there's an even higher level of Spell Check: you can check the entire project. If you elect to spell check the entire project, the following project components can be checked: all of the topics, the TOC, the Index, and the Glossary.

Student Activity: Use Spell Check

1. Open an existing RoboHelp project.

   ❒ from the **bottom left** of the Starter, click **Open Project**
   ❒ from within the **RoboHelp2017Data** folder, open **RoboHelpProjects**
   ❒ open the **content_editing** folder, and then open **contentediting.xpj**

2. Spell check a topic.

   ❒ from either the **Topic List** pod or the **Project Manager** pod, open the **About This Guide** topic

   There are a couple of typographic errors in the topic (a duplicate word and a misspelling).

   ❒ on the **Review** tab, **Proofing** group, click **Spell Check**

   The Spelling dialog box opens and an error is flagged—a duplicate word.

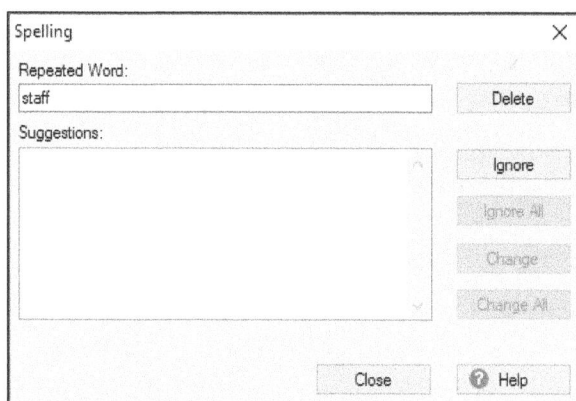

Spelling	✕
Repeated Word:	
staff	Delete
Suggestions:	
	Ignore
	Ignore All
	Change
	Change All
	Close ❓ Help

   ❒ click the **Delete** button

   The next flagged word is misspelled.

   ❒ select **immediately** from the list of Suggestions
   ❒ click the **Change** button

   You'll be notified that the spell check is complete.

   ❒ click the **OK** button

Spell Check Confidence Check

1. On the **Review** tab, click **Spell Check All Topics**.

2. Make any spelling corrections that you deem necessary (ignore any words or acronyms you are not sure about). Click the **Add** button for any words you'd like to have RoboHelp accept as properly spelled the next time you Spell Check.

3. On the **Review** tab, click **Spell Check Project**.

   The Spell Check Project menu item will go through your topics again, but this time the project's TOC entries are checked.

4. When you come across acronyms (such as FMLA), you can add them to the dictionary by clicking the **Add** button.

5. When the Spell Check is complete, on the **Review** tab, **Proofing** group, **Spelling Options**.

6. On the **Options** tab, click **Modify**.

7. If you used the **Add** button when you ran the Spell Check, the added words were placed on this dialog. If you want RoboHelp to no longer recognize a word, you can select the word and then click the **Delete** button.

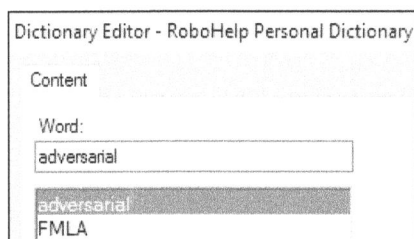

```
Dictionary Editor - RoboHelp Personal Dictionary

 Content

 Word:
 adversarial

 adversarial
 FMLA
```

8. Click the **OK** button, save, and close all topics. (You might also need to clean up your workspace because Spell Checking the project tends to open several pods.)

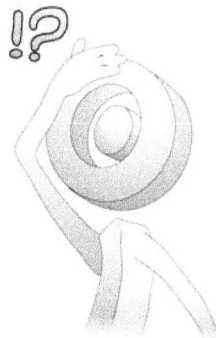

9. Save the project.

AutoCorrect

If you have specific words or phrases that you type frequently, RoboHelp's AutoCorrect feature will bring a smile to your face. Super Simplistic Solutions is simple to say... the words just seem to roll off the tongue. However, if your typing skills aren't sharp, Super Simplistic Solutions isn't much fun to type. Using the AutoCorrect feature, you can type **sss** and have the three letters change to Super Simplistic Solutions after you press [**spacebar**].

Student Activity: AutoCorrect Text

1. Ensure that the **contentediting** project is still open.

2. Set up AutoCorrect.

   ❑ open any topic
   ❑ On the **Review** tab, click **Spelling options**

   The Spelling Options dialog box opens.

   ❑ select the **AutoCorrect** tab
   ❑ in the **Replace** field, type **sss**
   ❑ in the **With** field, type **Super Simplistic Solutions** and then click the **Add** button

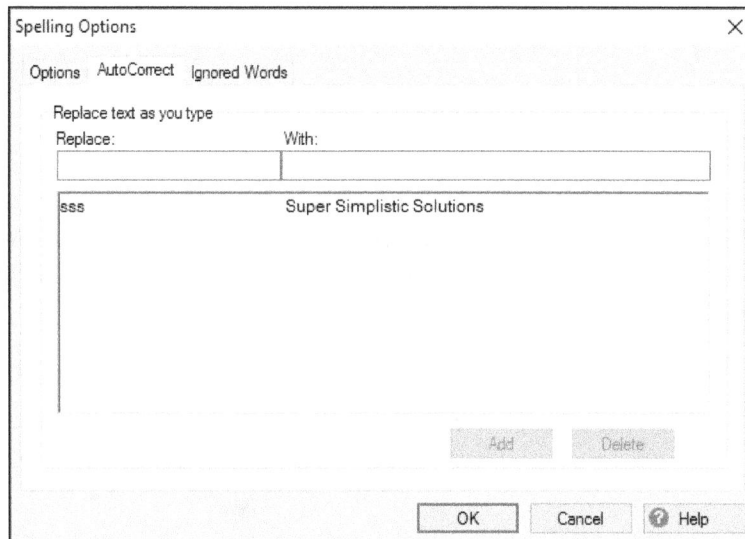

Spelling Options	✕
Options AutoCorrect Ignored Words	
Replace text as you type	
Replace: With:	
sss Super Simplistic Solutions	
Add Delete	
OK Cancel ❷ Help	

   ❑ click the **OK** button

3. Use the AutoCorrect feature.

   ❑ click at the end of the open topic and press [**enter**] to create a new line
   ❑ type **sss** and then press [**spacebar**]

   Thanks to the AutoCorrect entry you just set up, the letters **sss** are replaced with **Super Simplistic Solutions**.

4. Close the topic without saving.

The Thesaurus

We've had the same thesaurus for years. The book has gotten so much use, it's just about worn out. We'd be tempted to replace our thesaurus with a new one, but what's the point? Much like you'd expect to find in a word processor, RoboHelp has a built-in thesaurus that makes a hard-copy book obsolete.

Student Activity: Use the Thesaurus

1. Ensure that the **contentediting** project is still open.

2. Use the built-in Thesaurus.

   ❏ open the **About This Guide** topic
   ❏ highlight the word **assist** in the first sentence
   ❏ On the **Review** tab, **Proofing** group, click **Thesaurus**

   The Thesaurus dialog box opens.

   ❏ from the **Category** list, select **to give assistance <verb>**
   ❏ from the list of **Synonyms**, select **aid**

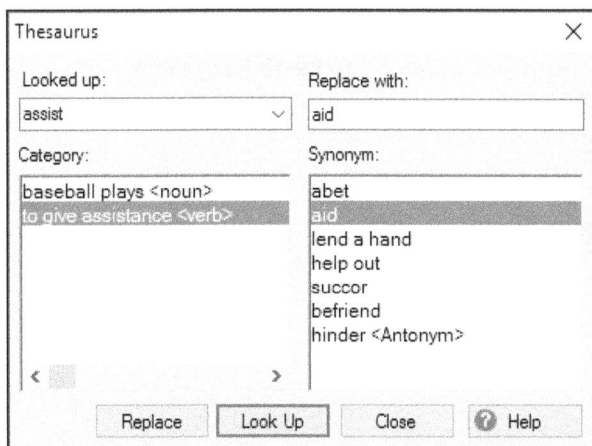

Thesaurus	✕
Looked up:	Replace with:
assist ⌄	aid
Category:	Synonym:
baseball plays <noun>	abet
to give assistance <verb>	aid
	lend a hand
	help out
	succor
	befriend
	hinder <Antonym>
‹ ›	
Replace Look Up Close ❷ Help	

   ❏ click the **Replace** button

   The Thesaurus closes and the word **assist** is replaced with **aid**.

3. Delete a few words from the topic.

   ❏ still in the **About This Guide** topic, delete the word **staff** in the first paragraph
   ❏ delete the first occurrence of **Super Simplistic Solutions** in the first paragraph

   The first paragraph should now read, "This guide has been developed to aid employees in understanding the general operation of Super Simplistic Solutions and its present policies and procedures."

Finding and Replacing Content

The Help System has a small problem that you need to fix, and it's in multiple topics. The company name, Super Simplistic Solutions, does not appear correctly in some of the topics. Someone used the acronym **SSS** instead of **Super Simplistic Solutions**. Thankfully, RoboHelp's Find and Replace in Files feature makes quick work out of what would otherwise be a laborious task.

Student Activity: Find and Replace Text

1. Save and close any open topics.

2. Open the Find and Replace pod.

   ❏ on the **Project** tab, click **Find and Replace**

   The Find and Replace pod appears at the far right of the window.

3. Go to the Find tab and specify what RoboHelp will find.

   ❏ in the **Find** field, **SSS**

4. Specify the current project as the project to be used during the search.

   ❏ from the **Look in** drop-down menu, choose **<Current Project>**

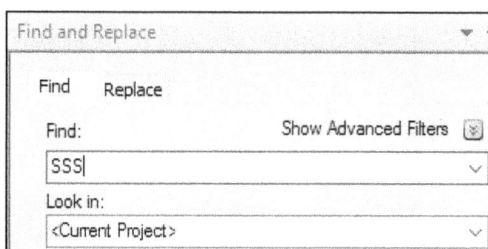

5. Find all occurrences of **SSS**.

   ❏ click the **Find All** button

   The project is searched and all occurrences of **SSS** are listed in the Find Results panel.

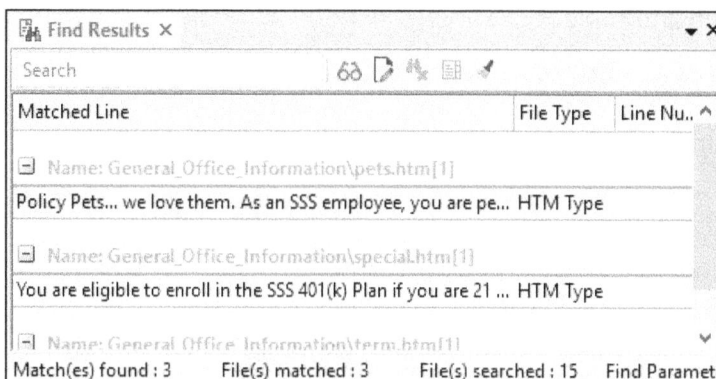

6. Replace all occurrences of **SSS** with **Super Simplistic Solutions**.

  ☐ go to the Replace tab.
  ☐ for the **Replace** field, fill in **Super Simplistic Solutions**
  ☐ from the **Look in** drop-down menu, choose **<Current Project>**
  ☐ click the **Replace All** button

You will be alerted that changes were made to three topics.

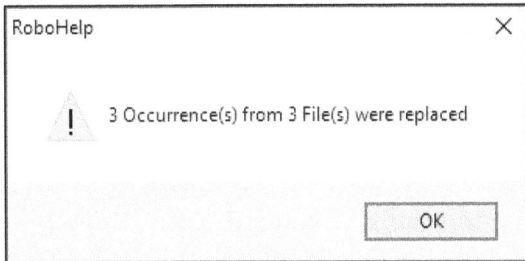

RoboHelp	✕
⚠ 3 Occurrence(s) from 3 File(s) were replaced	
	OK

  ☐ click the **OK** button

7. Save the project.

PDF Review

It's likely that at some point you'll be asked to share the content within your Help System with members of your team so that they can provide feedback. You could post your generated Help System on a web server somewhere, ask reviewers to use the Help System, and then provide feedback. The problem is what to do with and how to manage the feedback you are likely to receive.

RoboHelp's Create PDF for Review option lets you create a PDF that reviewers can open with the free Adobe Reader. Your reviewers can use Adobe Reader 9 or newer to add comments. Believe it or not, the PDF stores those comments, and you can import them directly into RoboHelp. Once the comments have been imported into RoboHelp, you can accept or reject the comments, just as if you were using the Track Changes feature in word processors like MS Word.

> **Note:** You will be able to create a PDF for Review only if **Acrobat 9 Professional** (or newer) is installed on your computer. If you don't have Acrobat Professional or newer, you can download a free trial from Adobe's website.

> **Another Note:** Once you've sent content from your RoboHelp project out for review via a PDF, don't make any changes to any of the content in your RoboHelp project until after you've imported the PDF comments. If you make changes to your project prior to importing the comments, the import process will likely fail.

Student Activity: Create a PDF for Review

1. Ensure that the **contentediting** project is still open.

2. Open the **Alcohol Policy** topic.

   Although you can send an entire project out for a PDF review, you'll just be sending this single topic out today. You'd like to find out if any of your colleagues have feedback or changes to the text.

3. Create a PDF for Review.

   ❑ on the **Review** tab, **PDF** group, click **Create PDF**

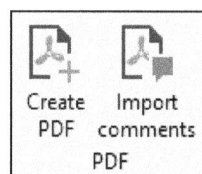

   The Create PDF for Review dialog box opens.

4. Ensure that the Project Manager files are displayed.

   ❑ from the **Show files from** area of the dialog box, select **Project Manager**

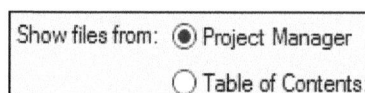

By default, every topic in the project is selected and would be sent for review. Because you want only a single topic to appear in the PDF, you need to deselect everything except the Alcohol Policy topic.

5. Select a specific file to be included in the review.

   ❐ from the top of the list of topics, remove the check mark from **All**
   ❐ from the **Drugs_and_Alcohol** folder, select **Alcohol Policy**

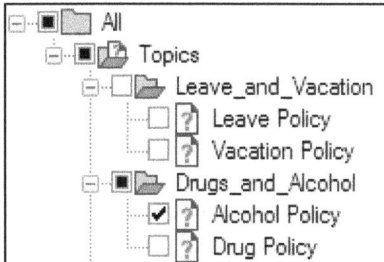

   ```
   ⊟ ▪■🗀 All
     ⊟ ▪■🗀 Topics
       ⊟ □🗀 Leave_and_Vacation
           □ ? Leave Policy
           □ ? Vacation Policy
       ⊟ ▪■🗀 Drugs_and_Alcohol
           ✔ ? Alcohol Policy
           □ ? Drug Policy
   ```

6. Select a PDF Setting.

   ❐ from the bottom of the dialog box, select **Save locally**

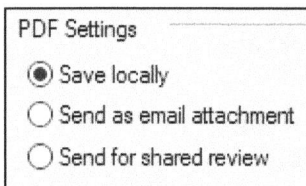

   ```
   PDF Settings
   ◉ Save locally
   ○ Send as email attachment
   ○ Send for shared review
   ```

7. Enable commenting.

   ❐ select **Enable commenting in Adobe Reader**

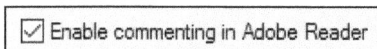

   ```
   ☑ Enable commenting in Adobe Reader
   ```

   Note: As mentioned earlier, you will be able to select **Enable commenting in Adobe Reader** only if you have Adobe Acrobat Professional installed on your computer. If you don't have Acrobat Professional, there is no need to finish creating the PDF. Instead, when instructed to add comments during the next step, use Acrobat or Adobe Reader to open **alcohol_review_with_annotations** from within the **content** folder of RoboHelp2017Data. You can add a few annotations to the file and then import them back into RoboHelp.

   ❐ from the **Save in** area, click the yellow folder at the right
   ❐ open the **RoboHelp2017Data** folder
   ❐ change the name of the PDF to **Alcohol** and click the **Save** button

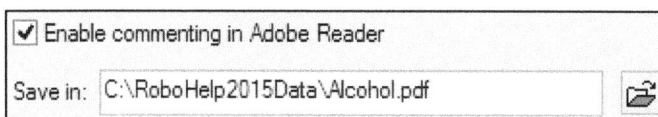

   ```
   ☑ Enable commenting in Adobe Reader
   Save in: C:\RoboHelp2015Data\Alcohol.pdf        📂
   ```

   ❐ click the **OK** button to create the PDF

❏ click **OK** to any alert dialog box that appears (there may be one or two)

Once the alcohol PDF has been created, you'll be prompted to give the review-enabled version of the PDF a name.

❏ name the review PDF **alcohol_review** and ensure it is saved to the RoboHelp2017DataData folder

Depending on what's installed on your computer, the PDF should open in either Adobe Acrobat or Adobe Reader.

8. Add some comments to the PDF.

❏ in the first sentence of the PDF, select the phrase **or condone** and its trailing space
❏ click the **Comment** button in the upper right of the PDF window
❏ from the **Annotations** area, select the **Strikethrough** tool

The selected text should now have a red line directly though the phrase.

not permit ~~or condone~~ intoxication

❏ still working in the first paragraph, select the word **duty**
❏ from the **Annotations** area, select the **Replace** tool

❏ type the word **work** into the **Comment panel** that appears

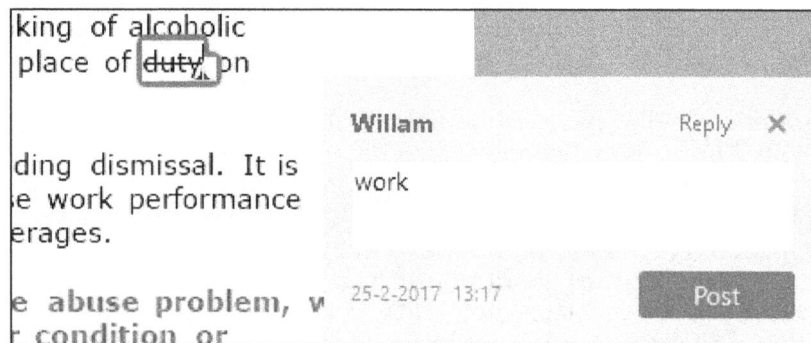

king of alcoholic
place of duty on

ding dismissal. It is
e work performance
erages.

e abuse problem, w
r condition or

Willam   Reply ✕

work

25-2-2017 13:17   Post

9. Save and close the PDF.

Student Activity: Import Comments From a PDF

1. Return to RoboHelp and ensure that the **contentediting** project is still open.

2. Import the comments/annotations from a PDF.

   ☐ on the **Review** tab, **PDF** group, click **Import Comments**

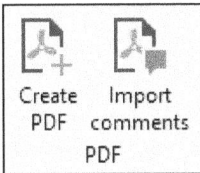

   The **Import comments from PDF** dialog box opens.

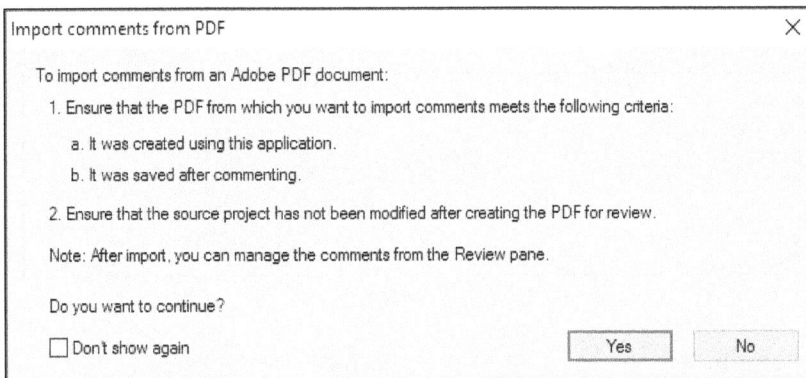

   Import comments from PDF   ✕

   To import comments from an Adobe PDF document:

   1. Ensure that the PDF from which you want to import comments meets the following criteria:

      a. It was created using this application.

      b. It was saved after commenting.

   2. Ensure that the source project has not been modified after creating the PDF for review.

   Note: After import, you can manage the comments from the Review pane.

   Do you want to continue?

   ☐ Don't show again   [Yes]   [No]

   ☐ review the information in the dialog box and then click the **Yes** button

   ☐ from the **RoboHelp2017Data** folder, open **alcohol_review.pdf** (or, if you were unable to add comments to your own PDF, open **alcohol_review_with_annotations** within the **content** folder of RoboHelp2017Data).

   The Import Comment Summary dialog box opens. This dialog box summarizes the number and type of comments that were added to the PDF.

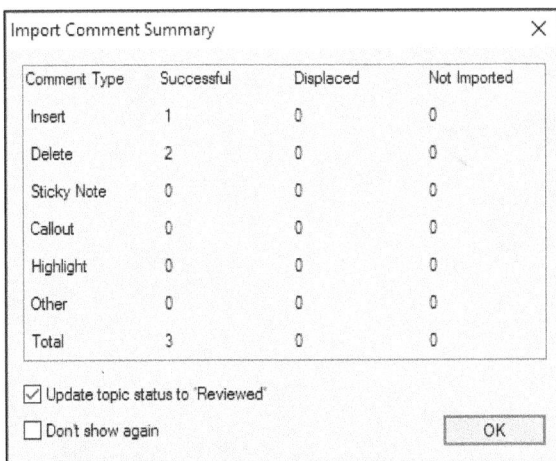

   Import Comment Summary   ✕

Comment Type	Successful	Displaced	Not Imported
Insert	1	0	0
Delete	2	0	0
Sticky Note	0	0	0
Callout	0	0	0
Highlight	0	0	0
Other	0	0	0
Total	3	0	0

   ☑ Update topic status to "Reviewed"
   ☐ Don't show again   [OK]

   ☐ click the **OK** button

3. Open the Alcohol Policy topic.

   The comments have been imported into the topic.

   > **Alcohol·Policy¶**
   >
   > Super·Simplistic·Solutions·does·not·permit·~~or·condone·~~
   > intoxication·or·drinking·of·alcoholic·beverages·on·the·premises·
   > of·the·company·or·at·an·employee's·assigned·place·of·
   > ~~duty~~work·on·company·time.¶

4. Show the Review Pane.

   ❑ on the **Project** tab, click **Pods** and choose **Review Pane**

	Reviewer	Modified	Details	Status	Type	Path
✖	Willam	25-2-2017 13:15:54	or condone		Deleted	Drugs_and_Alcohol
✖	Willam	25-2-2017 13:17:31	duty		Deleted	Drugs_and_Alcohol
↳	Willam	25-2-2017 13:18:06	work		Inserted	Drugs_and_Alcohol

5. Use the Review Pane to accept the comments from the reviewers.

   ❑ on the Review Pane, select the first comment (**or condone**)
   ❑ from the top of the Review Pane, click **Accept and Move to Next**

   > **Accept and Move to Next**
   >
   > Accept this change and move to the next change

Comments Confidence Check

1. Accept the remaining comments.

2. Save the project.

3. Close the project.

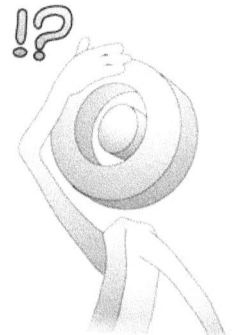

Module 5: Linking

In This Module You Will Learn About:

And You Will Learn To:

Linking to Content

You learned earlier how to import Word and FrameMaker documents into your project (beginning on page 32). When you imported the content, the text within the document was split (paginated) into new topics based on the styles used in the document and the way you mapped the Word styles (or FrameMaker formats) to RoboHelp project styles. After the import process, the original document has little value because its contents are copied into the RoboHelp project and become topics. Any changes you make to the imported text will not appear in the original Word document; any changes you make to the original Word document will not appear in RoboHelp. If you are alerted that significant changes have been made to the original Word document, your only choices are to make the identical changes to your content within RoboHelp or to delete the imported topic(s) from the RoboHelp project and re-import the updated content. Neither of these two scenarios is ideal.

If the Word or FrameMaker content you need to import into your RoboHelp project is a "moving target" and is constantly being updated by an author or subject matter expert (SME), consider linking to the source document instead of importing.

Student Activity: Link to a Word Document

1. Open an existing RoboHelp project.

   ❑ from the **bottom left** of the Starter, click **Open Project**
   ❑ from within the **RoboHelp2017Data** folder, open **RoboHelpProjects**
   ❑ open the **links** folder and then open **links.xpj**

2. Link to a Word document.

   ❑ on the **Project** tab, **Link** group, click **Word File**

   ```
   ⚙ Settings        ↻
   FM FM File
   W  Word File   Update
                     ▼
        Link
   ```

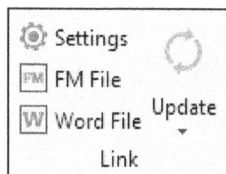

   ❑ from the **RoboHelp2017Data** folder, open the **content** folder
   ❑ open **HolidaySchedule.doc**

   The file is added to the **Project Files** folder on the **Project Manager** pod.

   ❑ on the **Project Manager** pod, open the **Project Files** folder

   The linked document appears on the Project Manager pod. There's a yellow warning mark on the icon because the content contained within the document has not yet been added to the project. You'll soon create content from the document. Prior to that, you need to set the conversion options for the Word document.

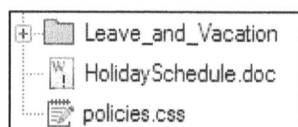

   ```
   ⊞ 📁 Leave_and_Vacation
      W  HolidaySchedule.doc
      📄 policies.css
   ```

3. Select a CSS for Style Mapping

   ❏ on the **Project** tab, **Link** group, click **Settings**
   ❏ select the **Import** tab
   ❏ from the **CSS for Style Mapping** drop-down menu, choose **policies.css**

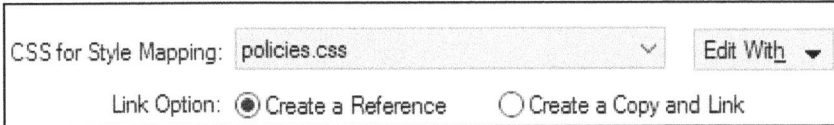

CSS for Style Mapping:	policies.css	∨	Edit With ▾
	Link Option: ⦿ Create a Reference ○ Create a Copy and Link		

   You created the policies.css file earlier in this book (page 54).

4. Edit the conversion settings for Word documents.

   ❏ from the **Word Document** area, to the right of **Edit the conversion settings for Word documents**, click the **Edit** button
   ❏ from the **Word Document Settings** area, double-click **Paragraph** to open the Paragraph group
   ❏ select **Heading 1**
   ❏ from the **RoboHelp Style** drop-down menu, choose **Heading 1**
   ❏ from the list of options in the middle of the dialog box, select **Pagination (Split into topics based on this style)**

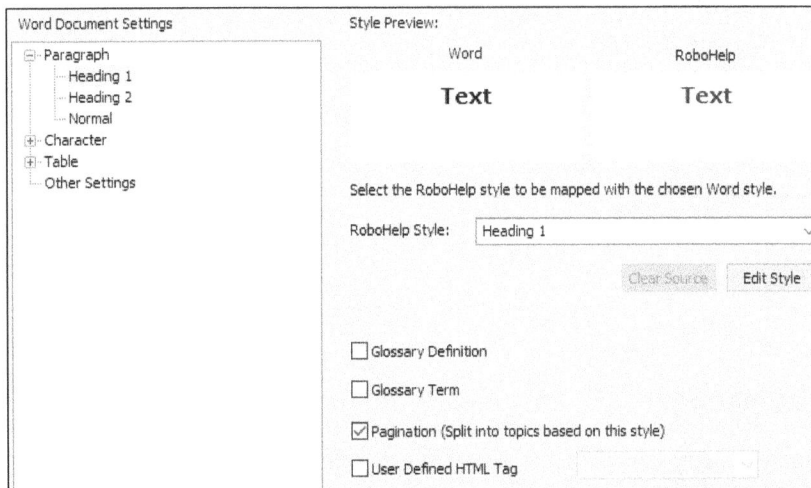

   Word Document Settings
   ```
   ⊟ Paragraph
       Heading 1
       Heading 2
       Normal
   ⊞ Character
   ⊞ Table
       Other Settings
   ```

   Style Preview:

Word	RoboHelp
Text	**Text**

   Select the RoboHelp style to be mapped with the chosen Word style.

   RoboHelp Style: Heading 1   ∨

   Clear Source   Edit Style

   ☐ Glossary Definition

   ☐ Glossary Term

   ☑ Pagination (Split into topics based on this style)

   ☐ User Defined HTML Tag

   As you learned on page 32, the Heading 1 style used in the Word document now uses a style of the same name in the RoboHelp project. In addition, selecting Pagination for the Heading 1 style forces RoboHelp to create a new topic every time it sees that a Heading 1 was used in the Word document.

   ❏ from the **Word Document Settings** area, select **Normal**
   ❏ from the **RoboHelp Style** area, select **Normal**
   ❏ click the **OK** button twice (once to close the Conversion settings dialog box and once to close the Project Settings dialog box)

5. Generate a Word document into a Help topic.

   ❏ on the **Project Manager pod**, right-click the reference to the **HolidaySchedule.doc** file and choose **Update > Generate**

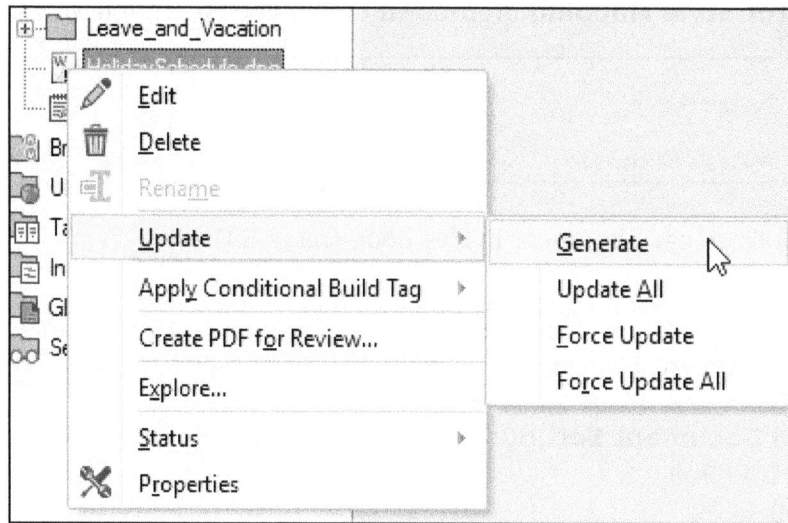

   Notice that there is now a **plus sign** to the left of the **Holiday Schedule.doc** reference—and the icon to the left of the reference is green (indicating that the linked content is up-to-date in the project).

   ❏ click the **plus sign** to the left of the HolidaySchedule.doc reference

   One topic has been created because only one paragraph in the Word document was using the Heading 1 style.

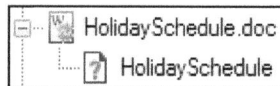

6. Open the new topic.

   ❏ on the **Project Manager** pod, double-click the **HolidaySchedule** topic

   The new topic has already been formatted using policies.css.

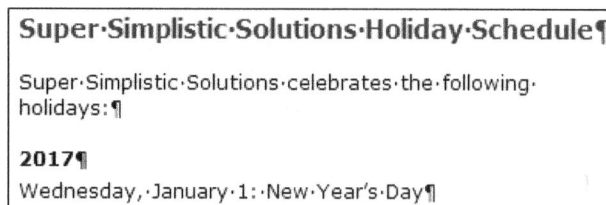

   Super·Simplistic·Solutions·Holiday·Schedule¶

   Super·Simplistic·Solutions·celebrates·the·following· holidays:¶

   2017¶
   Wednesday,·January·1:·New·Year's·Day¶

Student Activity: Edit a Linked Word Document

1. Edit the linked Word document.

   ☐ on the **Project Manager** pod, right-click **HolidaySchedule.doc** reference (not the HolidaySchedule topic) and choose **Edit**

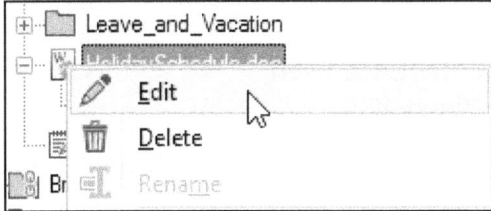

   ⊞ 📁 Leave_and_Vacation
   ⊟ 📄 HolidaySchedule.doc
       ✏️ **Edit**   ↖
       🗑️ **Delete**
   📇 Br ⌷ Rename

   The linked document opens in Microsoft Word.

   ☐ scroll down and change **2020** to **2019**

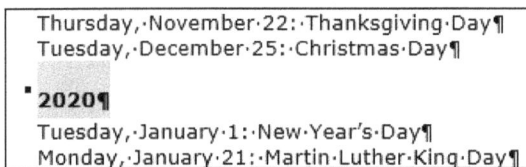

   > Thursday,·November·22:·Thanksgiving·Day¶
   > Tuesday,·December·25:·Christmas·Day¶
   >
   > ▪ **2020**¶
   > Tuesday,·January·1:·New·Year's·Day¶
   > Monday,·January·21:·Martin·Luther·King·Day¶

   ☐ highlight the **dates** under the 2017 heading
   ☐ select the **Home** tab and then click the **Bullets** tool

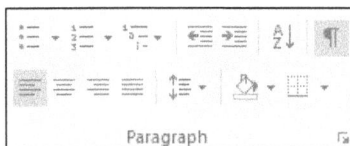

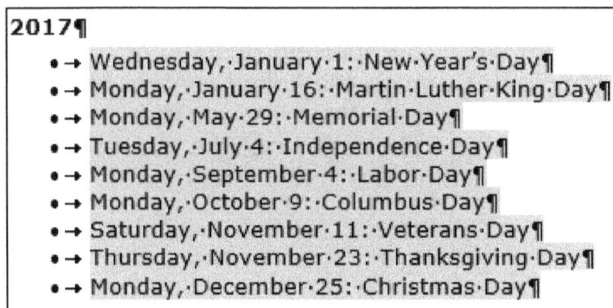

   > Paragraph

   > **2017**¶
   > • → Wednesday,·January·1:·New·Year's·Day¶
   > • → Monday,·January·16:·Martin·Luther·King·Day¶
   > • → Monday,·May·29:·Memorial·Day¶
   > • → Tuesday,·July·4:·Independence·Day¶
   > • → Monday,·September·4:·Labor·Day¶
   > • → Monday,·October·9:·Columbus·Day¶
   > • → Saturday,·November·11:·Veterans·Day¶
   > • → Thursday,·November·23:·Thanksgiving·Day¶
   > • → Monday,·December·25:·Christmas·Day¶

2. Save the Word document.

Word Linking Confidence Check

1. Apply bullets to the dates below the remaining date headings.

2. Save the document and then exit Microsoft Word.

3. Back in RoboHelp, observe the HolidaySchedule.doc reference. The yellow alert icon is back. This time, the icon is an indication that the source content has been changed and you need to bring the updates into RoboHelp.

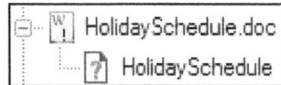

```
┌─ [W] HolidaySchedule.doc
│   [?] HolidaySchedule
```

4. Right-click the HolidaySchedule.doc reference and choose **Update > Update**.

5. If necessary, open the HolidaySchedule topic and notice that the changes you made in Word appear in the RoboHelp topic.

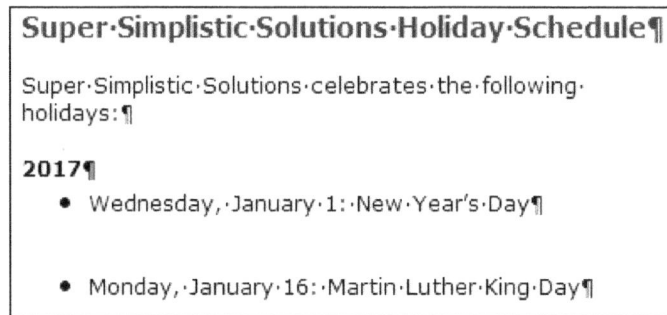

Super·Simplistic·Solutions·Holiday·Schedule¶

Super·Simplistic·Solutions·celebrates·the·following· holidays:¶

2017¶
- Wednesday,·January·1:··New·Year's·Day¶

- Monday,·January·16:··Martin·Luther·King·Day¶

---

6. Close the topic.

Note: When you link content from Word to RoboHelp (instead of importing the content), you should not change the linked content from within RoboHelp (the edits should be made in Word like you did above). If you edit the linked content in RoboHelp, you'll be alerted that your changes will be lost the next time the linked document is updated.

Hyperlinks

Hyperlinks give your users the ability to easily jump from one location to another. There are several types of hyperlinks you can create including standard links (links that typically jump from one Help topic to another), web address links (links that open a website or resource), email links (links that start the user's mail system, such as Outlook, and send an email to a recipient you specify), and links to a Multimedia file or other external file (such as a PDF or Word document not imported into or directly within the RoboHelp project).

Student Activity: Insert Hyperlinks

1. Ensure that the **links** project is still open.

2. Open the **Drug Policy** topic.

3. Add text to a topic.

   ☐ in the second paragraph ("If you are having difficulties resulting..."), click after the word **drug**
   ☐ press [**spacebar**] and then type **or alcohol**

   The sentence should now read "If you are having difficulties resulting from drug or alcohol use, Super Simplistic Solutions may request that you enter a rehabilitation program."

   > If·you·are·having·difficulties·resulting·from·drug·or·alcohol·use,·Super·Simplistic·
   > you·enter·a·rehabilitation·program.·Failure·to·enter·a·rehabilitation·program·or·to
   > constitutes·grounds·to·terminate·your·employment.¶

4. Insert a hyperlink to another topic in the project.

   ☐ double-click the word **alcohol** that you just typed (to highlight the word)
   ☐ on the **Insert** tab, **Links** group, click **Hyperlink**

   The Hyperlink dialog box opens. The topics in the Drugs_and_Alcohol folder appear in the **Select destination (file or URL)** area.

   ☐ from the **Select destination (file or URL)** area, select **Alcohol Policy**

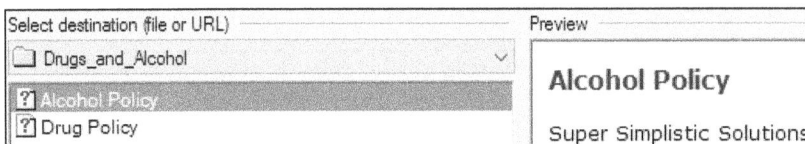

Select destination (file or URL)	Preview
📁 Drugs_and_Alcohol ⌄	**Alcohol Policy**
❓ Alcohol Policy	
❓ Drug Policy	Super Simplistic Solutions

   ☐ click the **OK** button and then deselect the text

   Now that you have made the word "alcohol" a hyperlink, the text takes on the traditional appearance of linked text (**blue** with an **underline**).

   > ·drug·or·alcohol·use,·Sup
   > to·enter·a·rehabilitation

5. Insert another link.

   ☐ press [**ctrl**] and click the text "alcohol" to open the **Alcohol Policy** topic
   ☐ at the end of the topic text, click after the last word and press [**enter**] to add a new paragraph
   ☐ change the style of the new paragraph to **Normal**
   ☐ type **See also:**
   ☐ find the **Drug policy** topic in the Project Manager pod
   ☐ drag and drop the topic after the text **See also:**

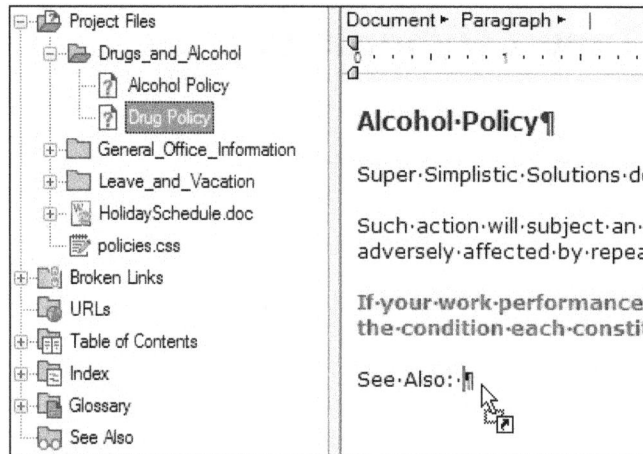

   Your project now has two hyperlinks to existing topics.

   Note: You can also insert a hyperlink into a topic by dragging a topic from the Topic List pod into a topic.

6. Save and close all topics.

7. Generate the Primary Output and test the hyperlinks.

   ☐ press [**ctrl**] [**m**] to Generate WebHelp
   ☐ click the **View Result** button when prompted
   ☐ open the **Drugs and Alcohol** book and then click the **Drug Policy** topic

   The word "alcohol" is blue and underlined, an indication that the text is a hyperlink.

   > If you are having difficulties resulting from drug or alcohol use, Super Simplistic Solutions may request that you enter a rehabilitation program. Failure to enter a rehabilitation program or to complete the program constitutes grounds to terminate your employment.

   ☐ click the word **alcohol**

   You should be sent to the Alcohol Policy topic.

   ☐ click the words **Drug Policy** at the bottom of the Alcohol Policy window

   You should be sent to the Drug Policy topic.

8. Close the browser and return to the RoboHelp project.

Hyperlinks Confidence Check

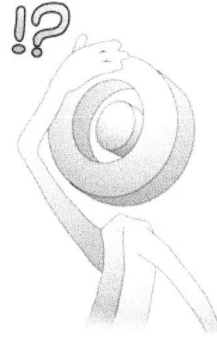

1. Open the **Payroll Policy** topic.

2. Add the following new paragraph at the end of the topic:
   See also: Overtime Policy.

3. Highlight the phrase "Overtime Policy" and Hyperlink the text to the following topic: **Overtime Policy**.

   Note: The keyboard shortcut to insert a Hyperlink on selected text is [**ctrl**] [**k**].

4. Open the **Overtime Policy** topic and add the following new paragraph at the end of the topic: **See also: Payroll Policy**.

5. Highlight the phrase "Payroll Policy" and Hyperlink the text to the following topic: **Payroll Policy**.

6. Save and close all of the topics.

7. Generate (remember, you can always press [**ctrl**] [**m**] to quickly Generate the project) and then View the results.

8. Open the **General Office Information** book. Test your new links. (You added links to the following topics: **Payroll Policy** and **Overtime Policy**.)

9. Close the browser when finished and return to the RoboHelp project.

10. *And now try this:* Let's assume that you made a mistake while creating one of your links. (Hey, it happens.) You are probably wondering how you would make changes to your links. Here's how:

    Open any topic with a link (you added a link in the **Payroll Policy** topic).

    Right-click the link to display a shortcut menu.

    Select **Hyperlink Properties** from the shortcut menu. You now could select the correct topic from your list of topics. If you made a mistake during this Confidence Check, spend a moment or two making corrections. If everything is perfect, click the Cancel button.

    And one more thing: Don't actually do this right now, but if you want to remove an unwanted link, find the unwanted hyperlink, right-click, and choose **Remove Hyperlink.**

11. Open the **Payroll Policy** topic.

12. Click after the Hyperlink to Overtime Policy and press [**spacebar**].

13. Type **or Vacation Policy**.

14. Hyperlink the words **Vacation Policy** to the Vacation Policy topic. (Vacation Policy is inside the **Leave_and_Vacation** folder.)

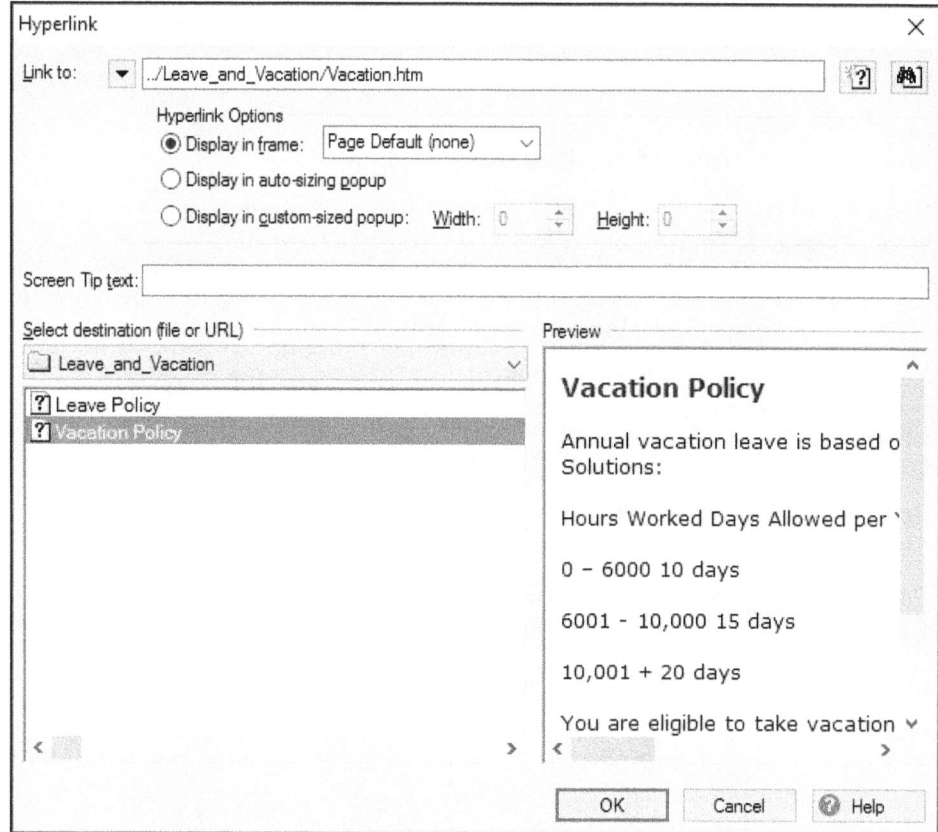

Hyperlink							✕

Link to: ▼ ../Leave_and_Vacation/Vacation.htm [?] [🔍]

Hyperlink Options
- ⦿ Display in frame: Page Default (none) ⌄
- ○ Display in auto-sizing popup
- ○ Display in custom-sized popup: Width: 0 ⤒ Height: 0 ⤒

Screen Tip text: [   ]

Select destination (file or URL)

📁 Leave_and_Vacation ⌄

[?] Leave Policy
[?] Vacation Policy

Preview

Vacation Policy

Annual vacation leave is based o
Solutions:

Hours Worked Days Allowed per `

0 – 6000 10 days

6001 - 10,000 15 days

10,001 + 20 days

You are eligible to take vacation ⌄

[OK] [Cancel] [?] Help

15. Save and close all topics.

16. Generate and then View the Primary Output.

17. Test your newest link in the Payroll Policy topic.

18. Close the browser when you are finished.

19. Return to the RoboHelp project.

20. Save and close all topics.

21. Keep the **links** project open.

Bookmarks

You can use bookmarks to create links to specific locations within a topic. For instance, you can create a bookmark in the middle of a large topic. You can create a link in a topic that jumps a user into the large topic and to the location you specify when you insert the bookmark. You can link to a bookmark from any other topic in your project or from an Index or TOC entries.

Student Activity: Insert Bookmarks

1. Ensure that the **links** project is still open.

2. Using the Topic List pod, open the **Termination Policy** topic.

3. Insert a Bookmark.

   ❏ at the top of the topic, click to the left of the word **Resignation** (do not highlight the word—click just in front of the word)
   ❏ on the **Insert** tab, **Links** group, click **Bookmark**

   The Bookmark dialog box opens. By default, the first line to the right of your insertion point always is used as the name of a new Bookmark. The name Resignation is appropriate, so there is no need to change the default name.

   ```
   Bookmark

   Name:  Resignation
   ```

   ❏ click the **OK** button

   A white flag appears to the left of the word Resignation. This is a visual indicator that a bookmark has been inserted.

   ```
   ⚐Resignation¶

   If·you·voluntarily·terminate·your·employment·with
   provide·a·written·statement·of·resignation.··The·cd
   ```

4. Insert a second Bookmark.

   ❏ click to the left of the second heading: **Disciplinary Policies and Procedures**
   ❏ on the **Insert** tab, **Links** group, click **Bookmark**

   ```
   Name:  Disciplinary_Policies_and_Procedures
   ```

   ❏ click the **OK** button

Bookmarks Confidence Check

1. Add a third bookmark in the Termination Policy topic for the last heading in the topic: **Unemployment Insurance**.

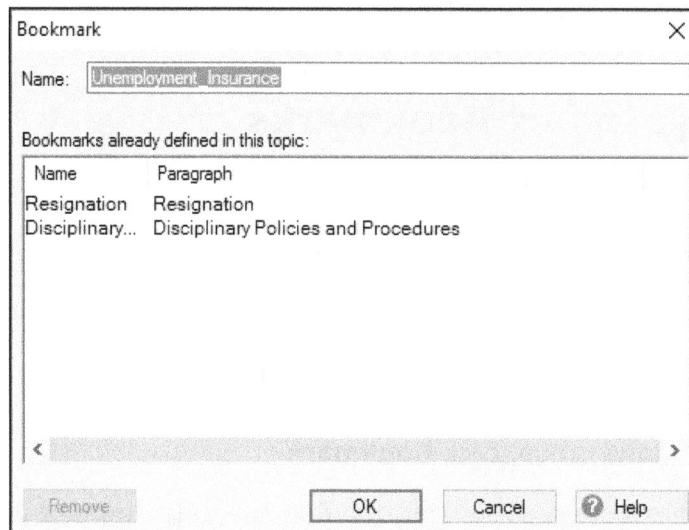

```
Bookmark                                              ×

Name:   [Unemployment_Insurance]

Bookmarks already defined in this topic:

 Name           Paragraph
 Resignation    Resignation
 Disciplinary... Disciplinary Policies and Procedures




 <                                                  >

 [Remove]              [    OK    ] [  Cancel  ] [? Help]
```

2. Still in the Termination Policy topic, click after the main heading (**Termination Policy**) and press [**enter**] to add a line between the main heading and subheading **Resignation**.

3. Type **Our Termination Policy consists of three main areas: Resignation, Disciplinary Policies and Procedures and Unemployment Insurance.**

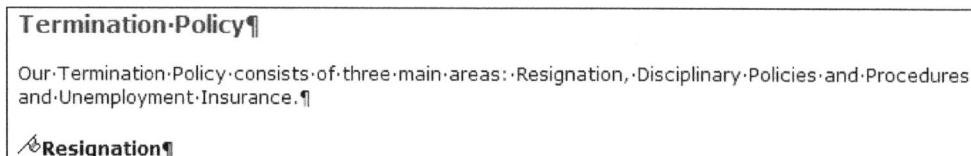

```
Termination·Policy¶

Our·Termination·Policy·consists·of·three·main·areas:·Resignation,·Disciplinary·Policies·and·Procedures·
and·Unemployment·Insurance.¶

⚓Resignation¶
```

4. Highlight the word **Resignation** in the text that you just typed.

5. Insert a Hyperlink.

6. From the **Select destination (file or URL)** area, select the bookmark **Resignation** from the Termination Policy topic and then click the **OK** button.

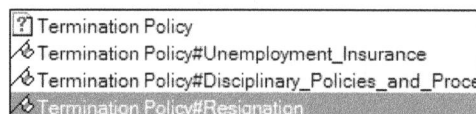

```
[?] Termination Policy
⚓Termination Policy#Unemployment_Insurance
⚓Termination Policy#Disciplinary_Policies_and_Proce
⚓Termination Policy#Resignation
```

7. Link the text **Disciplinary Policies and Procedures** and **Unemployment Insurance** to their respective bookmarks.

8. On the **Project** tab, **View** group, click **View item** to preview the topic.

9. Test the bookmarks (by clicking any of the links at the top of the page).

10. When finished, close the preview and then save and close all open topics.

Topic TOCs

In the previous exercise, we manually added bookmarks and links. While it is very useful to be able to jump to a specific section in a topic, can be a lot of work to manually create all the links. Fortunately, RoboHelp has a trick up its sleeve that will make linking easier: Topic TOCs. Topic TOCs allow you to display heading content directly within a topic. The content within the Topic TOCs is made up of hyperlinks, providing users not only a quick overview of longer topics but easy navigation to the information.

Student Activity: Add a Topic TOC

1. Ensure that the **links** project is still open.

2. Add a Topic TOC Placeholder within a topic.

   ☐ open the **Special Benefits** topic

   This is one of the longest topics in the Help System and has been formatted using Heading 1 and Heading 2 styles. You will use the contents of the Heading 2 styles in the Topic TOC.

   ☐ click in front of the **401(k) Plan** heading
   ☐ on the **Insert** tab, **Page Design** group, click **Topic TOC**

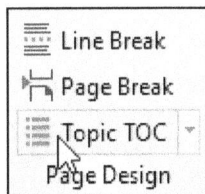

   The Topic TOC Options dialog box opens.

   ☐ click the **OK** button to accept the default settings

   The Topic TOC appears below the Special Benefits heading.

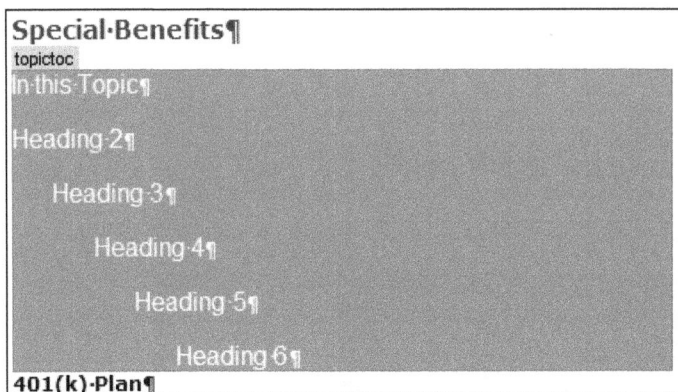

3. Format the Topic TOC.

❏ double-click the **Topic TOC** (inside the blue area)

The Topic TOC Options dialog box reopens.

❏ from the **Structure** area, select **Bulleted List**
❏ from the **Bulleted List** drop-down menu, ensure **default** is selected

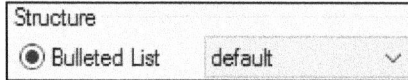

> Structure
> ⦿ Bulleted List   default   ∨

❏ at the bottom of the dialog box, **Format** area, **Apply formatting to** drop-down menu, ensure **Topic TOC** is selected
❏ change the Font to **Verdana**
❏ change the Font Size to **10pt**

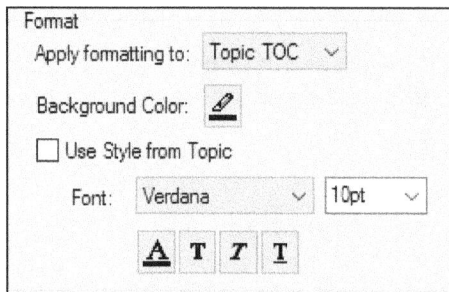

> Format
> Apply formatting to: Topic TOC ∨
>
> Background Color: ✎
> ☐ Use Style from Topic
> Font: Verdana ∨   10pt ∨
>
> **A** T *T* T

❏ at the bottom of the dialog box, **Format** area, **Apply formatting to** drop-down menu, choose **Caption**
❏ change the Font to **Verdana** and the Font Size to **11pt**

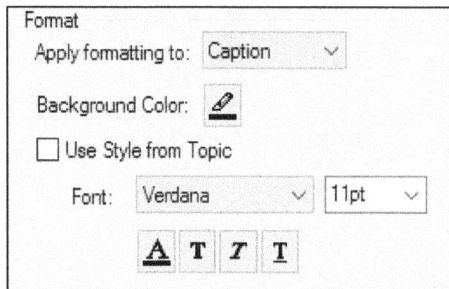

> Format
> Apply formatting to: Caption ∨
>
> Background Color: ✎
> ☐ Use Style from Topic
> Font: Verdana ∨   11pt ∨
>
> **A** T *T* T

❏ click the **OK** button

The Topic TOC should look like the picture below.

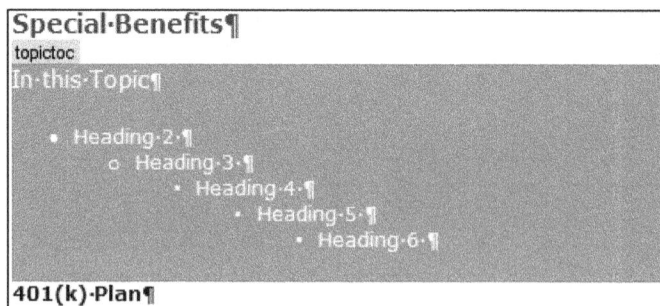

> **Special·Benefits¶**
> topictoc
> In·this·Topic¶
>
> • Heading·2·¶
>   ○ Heading·3·¶
>   • Heading·4·¶
>   • Heading·5·¶
>   • Heading·6·¶
>
> **401(k)·Plan¶**

4. Test the Topic TOC.

   ☐ on the **Project** tab, **View** group, click **View Item**

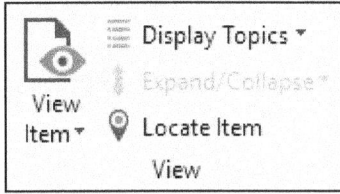

View Item ▾	Display Topics ▾
	Expand/Collapse ▾
	Locate Item
	View

   The Topic TOC, including its links, appears within the topic. You can click any of the links to jump around the topic. You can also click the word **Hide** to collapse the Topic TOC. Using this technique replaces the need to manually add bookmarks and links (you learned about that on page 87).

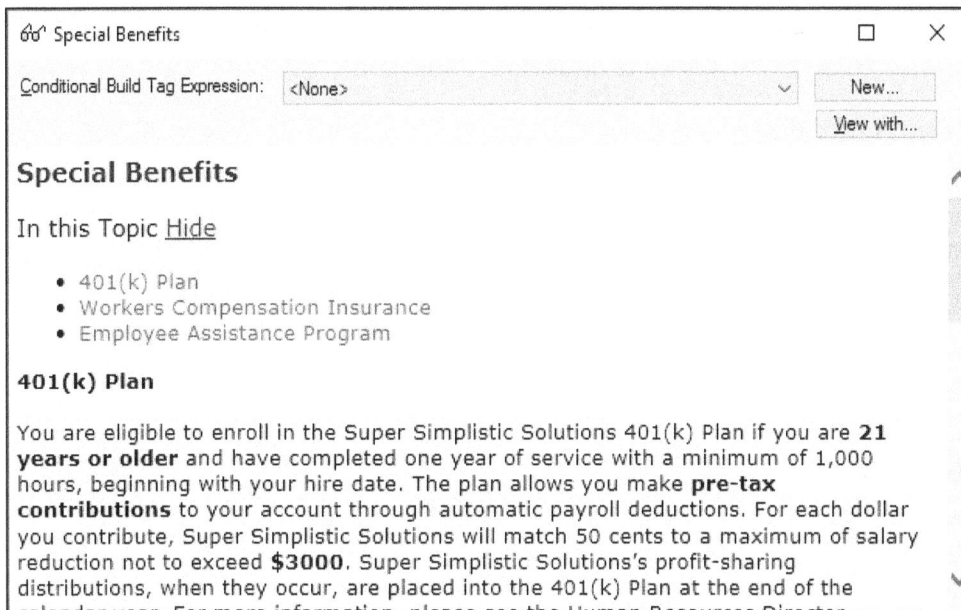

👓 Special Benefits	□ ✕
Conditional Build Tag Expression: <None> ⌄	New...
	View with...

   ## Special Benefits

   In this Topic <u>Hide</u>

   - 401(k) Plan
   - Workers Compensation Insurance
   - Employee Assistance Program

   401(k) Plan

   You are eligible to enroll in the Super Simplistic Solutions 401(k) Plan if you are **21 years or older** and have completed one year of service with a minimum of 1,000 hours, beginning with your hire date. The plan allows you make **pre-tax contributions** to your account through automatic payroll deductions. For each dollar you contribute, Super Simplistic Solutions will match 50 cents to a maximum of salary reduction not to exceed **$3000**. Super Simplistic Solutions's profit-sharing distributions, when they occur, are placed into the 401(k) Plan at the end of the

5. Close the preview.

Popup Hyperlinks

The hyperlinks you have added to topics have taken users from one topic to another. If you want users to hyperlink to a small window within a topic, popups are just the ticket. When users click the hyperlink, the content they link to can appear in either an auto-sizing popup (which is only as big as necessary to display the content) or a custom-sized popup (which appears in a window width that you control).

Student Activity: Insert Auto-Sizing Popups

1. Ensure that the **links** project is still open.

2. Insert an auto-sizing popup.

   ❑ open the **About This Guide** topic
   ❑ highlight the word **president** (the last word in the topic)
   ❑ on the **Insert** tab, **Links** group, click **Hyperlink**

   The **Hyperlink** dialog box opens.

   ❑ in the upper right of the dialog box, click **New Topic** 🔲

   The New Topic dialog box opens.

   ❑ change the Topic Title to **Our President**
   ❑ ensure that the File Name is **Our_President**

   ❑ click the **OK** button

   You should be back in the Hyperlink dialog box.

   ❑ from the Hyperlink Options area, select **Display in auto-sizing popup**

   ❑ click the **OK** button

3. Save the project.

Popup Hyperlink Confidence Check

1. Open the new **Our President** Topic.

2. Highlight the text "Type topic text here" and replace it with **The president of Super Simplistic Solutions is Biff Bifferson. Our tireless leader can be reached by dialing extension 123 or by sending an Email.**

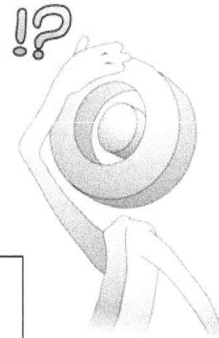

Our·President¶

The·president·of·Super·Simplistic·Solutions·is·Biff·Bifferson.·Our·tireless·
leader·can·be·reached·by·dialing·extension·123·or·by·sending·an·Email.¶

3. Select the text **Email** that you just typed.

4. Press **[ctrl] [k]** to insert a hyperlink.

5. From the **Link to** drop-down menu, choose **Email**.

6. Type **biffbiff@supersimplisticsolutions.com**.

Link to:	▼	mailto:biffbiff@supersimplisticsolutions.com

When clicked by your users, the Email link starts the user's email application and addresses the email to **biffbiff@supersimplisticsolutions.com**.

7. Click the **OK** button.

8. With the Our President topic still open, go to the **Edit** tab and use the **Assign Stylesheet** drop-down menu to select **policies.css**.

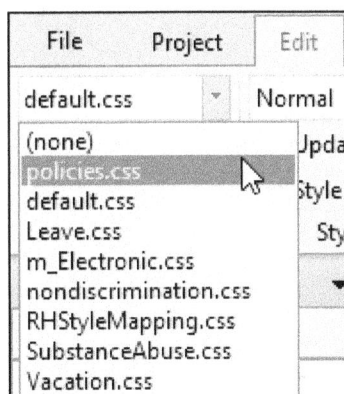

File	Project	Edit
default.css	▼	Normal
(none)		Upda
policies.css		Style
default.css		Sty
Leave.css		
m_Electronic.css		▼
nondiscrimination.css		
RHStyleMapping.css		
SubstanceAbuse.css		
Vacation.css		

9. Save the project and then close all topics.

10. Open the **About This Guide** topic.

11. Use the **View Item** tool to Preview the topic. (**Edit** tab, **View** group)

    Notice that the word "president" at the bottom of the topic is a hyperlink.

12. Click the hyperlink text to see the new popup.

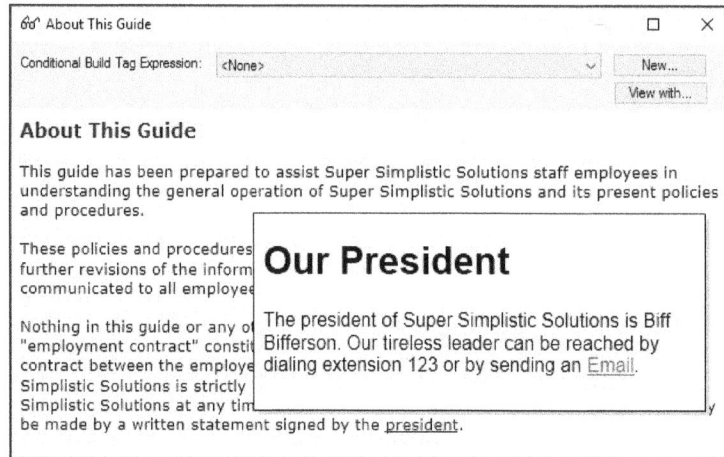

13. Click the popup to make it go away.

14. Close the preview.

15. Open the **Overtime Policy** topic.

16. Highlight the words **Human Resources** (in the "Authorization for Employees' Earned Compensatory Time" paragraph near the end of the topic).

17. On the **Insert** tab, **Links** group, click **Hyperlink**.

18. Select **Display in auto-sizing popup** and then click the **New Topic** button.

19. Give the topic the following Topic Title: **Human Resources**.

20. Give the file the following File Name: **hr** and then click the **OK** button.

Your Hyperlink options should now look like this (you can click the **OK** button when you are finished):

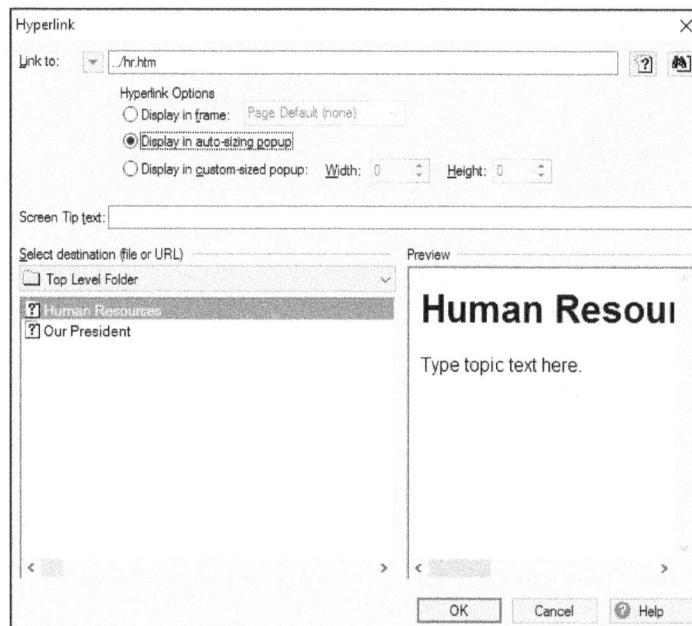

21. Open the Human Resources topic.

22. Replace the topic text with **Our Human Resources Director is Brandy McNeill at extension 552.**

> **Human·Resources¶**
>
> Our·Human·Resources·Director·is·Brandy·McNeill·at·extension·552.¶

23. Open the **Electronic Communications Policy** topic.

24. Scroll down and click after the last paragraph in the topic and press [**enter**] to add a new paragraph.

25. Type **See also: Information Services Director or Our Webmaster.**

26. Insert an auto-sizing popup hyperlink to the words "Information Services Director" that links to a New Topic with the Topic Title **Information Services Director** and has the following File Name: **IS.htm.**

Topic Title:	Information Services Directory	
Variables:	<Select a Variable to Insert in Topic Title>	Insert
File Name:	IS	

27. Open the new topic, **Information Services Director**, that you just created.

28. Replace the topic text with **Our Information Services Director is Travis DonBullian at extension 33.**

29. If necessary, reopen the **Electronic Communications Policy** topic.

30. Insert an auto-sizing popup hyperlink to the words "Our Webmaster" that links to a New Topic with the Topic Title **Webmaster** and has the following File Name: **webmaster.htm**.

General	✓ Status	[?] Appearance	Index	See Also	Advanced

Topic Title:	Webmaster	
Variables:	<Select a Variable to Insert in Topic Title>	Insert
File Name:	webmaster.htm	

31. Open the new topic, **Webmaster**, that you just created.

32. Replace the topic text with **Our Webmaster is Sandra Stimson. She can be reached at extension 34.**

33. Save and close all of the topics.

34. Generate and View the WebHelp layout.

35. Test some of the links and popups you've added.

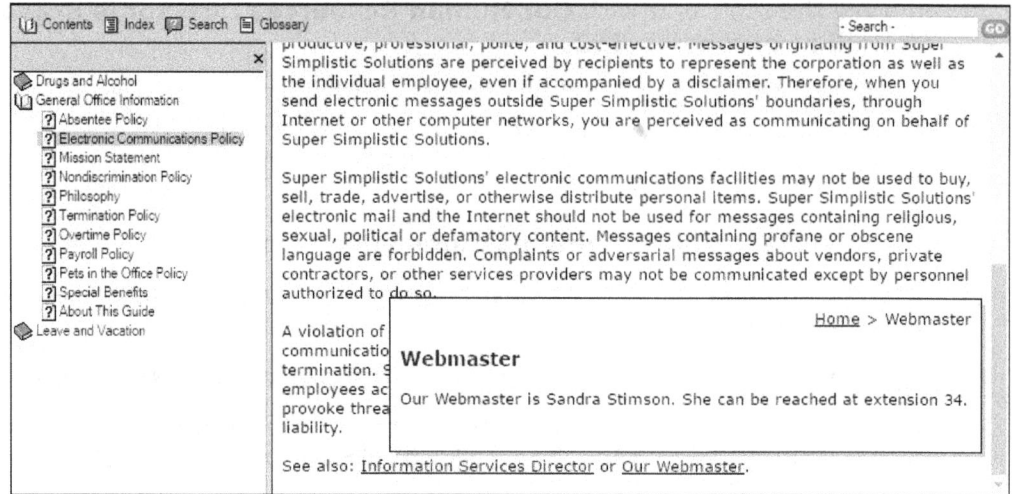

36. Close the web browser and return to the RoboHelp project.

Custom-Sized Popups

The popups added to the project have all been auto-sized—they will always be as big or small as they need to be to accommodate the topic contents. If you want your popups to be a specific size, you can create a custom-sized popup.

Student Activity: Insert Custom-Sized Popups

1. Ensure that the **links** project is still open.

2. Create a custom-sized popup link.

   ☐ open the **About This Guide** topic
   ☐ at the bottom of the topic, double-click the link you created to the word **president**

   The Popup dialog box opens.

   ☐ from the Hyperlink Options area, select **Display in custom-sized popup**
   ☐ change the Width to **325** and the Height to **375**

   ◉ Display in custom-sized popup: Width: 325 ▲▼   Height: 375 ▲▼

   ☐ click the **OK** button

3. Use a keyboard shortcut to Preview the topic.

   ☐ press [**ctrl**] [**w**]

4. Test the custom-sized popup.

   ☐ click the link to **president**

   Notice the size of your popup is 325 x 375 pixels. It's too large, but this demonstrates the kind of control you have over the appearance of popup windows.

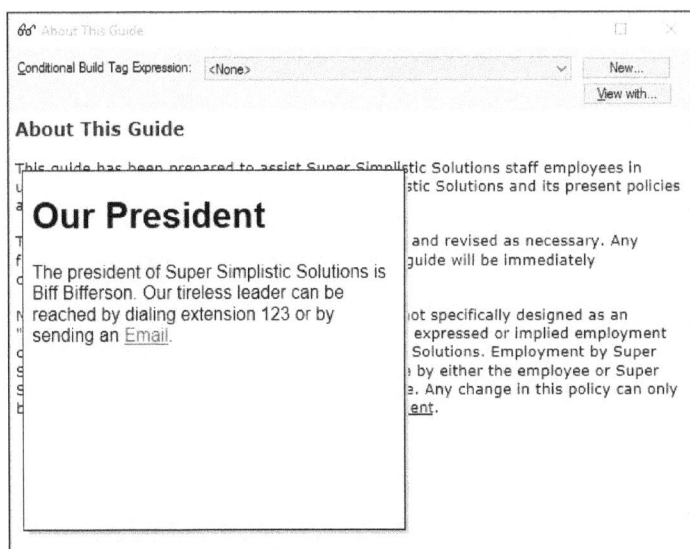

5. Close the preview window.

6. Return the link to an auto-sizing popup.

    ☐ still in the **About This Guide** topic, double-click the link to the word **president**

    ☐ select **Display in auto-sizing popup**

    ⊙ Display in auto-sizing popup

    ☐ click the **OK** button

7. Save the project.

8. Close all of the topics.

Text Popups

You learned how to create links to topics that force the topic to appear in a popup window (see page 92). Because the links point to topics in your project, the popup windows can be formatted using Style Sheets and contain images and multimedia effects. However, if you want to create a popup link to simple text that is not contained within a topic, you can create Text Popups. Because Text Popups do not link to project topics, you are limited to the amount of formatting you can control. In addition, Text Popups cannot contain images, audio, or other multimedia effects. One appropriate use of Text Popups would be for glossary terms, where you want the definition of a term to pop up when users click the term.

Student Activity: Insert a Text Popup

1. Ensure that the **links** project is still open.

2. Insert a Text Popup in a topic.

   ❑ open the **Electronic Communications Policy** topic
   ❑ from the middle of the last paragraph, highlight the word **indemnify**
   ❑ on the **Insert** tab, **Links** group, click **Text Popup**

   A yellow box appears near the word you selected.

   ❑ type **Compensate you for harm or loss.** into the yellow box
   ❑ click outside of the yellow box to close the Text Popup

3. Save your work.

4. Preview the topic and test the Text-only Popup.

   ❑ press [**ctrl**] [**w**]
   ❑ click the link to **indemnify** near the end of the last paragraph to display the Text-only Popup

   policy governing use of the electronic
   u to disciplinary action up to and including
   ill not d[   ]ise protect
   in the ev[Compensate you for harm or loss.]ivities
   her legal actions seeking civil or criminal

5. Close the preview.

Text Popup Confidence Check

1. Still working within the **Electronic Communications Policy** topic, double-click the word **indemnify** to display the Text Popup Properties.

2. Select **Verdana** from the Font menu.

3. Select any **Text** Color and Size you like.

4. Select any **Background color** you like.

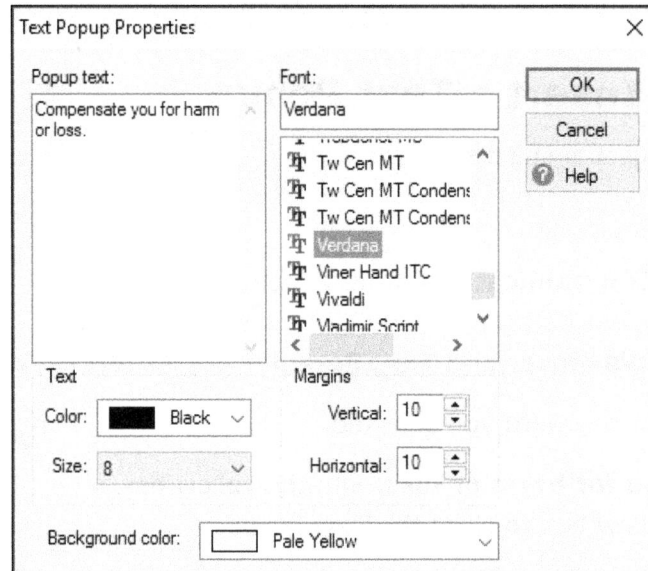

5. Click the **OK** button.

6. Preview the topic and test the changes you made to the Text Popup.

7. When finished, close the preview.

8. Save and close all topics.

Link View

RoboHelp's Link View pod allows you to look and move through the links in your project. While viewing the Link View pod, you can see where the links are going and where the links are coming from. Active topics appear in the center of the screen, and hyperlinks appear on the left and right sides of the active topics.

Student Activity: Use Link View

1. Ensure that the **links** project is still open.

2. Show the links for the Electronic Communications topic.

   ❏ on the **Topic List** pod, right-click the **Electronic Communications Policy** topic and choose **Show Topic Links** from the shortcut menu

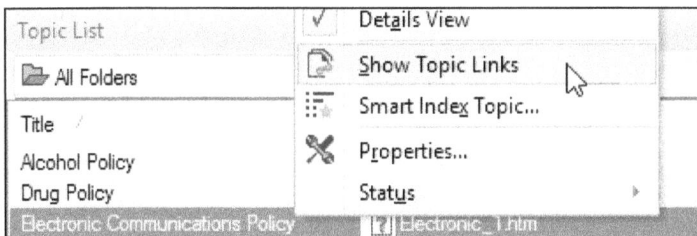

Topic List		
📂 All Folders	✓	Det**a**ils View
	📄	**S**how Topic Links
Title	📑	Smart Inde**x** Topic...
Alcohol Policy	✖	P**r**operties...
Drug Policy		Stat**u**s ▸
Electronic Communications Policy		Electronic_1.htm

   You will see icons in the Link View pod that show that the Electronic Communications topic is linked to other topics.

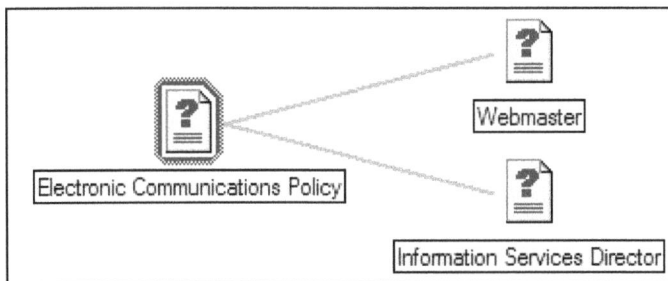

   Electronic Communications Policy — Webmaster, Information Services Director

   The color of the line and/on the shape of the icons you see mean the following: **Blue**=Normal Link, **Green**=Popup, and **Red**=Broken Link (you will learn about Broken Links next). Other colors and icons you may see include **Yellow**=Image Maps, **Blue Question Marks**=Local Topics, and **Globes**=Remote URLs.

3. Show the links for another topic.

   ❏ on the Topic List pod, right-click the **About This Guide** topic
   ❏ choose **Show Topic Links**

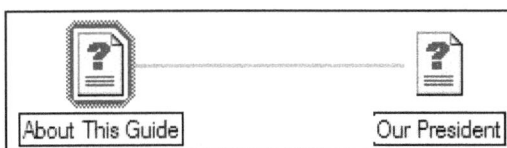

   About This Guide — Our President

Broken Links

A broken link occurs when the topic you are linking to has been deleted, renamed, or removed outside of RoboHelp. You are most likely to experience broken links when you import documents that no longer exist or have been moved.

Student Activity: Resolve Broken Links

1. Show the links for the Leave Policy topic.

   ❏ on the Topic List pod, right-click the **Leave Policy** topic
   ❏ choose **Show Topic Links**

   There is a red line coming from the Leave Policy topic. The topic is looking for a topic named **Ooops.htm** which does not exist. The red line is a visual indicator that the link from the Leave Policy topic is broken.

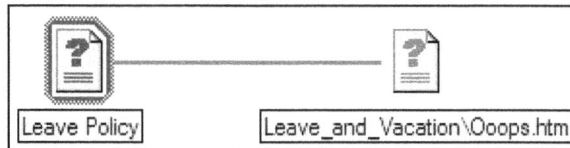

   ```
   [?]                        [?]
   Leave Policy     Leave_and_Vacation\Ooops.htm
   ```

2. View the contents of the Broken Links folder.

   ❏ on the **Project Manager** pod, open the **Broken Links** folder

   The Broken Links folder indicates that Ooops.htm, which is needed in a link in the Leave Policy topic, does not exist.

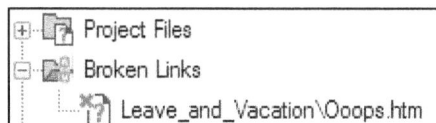

   ```
   [+] Project Files
   [-] Broken Links
          Leave_and_Vacation\Ooops.htm
   ```

3. Resolve Broken Links.

   ❏ on the **Project** tab, **Navigation** group, click **Broken Links**

   The Resolve Broken Links dialog box opens. According to the information shown in this dialog box, the Leave Policy topic contains a "Jump" (or link) that is looking for a missing topic ("Ooops.htm").

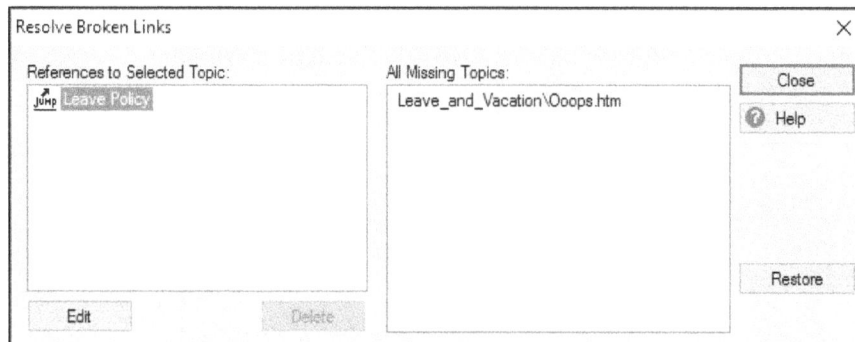

   ```
   Resolve Broken Links                                              ×

   References to Selected Topic:       All Missing Topics:          [  Close  ]
   JUMP Leave Policy                    Leave_and_Vacation\Ooops.htm
                                                                    [? Help ]




                                                                    [ Restore ]

   [  Edit  ]        [ Delete ]
   ```

❑ click the **Edit** button to open the Leave Policy topic

❑ scroll to the bottom of the topic and double-click the **Vacation Policy** hyperlink

❑ from the Leave_and_Vacation folder, select the **Vacation Policy** topic

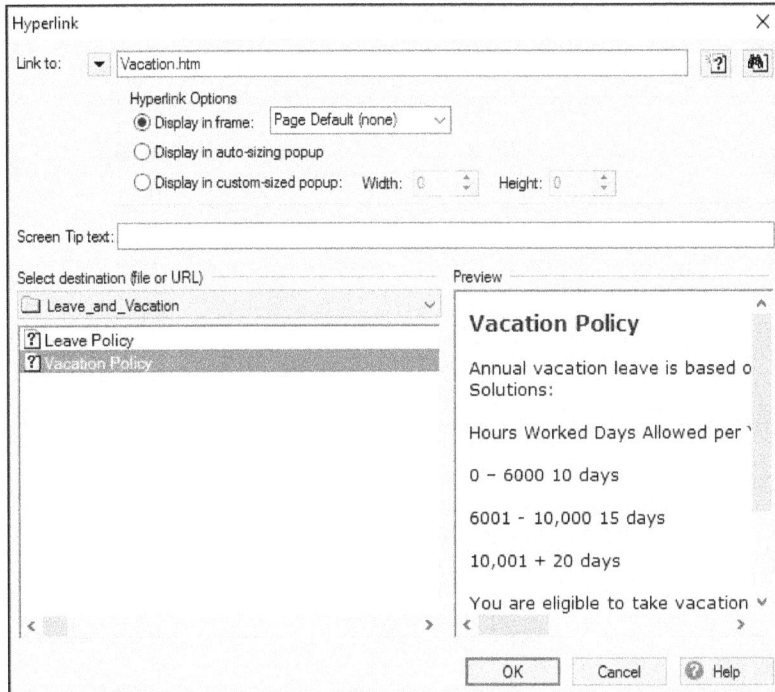

❑ click the **OK** button

4. Save the project.

   Once you have saved the project, the Broken Links folder on the Project Manager pod should show as empty. The project's broken links have been resolved.

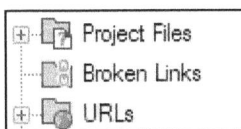

5. Close the project.

Notes

iCONLOGiC

"Skills and Drills" Learning

Module 6: Images and Multimedia

In This Module You Will Learn About:

And You Will Learn To:

Challenge Your New Skills:

Working with Images

Given today's often distracted and harried workers, people who use your Help System will be looking to find information as quickly as possible. Gone are the days when a Help System could survive on the text alone. We're a firm believer that Help topics should contain a minimal amount of text and be loaded with helpful images and interactive eLearning videos.

RoboHelp accepts the following graphic formats: **GIF, JPEG, BMP,** and **PNG**.

GIF (Graphic Interchange Format): This format is typically used for images that are black and white, or contain few colors as it only support 256 colors. It's ideal for simple artwork such as geometric shapes.

JPEG (Joint Photographic Expert Group): JPEG images are typically used for complex graphics (such as detailed photos) that are composed of more than 256 colors. JPEG images compress much better than GIFs.

BMP (Windows Bitmap): Bitmaps are created using dots—known as pixels—and the file size of a simple bitmap image can be very large. You can't directly import Bitmap images into your RoboHelp project. However, if you've used bitmaps in a RoboHelp for Word project and are converting the project into a RoboHelp project, all of your bitmaps will be converted to GIF. Bitmaps can be up to 24-bit color. Although many applications (such as Paint) let you create and save images as bitmaps, it is not recommended that you load your project with them.

PNG (Portable Network Graphics): PNG images are similar to GIFs. They are newer than GIFs and offer more colors. This makes the better suited for icons and screen shots than DIF.

Student Activity: Insert an Image

1. Open the **images_multimedia** RoboHelp project. (The project is located within the **RoboHelpProjects** folder.)

2. Open a topic and Insert an image.

   ❑ open the **Mission Statement** topic
   ❑ click to the left of the word **To** in the sentence "To continually create..." (confirm that your insertion point is now blinking **in front** of the sentence and that you have not selected any of the text)
   ❑ on the **Insert** tab, **Media** group, click **Image**

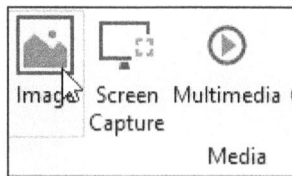

   The Image dialog box opens.

   ❑ on the **Image** tab, click the **yellow folder** in the **upper right** of the dialog box
   ❑ from the **RoboHelp2017Data** folder, open the **images** folder
   ❑ open the **LogoCropped.bmp** image file

The Image dialog box opens. A preview of the image appears in the Preview area.

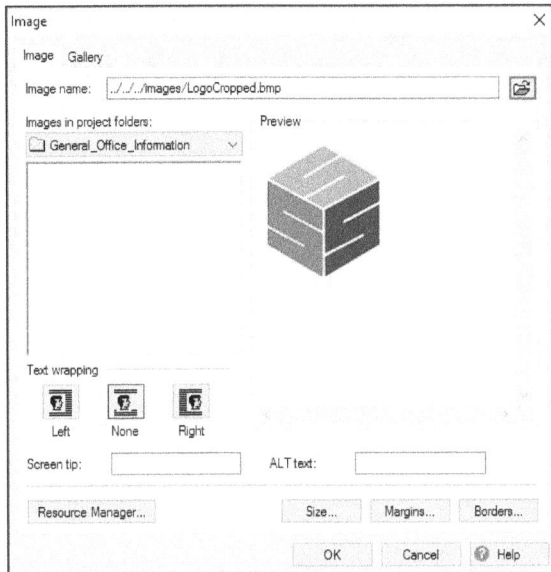

❒ click the **OK** button

The image appears in the topic at the exact location of the insertion point. You will change the alignment for the image next.

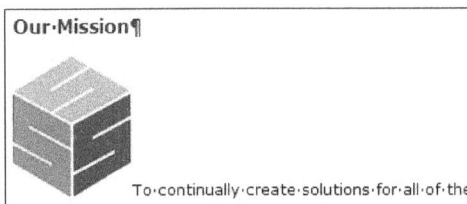

Note: Once you have inserted an image into a topic and saved your work, the Project Manager pod maintains a list of the images used in your project. If you want to use an image again, you do not need to choose **Insert > Image**; all you would need to do in the future is drag the logo from the Project Manager pod into a topic.

3. Change the Text wrapping for an image.

   ❒ double-click the logo you just inserted in the Mission Statement topic

   The Image dialog box re-opens.

   ❒ change the Text wrapping to **Right**

4. Add a Screen tip.

   ❒ click in the **Screen tip** area and type **Super Simplistic Solutions: Creative solutions to the world's problems.**

   The Screen tip appears when the user hovers the cursor over the image. Typically, a Screen tip is simply the image title.

5. Add ALT text.

❏ click in the **ALT text** field and type **The Super Simplistic Solutions Logo**

The ALT text appears when the image cannot be displayed. This happens when accessibility software such as screen readers read your content out loud or when Google reads your page to add it to its search index. Typically, ALT text is a brief description of the image. Some authors use the same text for both the Screen tip and the ALT text, which is fine. To make sure your content is accessible for impaired readers, always included an ALT text.

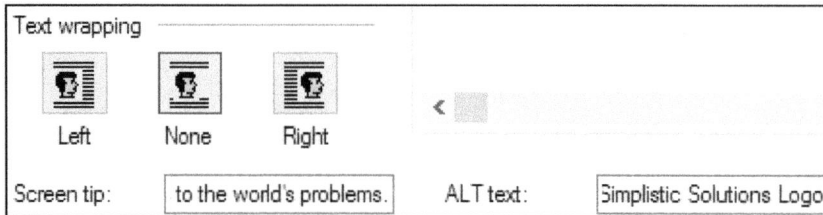

Text wrapping					
Left	None	Right		‹	
Screen tip:	to the world's problems.		ALT text:	Simplistic Solutions Logo	

❏ click the **OK** button

The Text wrapping changes and the image is now to the right of the text. But what's the role of the Screen tip?

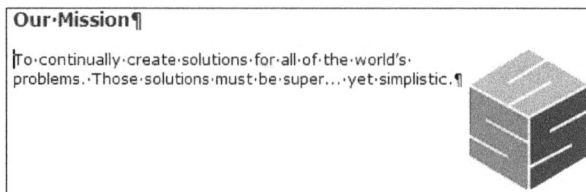

Our·Mission¶

To·continually·create·solutions·for·all·of·the·world's· problems.·Those·solutions·must·be·super...·yet·simplistic.¶

6. Test the Screen tip.

❏ press [**ctrl**] [**w**] to preview the topic
❏ slowly move your pointer over the logo

The Screen tip should appear as your mouse gets to the image and disappear a few seconds later.

world's problems. Those

Super Simplistic Solutions: Creative solutions to the world's problems.

7. Test how close text gets to the image.

   ☐ resize the preview window wider and then narrower

   As you resize the window, notice how close the text gets to the left edge of the logo. At times, the text gets very close. Next you will add white space to the left of the logo so that text can never get closer than 12 pixels.

8. Close the preview.

9. Save the project.

Student Activity: Add an Image Margin

1. Ensure that the **images_multimedia** project is still open.

2. Add white space to the left side of the SSS logo.

   ❑ still working within the **Mission Statement** topic, double-click the **logo** image

   The **Image** dialog box opens.

   ❑ click the **Margins** button (in the lower right of the dialog box)
   ❑ change the **Left** Margin to **12**

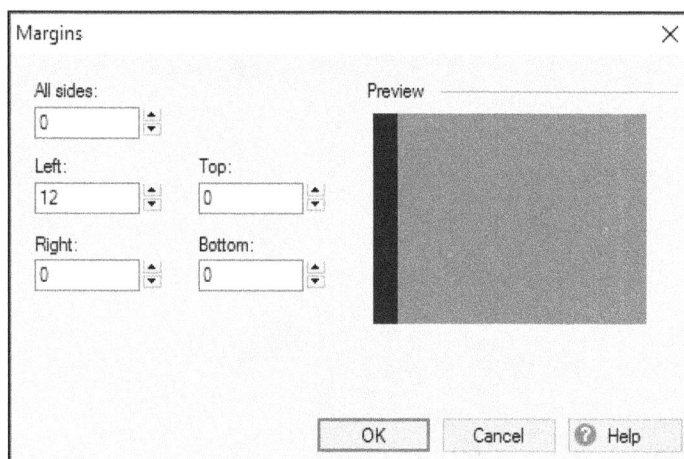

   Margins ✕

   All sides:
   0

   Left: Top:
   12   0

   Right: Bottom:
   0   0

   Preview

   OK   Cancel   ❓ Help

   ❑ click the **OK** button two times (to close both dialog boxes)

3. Preview the topic.

   ❑ press [**ctrl**] [**w**]

   You should see extra white space on the left side of the logo.

4. Close the preview.

5. Save the project.

Hyperlink Confidence Check

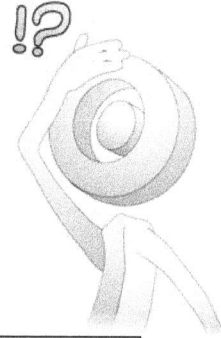

1. Still working within the Mission Statement topic, right-click the **logo** and choose **Insert Hyperlink**.

2. From the **Link to** drop-down menu choose **Web Address** and then add **www.supersimplisticsolutions.com** to the text field.

3. From the **Hyperlink Options** area, **Display in frame** drop-down menu, choose **New Window**.

Link to: ▼   http://www.supersimplisticsolutions.com

Hyperlink Options
⦿ Display in frame: New Window

By choosing **New Window** from the Hyperlink Options area, the web page opens in a new browser window or tab. If you don't select the New Window option, the resulting link will replace the current topic with the web page. We consider it a best practice to link into a New Window when the target of the link is an external web page.

4. Click the **OK** button and preview the topic.

5. Click one time on the **Super Simplistic Solutions logo**.

If you have an Internet connection, you will be taken to the Super Simplistic Solutions website. You can use the same link technique to link to anything from FTP sites to PDF files stored on a web server.

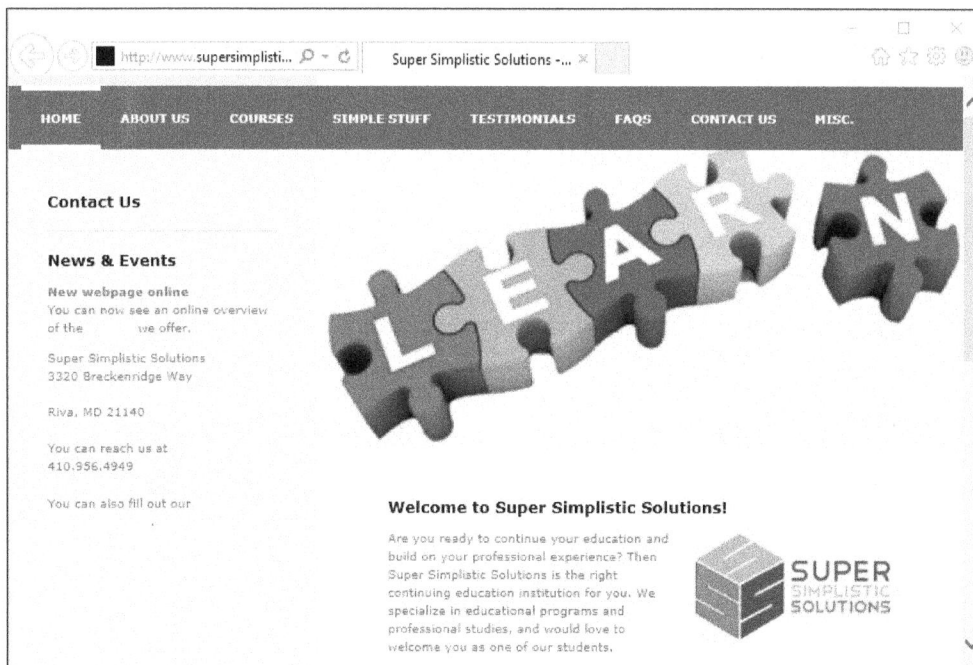

6. Close the browser window.

7. Close the preview window.

Background Images

Background images can be *very* cool. They can also be incredibly tacky. If you use a graphic as a background image, ensure that the graphic is a simple one that is not overly distracting to the user.

Student Activity: Add a Background Image

1. Ensure that the **images_multimedia** project is still open.

2. Add a background image to the CSS file.

   ❏ on the **Project Manager** pod, open the **Project Files** folder
   ❏ right-click **policies.css** and choose **Edit**

   The Styles dialog box opens.

   ❏ expand the **Other** group
   ❏ select **Background + Text (BODY)**

   The Background + Text (BODY) style controls the text, background images, background colors, and borders used in any topic that uses the policies style sheet. Because all of the topics in your project use the style sheet, they are affected by changes you make here. If you want to change the background image used in just a single topic, you would not modify the CSS. Instead, open the topic and, on the **Edit** tab, **Paragraph** group, click the **More dots** and choose **Topic Borders and Shading**. Any changes you make affect only the open topic.

   ❏ from the lower left of the dialog box, click the **Format** button and choose **Borders and Shading**

   The Borders and Shading dialog box opens.

   ❏ click the **Shading** tab
   ❏ in the **Pattern** area, click the **Browse** icon 📖
   ❏ in the **Image name** area, click the folder at the right
   ❏ from the **RoboHelp2017Data/images** folder, open **back.gif**
   ❏ click the **OK** button three times to close all three dialog boxes

   The graphic is "tiling" and filling up the background of every topic in your project. In fact, every topic has been affected because all of the topics in your project are using the policies.css file you edited.

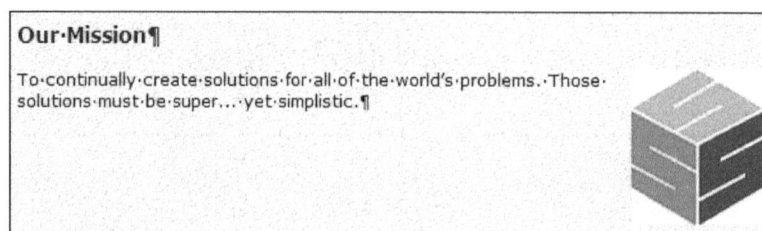

3. Save your work.

Images Confidence Check

1. Instead of the **back.gif** graphic, use the following graphic as the background: **cat.gif**.

   Need help? Edit the **policies.css** style sheet. Edit the **Background + Text** style, **Borders and Shading** format. Then open **cat.gif** from the images folder.

   When finished, the cat image should be filling up the background of every topic. We think you will agree that the cat image is not appropriate for use as a background image. Because background images "tile" by default to fill up the screen, the image makes it nearly impossible to read the text.

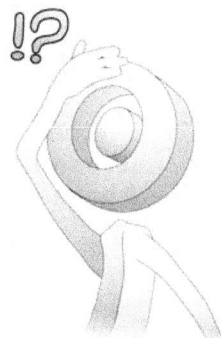

2. Remove the background image from the CSS.

   Need help? Edit the **policies.css** style sheet again. Specifically, edit the **Background + Text** style and, from the **Borders and Shading**, **Shading** tab, remove the **cat.gif** reference from the Image field.

3. Open the **Our President** topic and click to the left of the text "The president of Super Simplistic Solutions is Biff Bifferson."

4. Insert the following image: **biff_baby.jpg**. (**Note:** Don't edit the style sheet this time. Instead, on the **Insert** tab, **Media** group, click **Image** and open the graphic.) Then click the **OK** button.

5. Edit the graphic you just inserted. Change its Text wrapping to **Right** and add the following as both a Screen tip and ALT text: **Our President, Biff Bifferson**.

6. Click the **Size** button and change the Preferred height to **90**. (Then click the **OK** button two times.)

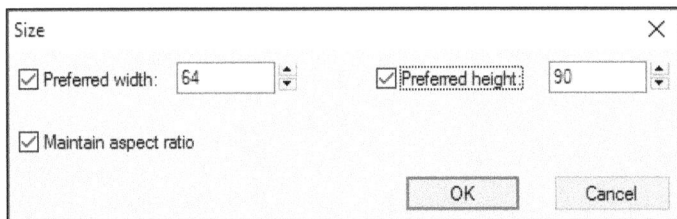

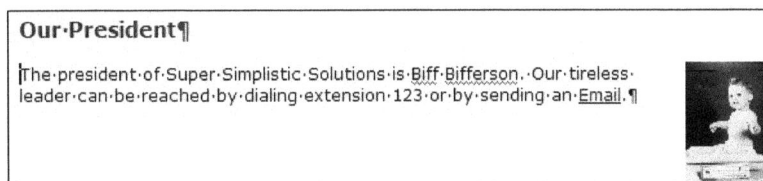

Size		×
☑ Preferred width: 64 ⬍	☑ Preferred height: 90 ⬍	
☑ Maintain aspect ratio		
	OK	Cancel

Our·President¶

The·president·of·Super·Simplistic·Solutions·is·Biff·Bifferson.··Our·tireless· leader·can·be·reached·by·dialing·extension·123·or·by·sending·an·Email.¶

7. Open the **Webmaster** topic.

8. Click to the left of the text "Our Webmaster is Sandra Stimson" and insert the following graphic: **sandra_baby.jpg**.

9. Edit the graphic. Change its Text wrapping to **Right**. Add the following **Screen tip** and **ALT text** to the image: **Our Webmaster, Sandra Stimson**. Change its Preferred height to **90**.

10. Open the **Human Resources** topic.

11. Click to the left of the text "Our Human Resources Director is Brandy McNeill at extension 552" and insert the following graphic: **brandy_baby.jpg**.

12. Edit the graphic. Change its Text wrapping to **Right**. Add the following **Screen tip** and **ALT text** to the image: **Our HR Director, Brandy McNeill.** Change its Preferred height to **90**.

13. Open the **Information Services Director** topic.

14. Click to the left of the text "Our Information Services Director is Travis DonBullian at extension 33" and insert the following graphic: **travis_baby.jpg**.

15. Edit the graphic. Change its Text wrapping to **Right**. Add the following **Screen tip** and **ALT text** to the image: **Travis and his big sister, Matilda.** Change its Preferred height to **90**.

16. Save and close all of your topics (keep the project open).

Image Maps

Image Maps allow the user to click on a particular area (hotspot) of an image and jump to a different area of your Help System. Image Maps are made up of two elements: an image and multiple hotspots. Hotspots (also known as clickable regions) can target websites, topics, bookmarks, email addresses, or files. You can create circle, polygon, or rectangle clickable regions.

Student Activity: Add Hotspots to a Graphic

1. Ensure that the **images_multimedia** project is still open.

2. Insert an image within a topic to be used as the image map.

   ❏ open the **Mission Statement** topic
   ❏ click at the end of the text and press [**enter**] to create a new paragraph
   ❏ type **Use the image below to move around this Help System.**
   ❏ press [**enter**] to create a new paragraph
   ❏ on the **Insert** tab, **Media** group, click **Image**
   ❏ open **blocks.gif** from the **images** folder
   ❏ type **Site Map** as both the Screen tip and the ALT text

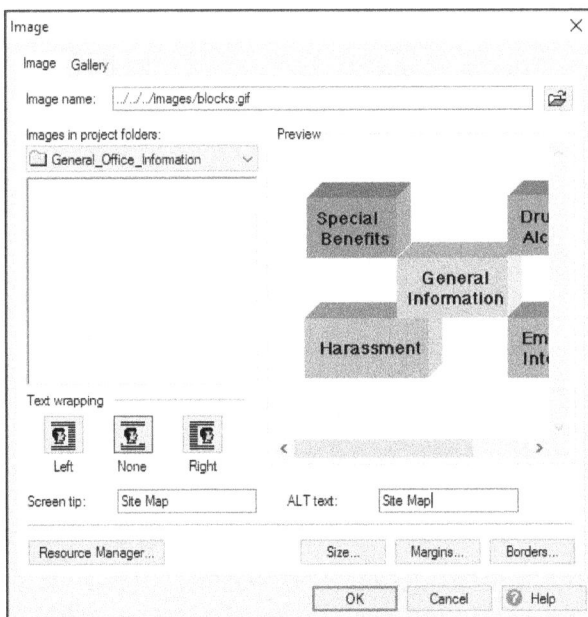

   ❏ click the **OK** button

3. Add a hotspot to the blocks image.

   ❏ select the **blocks** graphic you inserted
   ❏ on the **Insert** tab, **Links** group, click **Image Map > Rectangle**

   Your mouse pointer takes on the appearance of a cross. With your mouse pointer looking like this, you can use it to draw a rectangular hotspot on the blocks image.

❑ draw a box over the square containing the words **Special Benefits**

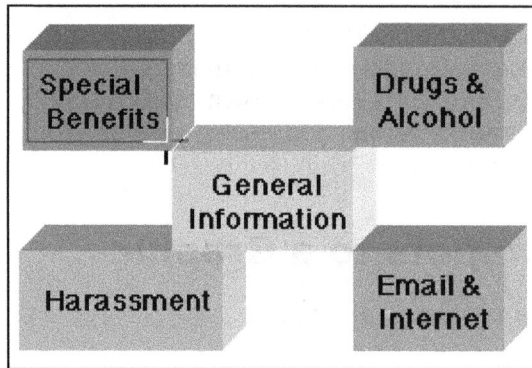

The instant you finish drawing what appears to be a rectangle over the image, the Image Map dialog box opens.

❑ select **Special Benefits** from the list of Topics

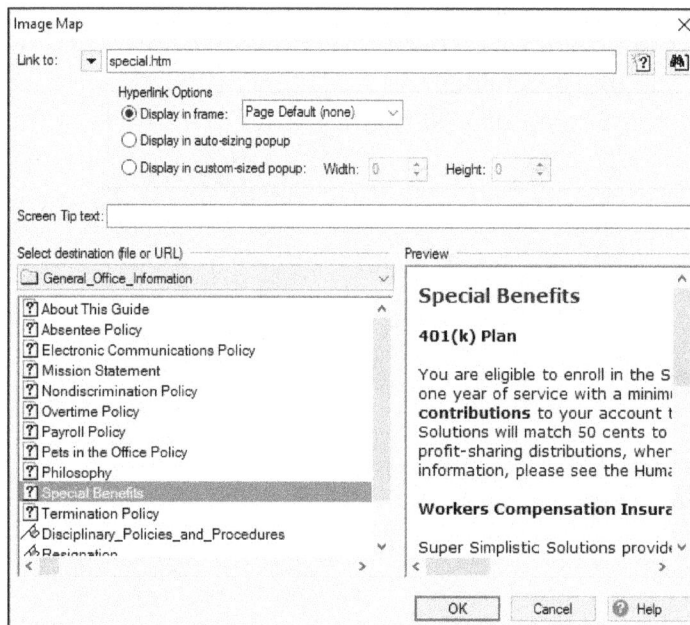

❑ click the **OK** button

A red box (a hotspot) surrounds the Special Benefits area of the image. You can move the red box, resize it, or delete it. If you need to change the hyperlink, you can double-click the red box and change it.

Image Map Confidence Check

1. Select the blocks image and insert a rectangular image map around the words **Drugs & Alcohol**.

2. Link the shape to the **Drug Policy** topic (the topic is inside the Drugs_and_Alcohol folder).

   Note: If you accidentally select the wrong target topic, double-click the box you drew around the block and select a different topic.

3. Draw a rectangle around the word **Harassment** that targets the following topic: **Nondiscrimination Policy**.

4. Draw a rectangle around the words **Email & Internet** that target the following topic: **Electronic Communications Policy**.

5. Draw a rectangle around the words **General Information** that targets the following topic: **About This Guide**.

6. Save the project.

7. Generate the Primary Output and View the results.

   When you click on any of the blocks in the Mission topic, you should be taken to the topic you targeted for each block. If you would like to go back to the Mission topic, click the **Back** button on the browser toolbar.

8. When finished, close the browser and return to the RoboHelp project.

eLearning Integration

If you have created an eLearning courses using eLearning tools such as Adobe Captivate, TechSmith Camtasia, or Articulate Storyline, you can insert the content directly into a RoboHelp topic. When the topic displays in a web browser, the eLearning lesson automatically plays. Beyond eLearning, streaming video and audio (multimedia files that begin playing as they are downloaded) are also supported in RoboHelp.

During the lessons that follow, you will import Adobe Captivate eLearning lessons and a TechSmith Camtasia video into a topic. RoboHelp supports both Flash (SWF) and HTML5 output. (Flash output works on desktop computers and laptops, but is not supported on most mobile devices (tablets and smart phones). Because HTML5 output works on most mobile devices but not older desktop browsers, it's a good idea to include both Flash and HTML5 eLearning content in your RoboHelp project.

Student Activity: Insert a Captivate Simulation

1. Ensure that the **images_multimedia** project is still open.

2. Import a Captivate SWF file and Captivate HTML5 output.

   ❏ open the **The Learning Center** topic
   ❏ click after the first subhead (Start an Application) and press [**enter**] to add a paragraph
   ❏ on the **Insert** tab, **Media** group, click **Captivate**

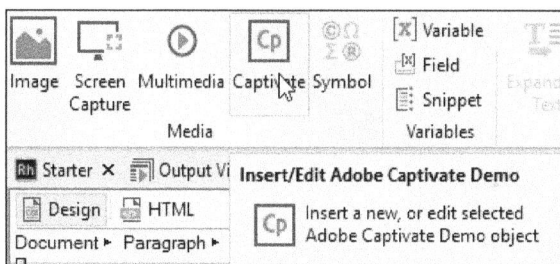

   ❏ click the **yellow folder** to the right of **HTML5 Output** and open the **RoboHelp2017Data** folder
   ❏ open the **eLearning** folder and then open the **StartNotepad_RH** folder
   ❏ open the **HTML5** folder and then open **index.html**
   ❏ click the **yellow folder** at the right of **Multimedia Name**
   ❏ go up one level, open the **Flash** folder, and open **StartNotepad_RH.swf**

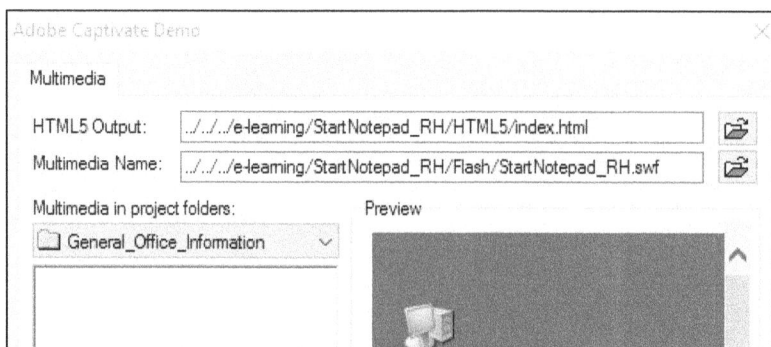

❑ click the **OK** button

The animation appears in the topic as a large gray box with a video icon. You'll need to preview the topic to see and interact with the eLearning lesson.

3. Preview the topic and interact with the simulation when prompted.

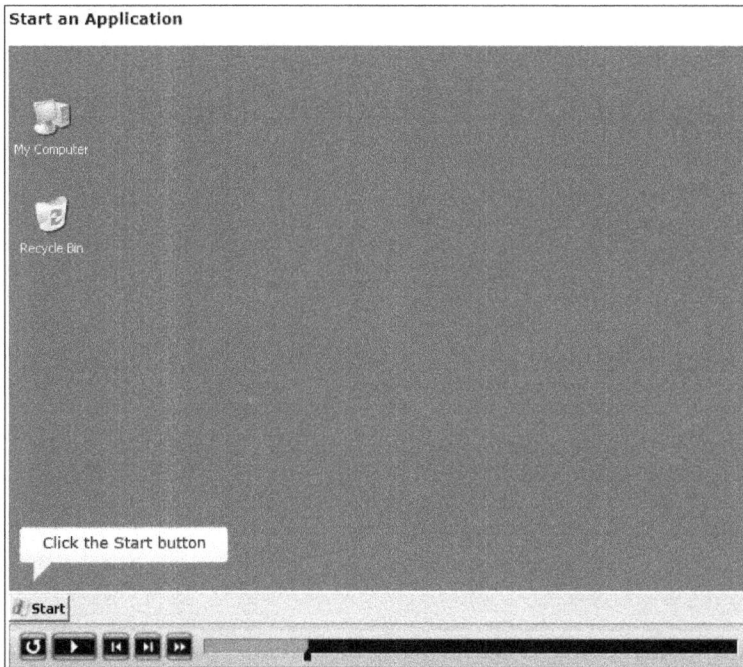

4. When finished, close the preview.

eLearning Confidence Check

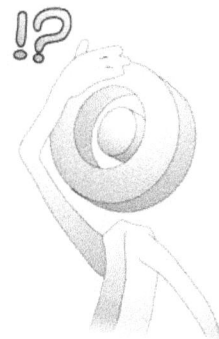

1. Still working within The Learning Center topic, add a paragraph after the **Save a File** subhead.

2. From the **CaptivateProjects\SaveNotepad_RH** folder, insert the **SaveNotepad_RH.swf** and **index.html** Captivate demos.

3. Add a paragraph after the **Copy and Paste Content Between Applications** subhead.

4. From the **CaptivateProjects\UseCharmap_RH** folder, insert the **UseCharmap_RH.swf** and **index.html** Captivate demos.

5. Preview **The Learning Center** topic and interact with all three of the eLearning lessons.

6. Close the preview window.

Student Activity: Insert a Video

1. Ensure that the **images_multimedia** project is still open.

2. Create a welcome heading

   ❏ within **The Learning Center** topic, click in front of the "Start an Application" heading and type **Welcome**

   ❏ press [**enter**] two times

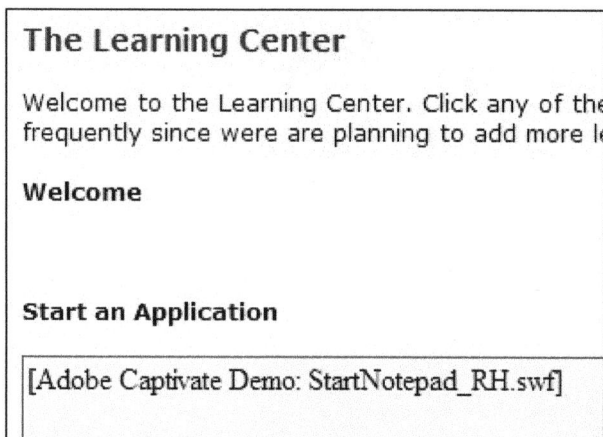

3. Import a Camtasia video

   ❏ on the **Insert** tab, **Media** group, click **Multimedia**

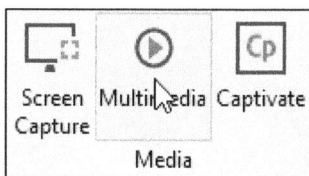

   ❏ click the **yellow folder** to the right of **Source** and open the **RoboHelp2017Data** folder

   ❏ open the **eLearning** folder

   ❏ select the **welcomeToLesson.mp4** file

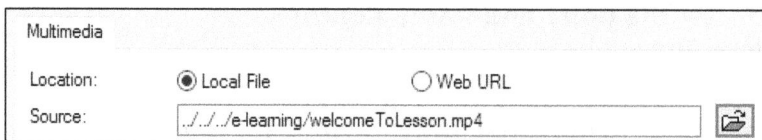

4. Set the height and width of the video

    ❏ click the **Appearance** button and choose **Size**
    ❏ deselect **Maintain aspect ration**
    ❏ set the **Preferred width** to **540px**
    ❏ set the **Preferred height** to **720px**

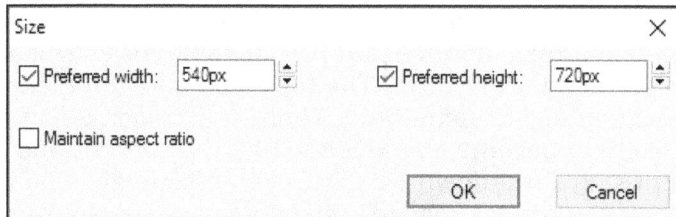

Size		×
☑ Preferred width: `540px`	☑ Preferred height: `720px`	
☐ Maintain aspect ratio		
	OK	Cancel

    ❏ click OK twice to close both dialog boxes and return to the topic

5. Preview the topic and view the video

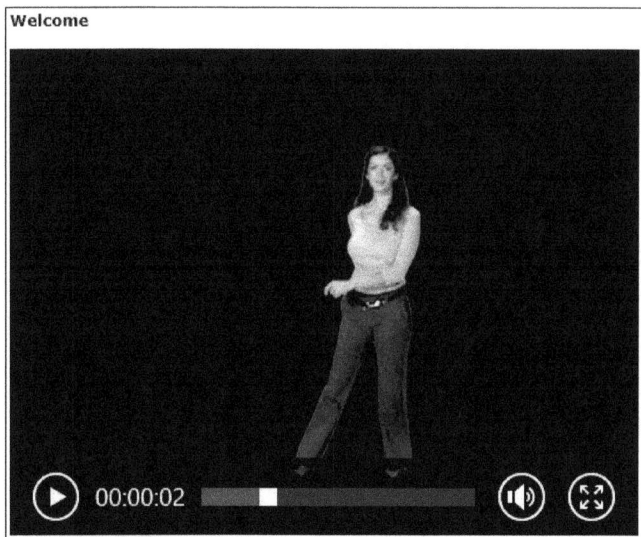

    Welcome

    ▶ 00:00:02 ▭▭▭▭ 🔊 ⤢

Dynamic HTML

Dynamic HTML (DHTML) gives you the ability to add PowerPoint-like effects to your topics. RoboHelp provides Dynamic HTML formatting of topic elements via the Insert tab. Effects added to text or graphics makes things fly onto the screen, fade in, change color, glow, and much more.

One of the most popular DHTML effects is Drop-down Text. Using this effect, you can quickly take a long, overwhelming topic and make it manageable for your learners. For instance, consider The Learning Center topic. The topic contains three eLearning lessons that appear on the screen at the same time. There is so much going on within the topic, users are likely to become overwhelmed by the content and spend little or no time in the topic. Using Drop-down Text, you can effectively hide the eLearning lessons with each of the three subheads. As users click the appropriate subhead, the eLearning lesson appears.

Student Activity: Create Drop-Down Text

1. Ensure that the **images_multimedia** project is still open.

2. If necessary, open the **The Learning Center** topic.

3. Insert a Drop-down Text DHTML effect.

   ❏ right-click the first video (welcomeToLesson) and choose **Cut**

   The video has not been deleted. Instead, it's hanging out on the clipboard. You'll paste it back within the topic shortly.

   ❏ delete the white space between the two subheads
   ❏ highlight the **Welcome** subhead
   ❏ on the **Insert** tab, **DHTML** group, click **DropDown Text**

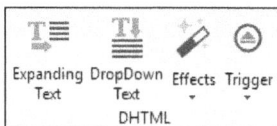

   The Drop-down Text Editor appears with some placeholder text.

   ❏ highlight the placeholder text ("Type your drop-down text here.") and paste the video in place of the text

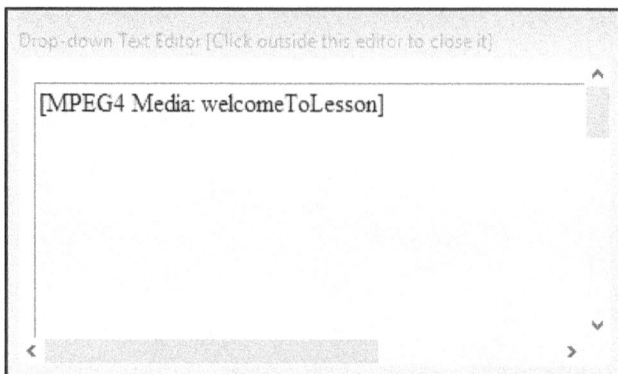

❏ click outside of the text editor to close the window

The selected subhead takes on the appearance of linked text.

4. Test the DHTML effect.

❏ press [**ctrl**] [**w**] to preview the topic
❏ click the **Welcome** heading

The video appears.

❏ click the **Welcome** heading again

The video disappears. How slick is that? Using this effect, you can quickly make some of your longer topics more manageable for users.

❏ close the preview window

5. Use the Drop-down Hotspot and Text effect again.

❏ right-click the Captivate simulation (StartNotepad_RH.swf) and choose **Cut**

Once again, the content has been moved to the clipboard.

❏ delete the white space between the second and third subheads
❏ highlight the **Start an Application** subhead
❏ on the **Insert** tab, **DHTML** group, click **DropDown Text**

The Drop-down Text Editor appears again.

❏ highlight the placeholder text ("Type your drop-down text here.") and paste the second Captivate lesson in place of the text

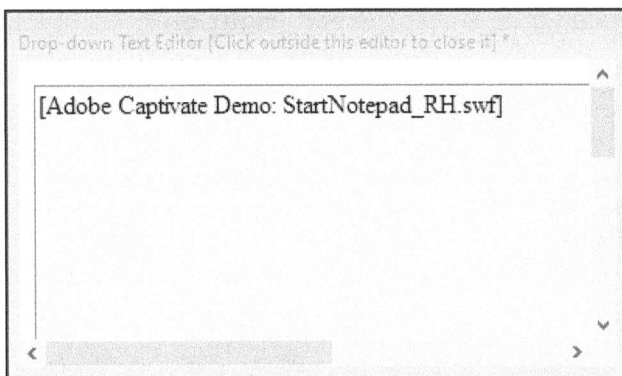

Drop-down Text Editor [Click outside this editor to close it] *

[Adobe Captivate Demo: StartNotepad_RH.swf]

❏ click outside of the text editor to close the window

The second subhead takes on the appearance of linked text.

To make these Drop-downs really useful, we need to make their behavior more predictable to users. At this moment, it is not immediately clear whether a link is just a regular hyperlink or one of these very cool Drop-downs items. And there is no way to indicate whether some content is shown or hidden when the link is clicked. Enter twisties! Twisties are small icons that indicate that a link will show or hide content.

Student Activity: Set Twisties

1. Add a twisty image to Drop-down text

    ❑ on the **Project Manager** pod, open the **Project Files** folder
    ❑ right-click **policies.css** and choose **Edit**

    The Styles dialog box opens.

    ❑ expand the **Hyperlink** group
    ❑ select **Drop-down hotspot**

    The Drop-down hotspot style controls the link for the Drop-down text. To make it easier for a user to understand the behavior of Drop-down text, you will be adding twisty images to indicate whether a Drop-down is closed or open.

    ❑ at the right of the dialog box, click the **Set Twisties** button

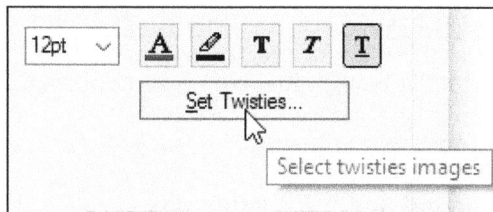

    The Select Twisties Images dialog box opens.

    ❑ click the **yellow folder** at the right of **Close image**

    The image dialog box opens

    ❑ click the **Gallery** tab
    ❑ from the lower left of the dialog box, select the **red_right.gif**

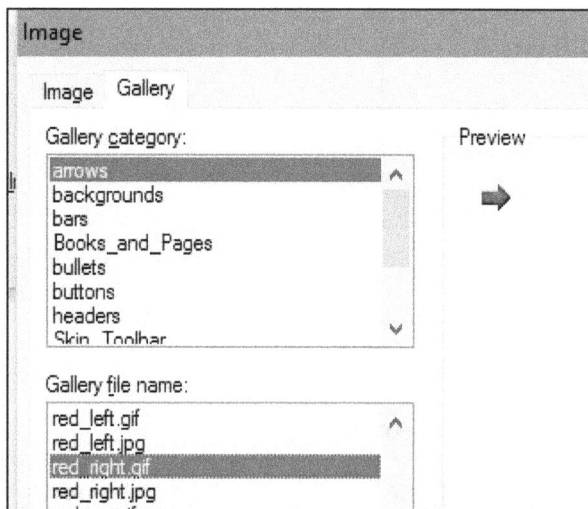

    ❑ click the **OK** button to close the dialog box
    ❑ click the **yellow folder** at the right of **Open image**

    The image dialog box opens

❏ click the **Gallery** tab

❏ from the lower left of the dialog box, select **red_down.gif**

❏ click the **OK** button three times to close all open dialog boxes

The Drop-down text in the topic looks unchanged. You'll need to preview the topic to see the Twisties.

2. Preview the topic and expand and collapse the Drop-down text to see the Twisties.

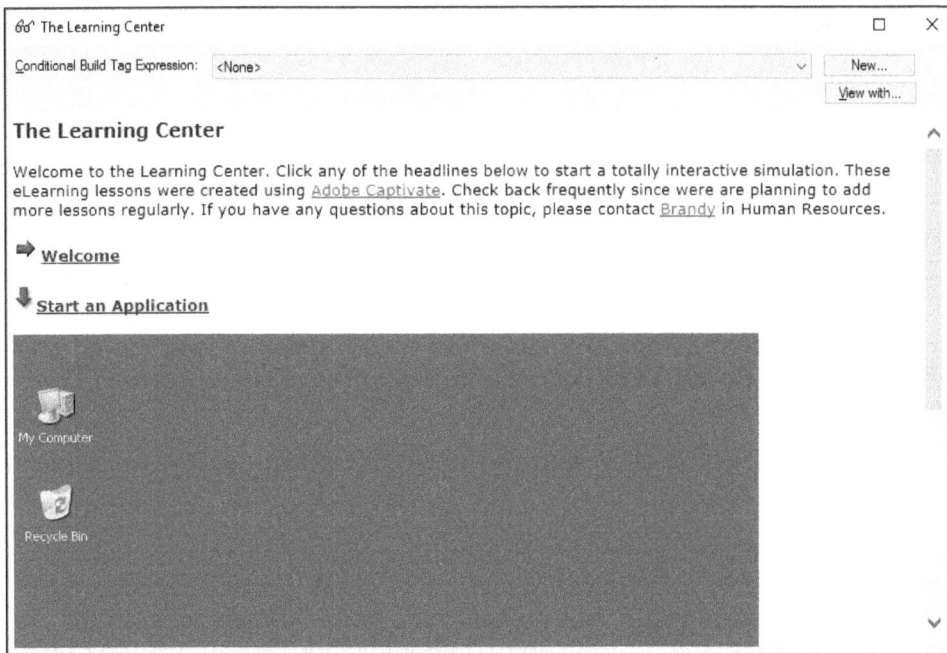

3. When finished, close the preview.

DHTML Confidence Check

1. Cut the last eLearning lesson to the clipboard.

2. Highlight the next subhead (Save a File) and create a **Drop-down Text** DHTML effect. (Paste the third eLearning lesson into the Text Editor window.)

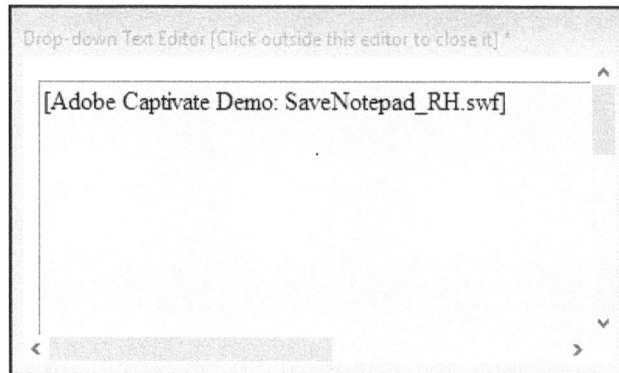

> Drop-down Text Editor [Click outside this editor to close it] *
>
> [Adobe Captivate Demo: SaveNotepad_RH.swf]

3. For the last subhead (Copy and Paste Content Between Applications) create one more **Drop-down Text** DHTML effect and move the eLearning lesson to the Drop-down.

4. Preview the topic and test all four of the DHTML effects you've added to the three subheads.

    Note: If you receive the error message shown below when Previewing, click the **Yes** button to dismiss the alert. The alert has been posted as a bug on multiple websites, but no solutions have been suggested to date. Nevertheless, the drop-down text should work for you despite the error message.

> **Script Error** ✕
>
> ⚠ An error has occurred in the script on this page.
>
> Line: 4258
> Char: 2
> Error: Unable to get property 'alpha' of undefined or null reference
> Code: 0
> URL: file:///C:/Program%20Files%20(x86)/Adobe/Adobe%20RoboHelp%202015/RoboHTML/ehlpdhtm.js
>
> Do you want to continue running scripts on this page?
>
> [Yes] [No]

5. When finished, close the preview.

6. Open the Pets in the Office Policy topic.

7. Change the **Text wrapping** of the dog image to **right**. (Need help? You learned how to do this on page 107.)

8. Change the **Preferred height** of the dog image to **120**. (Need help? You learned how to do this on page 113.)

9. Preview the topic.

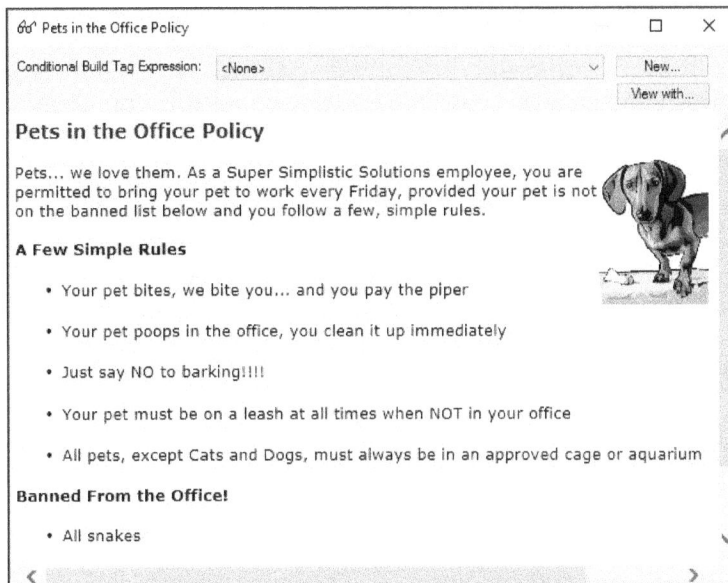

10. Close the preview.

11. Save and then close the project.

Student Activity: Midcourse Project

If you are using this book as part of an official RoboHelp training course, your instructor may review the project you create following the steps below (and the steps on page 286) to determine your final grade for this course.

❏ Create a new blank project and name it **YourFirstNameRoboHelpProject**. (When you create the project, pay particular attention where you save it. You will be adding to the project beginning on page 286.) *Need Help?* Refer to page 24.

❏ Create 10-12 new topics. The topics can be about anything you like. *Need Help?* Refer to page 27.

❏ Add books to the default TOC that contain your topics. Although the names can be anything you like, they should support your new topics. Each of the new books should be books with no Links. *Need Help?* Refer to page 44.

❏ Put a few topics into each book. *Need Help?* Refer to page 46.

❏ Create your own CSS file called **yourname.css**. *Need Help?* Refer to page 54.

❏ Format the styles within your CSS as you see fit. *Need Help?* Refer to page 54.

❏ Apply your CSS to all of your topics. *Need Help?* Refer to page 49.

❏ Insert hyperlinks in your topics so the topics are linked to each other. *Need Help?* Refer to page 83.

❏ Insert images into some of your topics as appropriate. (You can use any images available to you on your hard drive or network drives. You can also search the Internet for appropriate images.) *Need Help?* Refer to page 106.

❏ Generate WebHelp and view the results. *Need Help?* Refer to page 17.

iCONLOGiC
"Skills and Drills" Learning

Module 7: Reusing Content

In This Module You Will Learn About:

- Build Tags, page 130
- Content Categories, page 139
- Dynamic Filters, page 145
- User Defined Variables, page 152
- Snippets, page 155
- Sharing Resources, page 158

And You Will Learn To:

- Create a Conditional Build Tag, page 130
- Apply a Conditional Build Tag, page 132
- Create a Build Tag Expression, page 134
- Create a New TOC, page 139
- Apply Topic-Level Tags, page 141
- Create Content Categories, page 142
- Create Tags for Dynamic Filters, page 145
- Add Dynamic Filters to a Layout, page 147
- Tag Selected Content for a Build Expression, page 150
- Work With Variables, page 152
- Work With Snippets, page 155

Build Tags

A project can easily contain thousands of topics. When you generate an output, all of the topics are generated. But what if you want to exclude several topics from being generated? Using conditional tags, you can tag topics or topic content. When the time comes to generate, you can choose to create conditions that control which tagged content is generated. Using conditions, you can maintain one large project but generate multiple outputs; each output can have unique content. Content that is excluded from a output is not seen by your users.

Student Activity: Create a Conditional Build Tag

1. Open the **conditional_build_tags.xpj** RoboHelp project file. (The project is located within the **RoboHelpProjects** folder.)

2. View the Conditional Build Tags pod.

   ❏ on the **Project** tab, click **Pods** and choose **Conditional Build Tag**

   On the Conditional Build Tags pod, notice there are already two build tags (Online and Print). These tags are default tags that appear in every new RoboHelp project. You can elect to use the existing tags, delete them, or ignore them. For this project, you'll be ignoring them and creating your own.

3. Create a Conditional Build Tag.

   ❏ at the top of the **Conditional Build Tags** pod, click the **Create a conditional build tag** tool

   The New Conditional Build Tag dialog box opens.

   ❏ replace the existing tag name with **Biff**

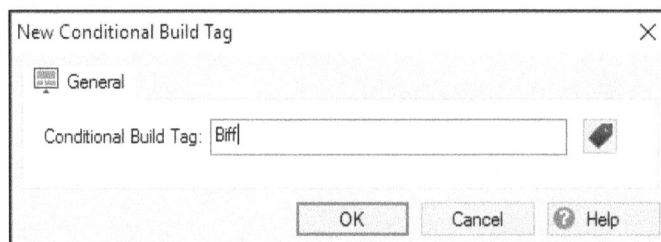

   ❏ click the **OK** button

   The new Conditional Build Tag 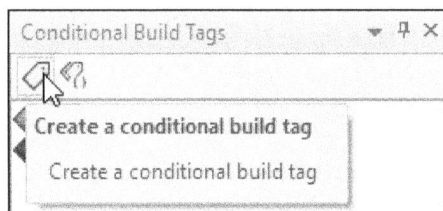 is now listed in the Conditional Build Tags folder.

4. Create another Conditional Build Tag.

   ❑ at the top of the **Conditional Build Tags** pod, click the
   Create a conditional build tag tool

   The New Conditional Build Tag dialog box reopens.

   ❑ replace the existing tag name with **AJ**

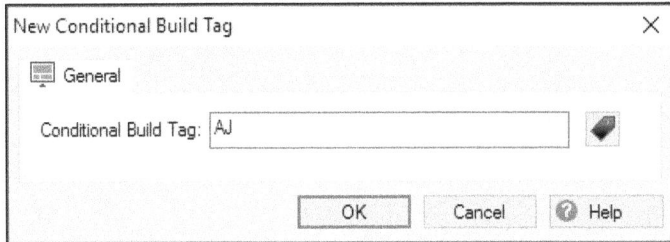

New Conditional Build Tag	×
General	
Conditional Build Tag: AJ	
	OK Cancel ⓘ Help

   ❑ click the **OK** button

   Your Conditional Build Tags pod should look like this:

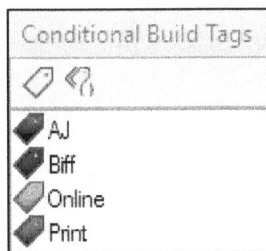

   Conditional Build Tags

   AJ
   Biff
   Online
   Print

5. Save the project.

Student Activity: Apply a Conditional Build Tag

1. Apply a Conditional Build Tag to text within a topic.

   ❑ open the **Our President** topic

   Because the topic is serving two presidents (AJ and Biff), the topic is an absolute mess.

   Our·President¶

   The·president·of·Super·Simplistic·Solutions·is·Biff·BiffersonAJ·George.··Our·tireless·leader·can·be·reached·by·dialing·extension·123456·or·by·sending·an·Email·to·himher.¶

   Here's the scenario: Super Simplistic Solutions has gotten so big, the company has been split into two independent companies: Super Simplistic Solutions East and Super Simplistic Solutions West. The two companies have different presidents (Biff in the East; AJ in the West) but share many of the original corporate policies and procedures. Beyond personnel, the differences between the two companies is largely regional. For instance, SSS East isn't near the water; SSS West is located near the beach and employees routinely take their surfboards out during the lunch hour. SSS West management has recently installed surfboard racks. Information about the surfboard racks is relevant if you work at SSS West but not if you work at SSS East. You will use Conditional Build Tags and Expressions to ensure that employees in the East see only information relevant to them, likewise for the employees in the West.

   ❑ highlight the words **Biff Bifferson**
   ❑ on the **Edit** tab, **Tags** group, click **Biff**
   ❑ highlight the email link for **him**
   ❑ on the **Edit** tab, **Tags** group, click **Biff**

2. Click away from the text.

   Notice that the text that received the conditions now has a colored line above it. This is a visual indicator that the text is conditional.

   Our·President¶

   The·president·of·Super·Simplistic·Solutions·is·Biff·BiffersonAJ·George.··Our·tireless·leader·can·be·reached·by·dialing·extension·123456·or·by·sending·an·Email·to·himher.¶

   Note: If you don't see the visual indicators for the applied conditions, you can go to the **Edit** tab, **View** group, and click **Show/Hide > Conditional Areas** to make them appear.

3. Save the project.

Build Tags Confidence Check

1. In the **Our President** topic, the picture at the right is **Biff**.

2. Select the picture and apply the **Biff** Conditional Build Tag to the picture.

3. Apply the **Biff** Conditional Build Tag to the numbers **123**.

4. Apply the AJ Conditional Build Tag to the words **AJ George**, **456**, the **her** email link, and the picture at the left.

Our·President¶

The·president·of·Super·Simplistic·Solutions·is·Biff·BiffersonAJ· George.·Our·tireless·leader·can·be·reached·by·dialing·extension· 123456·or·by·sending·an·Email·to·himher.¶

Note: You can remove a Conditional Area by applying the build tag a second time.

5. Save the project.

Student Activity: Create a Build Tag Expression

1. Preview the Our President topic.

   ❏ ensure the **Our President** topic is still open

   ❏ right-click within the topic and choose **Preview Topic**

   Because you have not yet defined a Build Tag Expression, both presidents appear in the preview, and the topic is a mess.

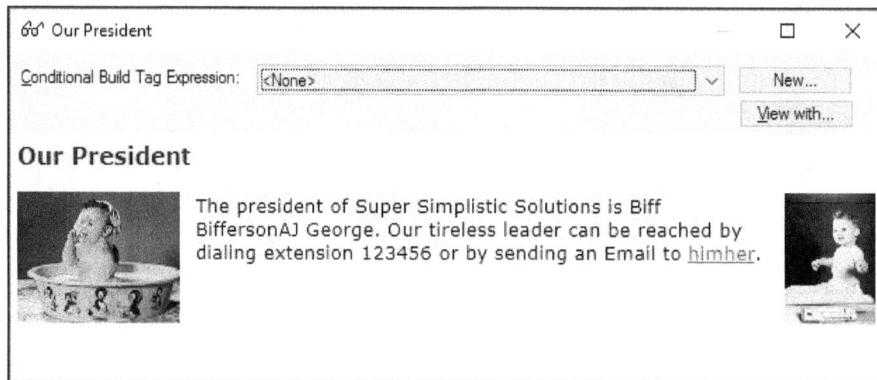

👓 Our President	▢ ✕	
Conditional Build Tag Expression: <None> ▢	New...	
	View with...	

   Our President

   The president of Super Simplistic Solutions is Biff BiffersonAJ George. Our tireless leader can be reached by dialing extension 123456 or by sending an Email to himher.

2. Define a Conditional Build Tag Expression.

   ❏ in the upper right of the preview window, click the **New** button

   The Define Conditional Build Tag Expression dialog box opens.

   ❏ double-click **Biff** to move Biff into the **Exclude from output** column

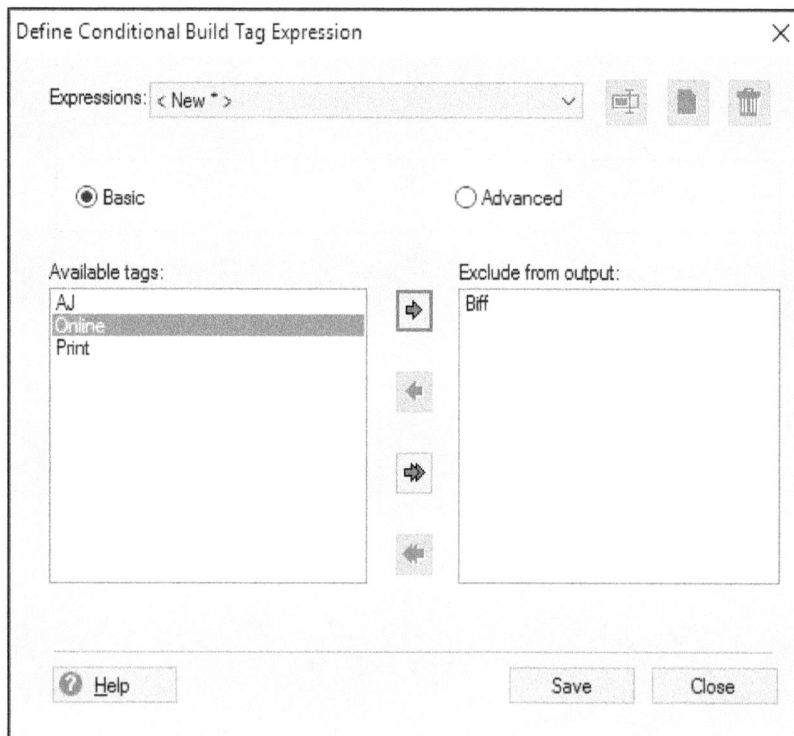

   Define Conditional Build Tag Expression ✕

   Expressions: < New * >

   ◉ Basic   ○ Advanced

   Available tags:
   AJ
   Online
   Print

   Exclude from output:
   Biff

   ❓ Help   Save   Close

   ❏ click the **Save** button

The **Create New Expression** dialog box opens. With this dialog you provide an easy to remember name for the new expression. Biff is the president of the East coast office. By excluding Bill we are showing content for the West coast office.

❏ replace the existing expression name with **SSSWest**

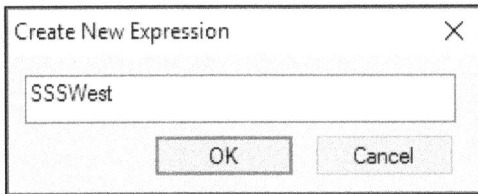

Create New Expression   ✕

SSSWest

                    OK   Cancel

❏ click the **OK** button
❏ click the **Close** button to close the dialog

At the top of the preview, notice that the Conditional Build Tag Expression **SSSWest** has been selected for you. And check out the topic—no mention of Biff or his email address.

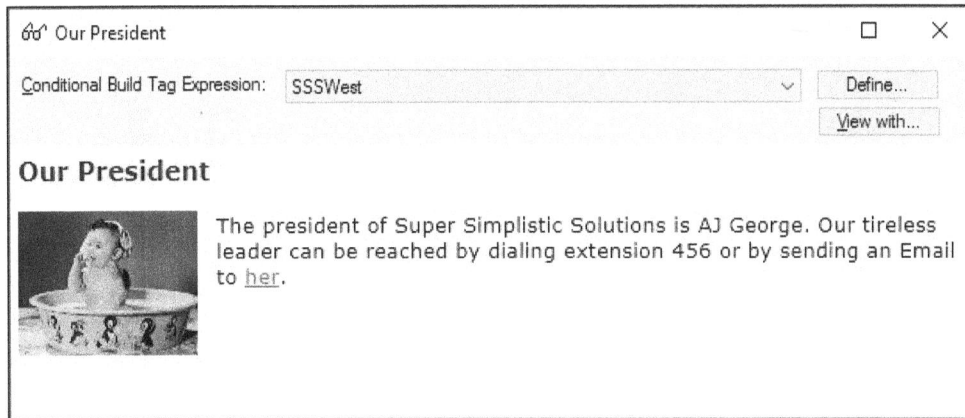

𝟞𝟞ʼ Our President   ☐   ✕

Conditional Build Tag Expression: SSSWest   ⌄   Define...
                                                                      View with...

Our President

The president of Super Simplistic Solutions is AJ George. Our tireless leader can be reached by dialing extension 456 or by sending an Email to her.

3. Define another Conditional Build Tag Expression.

❏ with the **Preview** window still open, click the **Define** button
❏ click the **Create new expression** button

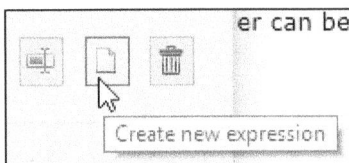

er can be

Create new expression

❏ double-click **AJ** to move AJ into the **Exclude from output** column

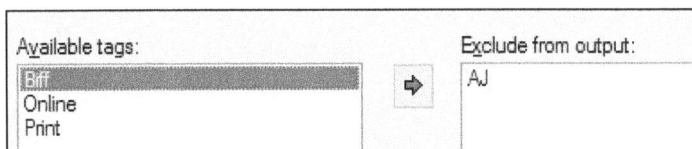

Available tags: Exclude from output:
Biff   AJ
Online   ➡
Print

❏ click the **Save** button

The Create New Expression dialog expression opens.

❒ replace the existing expression name with **SSSEast**

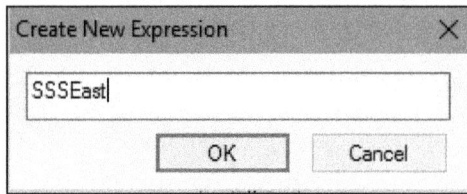

Create New Expression   ✕

SSSEast|

OK   Cancel

❒ click the **OK** button

❒ click the **Close** button

❒ from the **Conditional Build Tag Expression** drop-down menu, choose **SSSEast**

Now the preview shows Biff as the president with no mention of AJ.

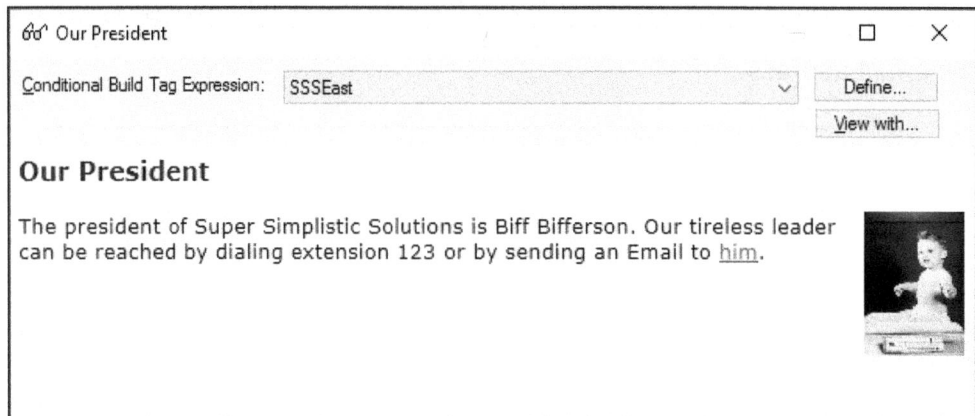

ᐁᐁ Our President   ☐   ✕

C̲onditional Build Tag Expression: [SSSEast   ∨]   [Define...]

[V̲iew with...]

Our President

The president of Super Simplistic Solutions is Biff Bifferson. Our tireless leader can be reached by dialing extension 123 or by sending an Email to <u>him</u>.

Build Expressions Confidence Check

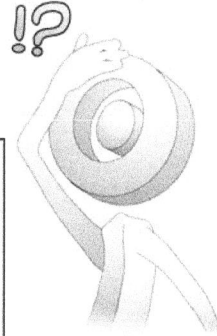

1. From the Conditional Build Tag Expression drop-down menu, choose **SSSWest**.

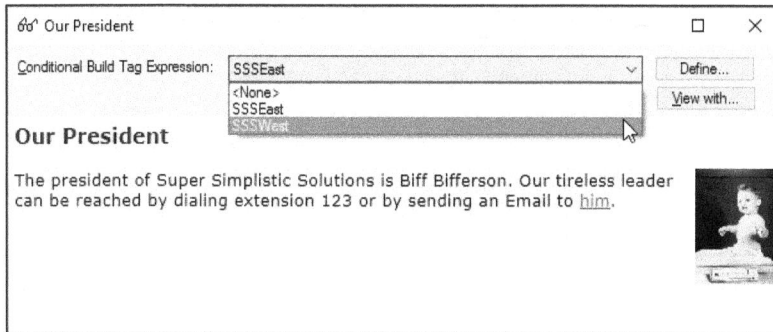

AJ is once again the president. Thanks to the build tags and the build tag expressions, you've essentially created two topics out of one. *How cool is that?*

2. Close the preview.

3. On the **Outputs(SSL)** pod, (**Project** tab > **Pods**), right-click **WebHelp (Primary Output)** and choose **Duplicate Output**.

4. Change the output Name to **SSSWest** and click the **OK** button.

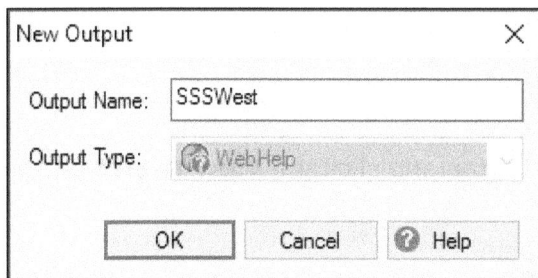

5. On the Outputs(SSL) pod, double-click **SSSWest** to open the output.

6. Open the **Content Categories** group and select **Content (Default)**.

7. From the **Conditional Build Expression** area, select **SSSWest**.

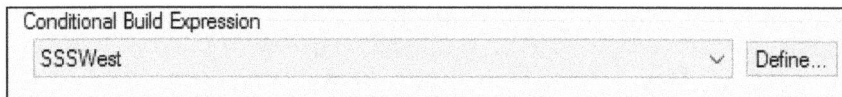

8. Click the **Save and Generate** button.

9. When the output is finished generating, click the **View Result** button.

10. Open the **About This Guide** topic.

11. Click the **president** link.

Because you selected **SSSWest** as the **Conditional Build Expression**, Biff does not appear, and AJ is shown as the president.

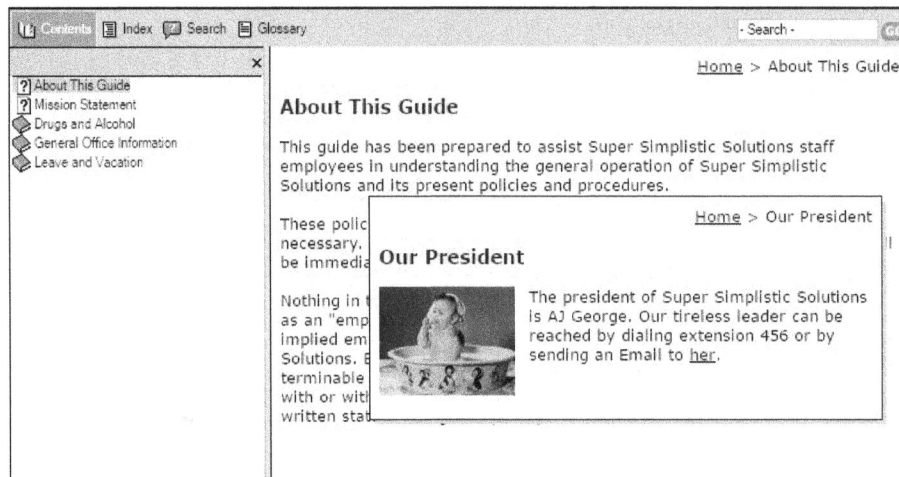

12. Close the web browser and return to the RoboHelp project.

13. On the **Outputs(SSL)** pod, duplicate the **SSSWest** output and give the duplicate output the name **SSSEast**.

14. Show the **Properties** of the **SSSEast** output and, from the Content group, change the Conditional Build Expression to **SSSEast**.

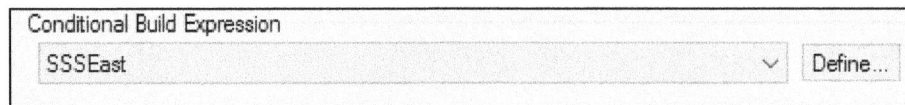

Conditional Build Expression

SSSEast   ∨   Define...

15. Click the **Save and Generate** button and click the **View Result** button when prompted.

16. Open the **About This Guide** topic.

17. Click the **president** link.

Because you selected **SSSEast** as the **Conditional Build Expression**, AJ does not appear, and Biff is the president.

18. Close the web browser and return to the RoboHelp project.

19. Save and then close the project.

Content Categories

You have learned how to create conditional build tags and expressions (page 134) and how to generate multiple outputs from one project (each containing potentially unique content). But what if you want to generate both outputs, combine them into one, and then let the users decide which output they want? During the activities that follow, you will add two new TOCs, create Content Categories (also known as **Dynamic User-Centric Content**), and then generate one output that contains information for both SSS divisions. A user is then able to pick the appropriate Help System from a drop-down menu.

Student Activity: Create a New TOC

1. Open the **content_vars_snipps.xpj** RoboHelp project file.

2. On the **Project Manager** pod, open the **Table of Contents** folder.

   The project currently has two TOCs: **content_vars_snipps** and **policies**. You're about to add a third.

3. Create a New Table of Contents.

   ❏ right-click the **Table of Contents** folder and choose **New Table of Contents**
   ❏ name the new TOC **SSS_East** and then select **Copy existing Table of Contents**
   ❏ click the **Browse** button at the far right of the dialog box (circled below)

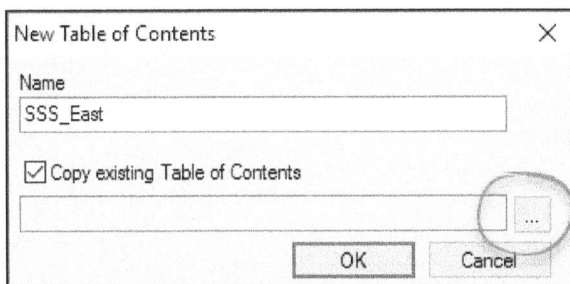

   ❏ from the **content_vars_snipps** project folder, open **policies.hhc**

   The policies.hhc file contains the TOC structure of the default policies TOC already in the project.

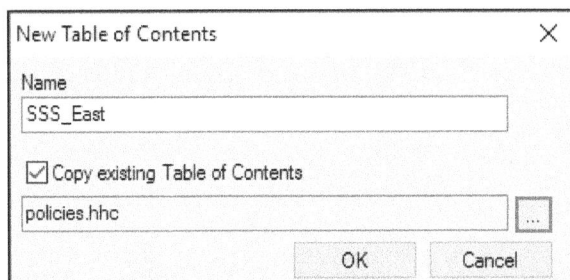

   ❏ click the **OK** button

   For the moment, your new TOC is identical to the original policies TOC.

Multiple TOC Confidence Check

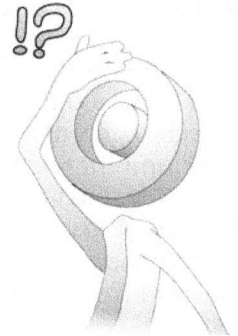

1. If necessary, open the **SSS_East** TOC.

2. Right-click the Drugs and Alcohol book and rename it **Substance Abuse**.

3. Arrange the books until the SSS_East TOC looks like the picture below at the right. (The two images below show the original TOC at the left and your new SSS_East TOC.)

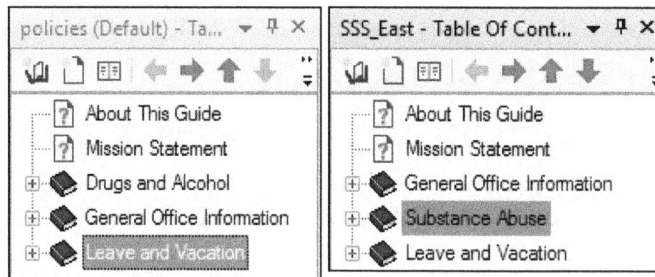

policies (Default) - Ta... ▼ ⏷ ×	SSS_East - Table Of Cont... ▼ ⏷ ×
🔲 ▢ 🔳 ⬅ ➡ ⬆ ⬇	🔲 ▢ 🔳 ⬅ ➡ ⬆ ⬇
? About This Guide	? About This Guide
? Mission Statement	? Mission Statement
📖 Drugs and Alcohol	📖 General Office Information
📖 General Office Information	📖 Substance Abuse
📖 Leave and Vacation	📖 Leave and Vacation

4. Create a New TOC called **SSS_West** (copy the new TOC from **policies.hhc**).

5. From within the **SSS_West** TOC, change the name of the Leave and Vacation book to **Time Off**.

6. Move the Drugs and Alcohol book to the bottom of the TOC.

   Your two new TOCs should look like this.

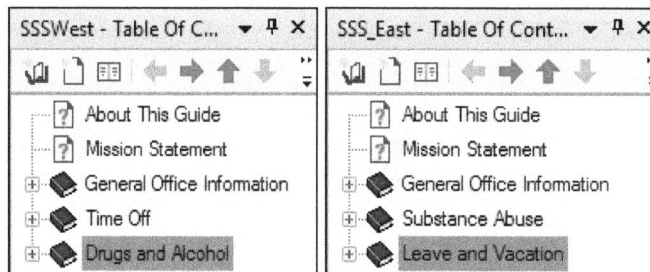

SSSWest - Table Of C... ▼ ⏷ ×	SSS_East - Table Of Cont... ▼ ⏷ ×
🔲 ▢ 🔳 ⬅ ➡ ⬆ ⬇	🔲 ▢ 🔳 ⬅ ➡ ⬆ ⬇
? About This Guide	? About This Guide
? Mission Statement	? Mission Statement
📖 General Office Information	📖 General Office Information
📖 Time Off	📖 Substance Abuse
📖 Drugs and Alcohol	📖 Leave and Vacation

Student Activity: Apply Topic-Level Tags

1. Ensure that the **content_vars_snipps** project is still open.

2. Apply a Conditional Build Tag to a topic.

   ☐ on the **Topic List** pod, right-click the **Surfboards** topic and choose **Properties**

   ☐ select the **Advanced** tab

   ☐ from the **Conditional Build Tags** area, select **AJ** (put a check in the box)

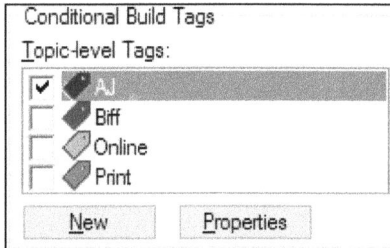

   By assigning the AJ tag to the Surfboards topic, the topic appears *only* in the SSSWest output. Because surfing is not a big event on the East Coast (home of SSS East), the topic does not need to appear in the SSSEast output.

   ☐ click the **OK** button

3. Save the project.

Student Activity: Create Content Categories

1. Create a new Content Category for SSSEast.

   ☐ on the **Outputs(SSL)** pod, right-click **WebHelp** and choose **Properties**
   ☐ from the left of the dialog box, select **Content Categories**
   ☐ click the **New** button
   ☐ change the name to **SSSEast** (don't use spaces in Category names)
   ☐ press [**enter**]

   > Content<Default>
   > SSSEast

2. Change the Content Title for the SSSEast Content Category.

   ☐ at the upper left of the dialog box, click the **plus sign** to the left of Content Categories
   ☐ select **SSSEast**
   ☐ change the Content Title to **SSS East**

   Note: Although spaces are not permitted in Content Category names, they are permitted within Titles.

3. Assign a TOC to the SSSEast Content Category.

   ☐ from the **Table of Contents** drop-down menu, choose **SSS_East**

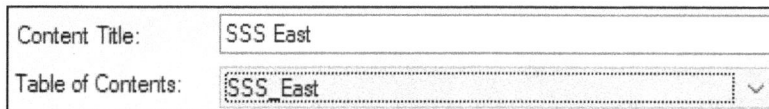

Content Title:	SSS East
Table of Contents:	SSS_East

4. Ensure that information about the president as SSS West does not appear in the policies for SSS East.

   ☐ from the Conditional Build Expression drop-down menu, choose **SSSEast**

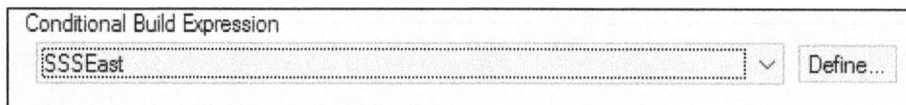

Conditional Build Expression		
SSSEast		Define...

   ☐ click the **Save** button

5. Save the project.

Content Categories Confidence Check

1. Create another Content Category named **SSSWest** within the WebHelp output that matches the specs shown below.

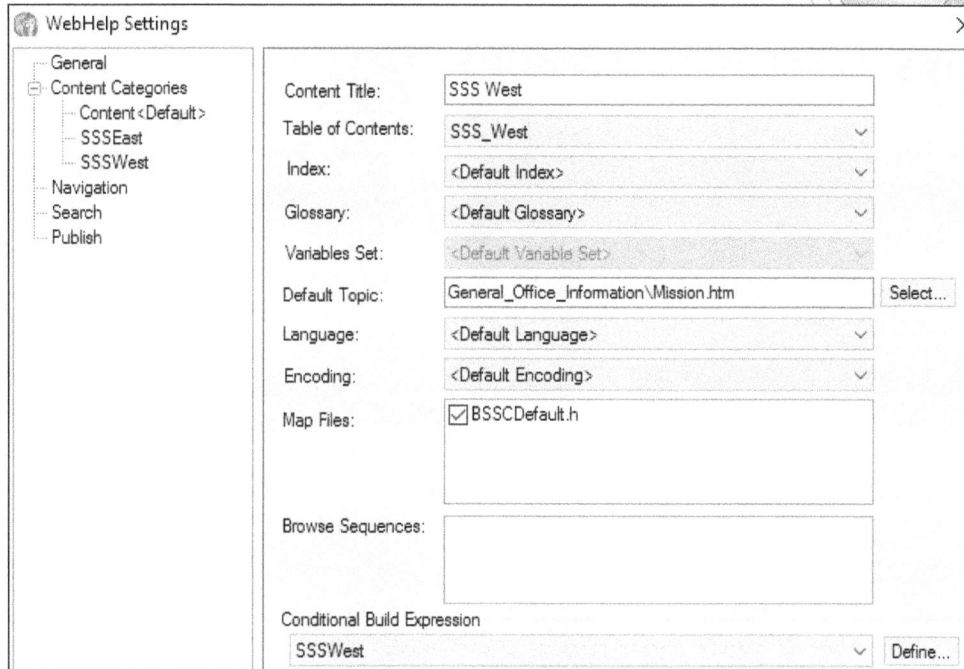

```
WebHelp Settings                                                    ×

 General                    Content Title:      SSS West
 Content Categories
   Content<Default>         Table of Contents:  SSS_West                    ⌄
   SSSEast
   SSSWest                  Index:              <Default Index>             ⌄
 Navigation
 Search                     Glossary:           <Default Glossary>          ⌄
 Publish
                            Variables Set:      <Default Variable Set>      ⌄

                            Default Topic:      General_Office_Information\Mission.htm   Select...

                            Language:           <Default Language>          ⌄

                            Encoding:           <Default Encoding>          ⌄

                            Map Files:          ☑ BSSCDefault.h



                            Browse Sequences:



                            Conditional Build Expression
                            SSSWest                                    ⌄   Define...
```

2. From the left of the dialog box, select **Content Categories**.

3. Select **SSSEast** and then click **Set As Default**.

```
Content<Default>                          Up
SSSEast
SSSWest                                   Down

                                      Set As Default
```

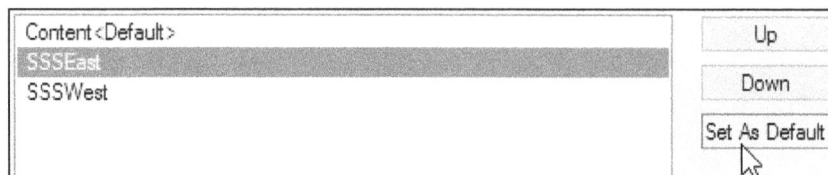

4. Select and **delete** the original Content Category named **Content** (leaving you with just two categories: **SSSEast** and **SSSWest**).

5. Save and generate the WebHelp output, then view the results.

6. From the upper left of the Navigation pane, notice that SSS East is the default category.

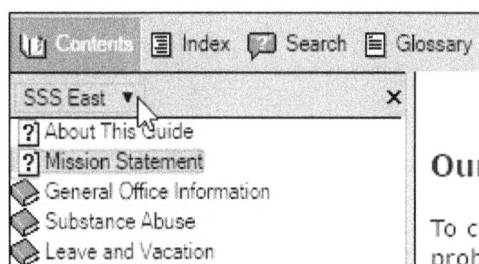

```
📖 Contents  📑 Index  💬 Search  📑 Glossary

SSS East ▼                           ×
 ❓ About This Guide
 ❓ Mission Statement              Our
 📓 General Office Information
 📓 Substance Abuse               To c
 📓 Leave and Vacation            prob
```

7. With the SSS East category selected, type **surfboards** into the Search field and then press [**enter**].

Because the Surfboards topic was assigned only to the SSS West output, no surfboard topics are found in the SSS East content.

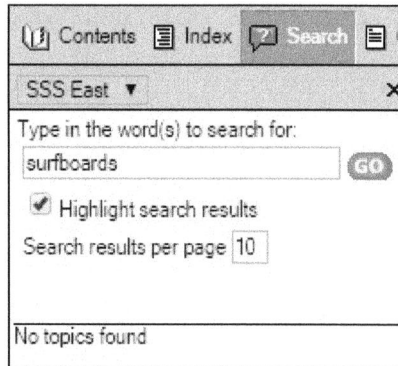

Contents	Index	Search	
SSS East ▼			×

Type in the word(s) to search for:

surfboards   GO

☑ Highlight search results

Search results per page 10

No topics found

8. Change the Content Category to **SSSWest**.

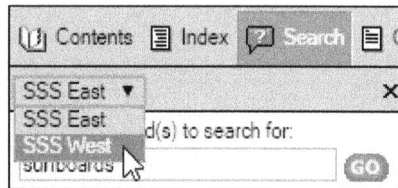

Contents	Index	Search	
SSS East ▼			×

SSS East
SSS West
d(s) to search for:
surfboards   GO

9. With the SSS West category selected, type **surfboards** into the Search field and press [**enter**].

This time, information about surfboards is found within the Help System.

Contents	Index	Search	
SSS West ▼			×

Type in the word(s) to search for:

surfboards   GO

☑ Highlight search results

Search results per page 10

Total Number of Search Results : 1

Title	Rank △
Surfboards Surfboard racks have been installed just outside the beach entrance on Riva Road. Please "park" you ...	1

10. Close the browser window.

11. Return to the RoboHelp project.

Dynamic Filters

Content Categories make it easy to combine multiple outputs using WebHelp. But you can make Conditional Build tags even more powerful with Responsive HTML5's Dynamic Filters. These filters allow a user to change the content being shown in real time. Although Content Categories are limited to a single conditional expression, Dynamic Filters allow you to use several conditional expressions at once.

Student Activity: Create Tags for Dynamic Filters

1. Ensure that the **content_vars_snipps** project is still open.

2. Create three Conditional Build Tags.

   ❏ show the **Conditional Build Tags** pod
   ❏ click the **Create a conditional build tag** tool

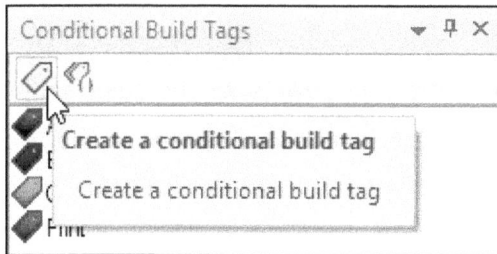

   ❏ name the tag **1_year**

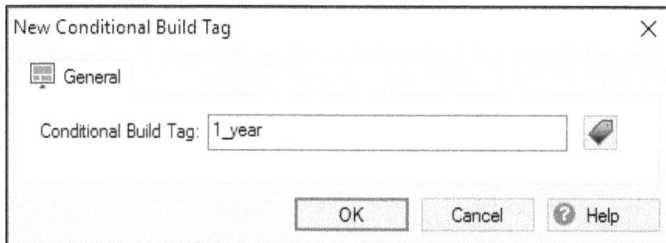

   ❏ click the **OK** button
   ❏ click the **Create a conditional build tag** tool
   ❏ name the tag **2_years** and click the **OK** button
   ❏ click the **Create a conditional build tag** tool
   ❏ name the tag **5_years**
   ❏ click the **OK** button

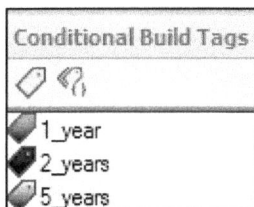

3. Save your work.

Dynamic Filters Confidence Check

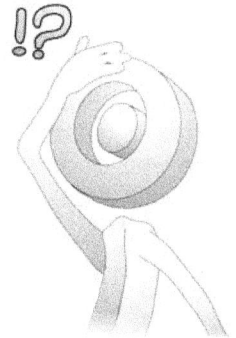

1. Open the **Unique Benefits** topic.

   The Unique Benefits topic contains benefits that are awarded to employees based on the number of years on the job. Currently, all of the benefits are visible. By applying filters, the user can choose which benefits to view.

2. Click anywhere in the list item **1 week of paid vacation**.

3. From the **Tag List** at the top of the topic, click **Item** (to select the bulleted item).

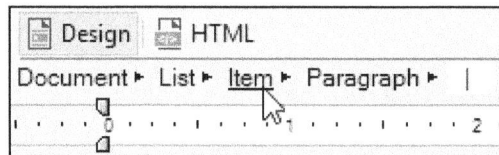

📄 Design	🖼 HTML

   Document ▸ List ▸ Item ▸ Paragraph ▸ |

4. From the **Conditional Build Tags** pod, drag **1_year** over the selected text.

   If you deselect the text, you'll see that there is a green line above the text indicating a tag has been applied.

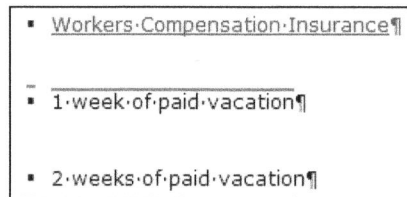

   - Workers·Compensation·Insurance¶

   - 1·week·of·paid·vacation¶

   - 2·weeks·of·paid·vacation¶

5. Go through the remaining items in the list and tag them as **1-year**, **2-year**, or **5-year** benefits, as you see fit.

6. Save your work.

Student Activity: Add Dynamic Filters to a Layout

1. Ensure that the **content_vars_snipps** project is still open.

2. Add Dynamic Filters to output.

   ❑ go to the **Outputs(SSL)** pod
   ❑ double-click the **Responsive HTML5** layout

   The Responsive HTML5 Settings dialog box opens.

   ❑ from the list at the left, select the **General** tab
   ❑ from the **Dynamic Content Filter** area, select **Use Dynamic Content Filter in the output**

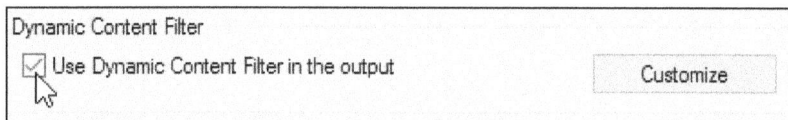

Dynamic Content Filter
☑ Use Dynamic Content Filter in the output   Customize

   The Dynamic Content Filter dialog box opens.

   ❑ in the **Title (Display in output)** field, type **Years employed**

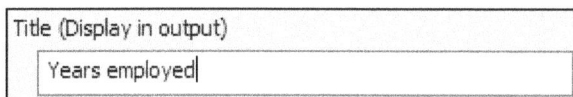

Title (Display in output)
Years employed|

   ❑ from the **Define** area, click the **Add Criteria** tool 🔗

   The Tags and Expressions dialog box opens, displaying the tags you created earlier.

   ❑ from the **Available Tags** area, select the **1_year**, **2_years**, and **5_years**

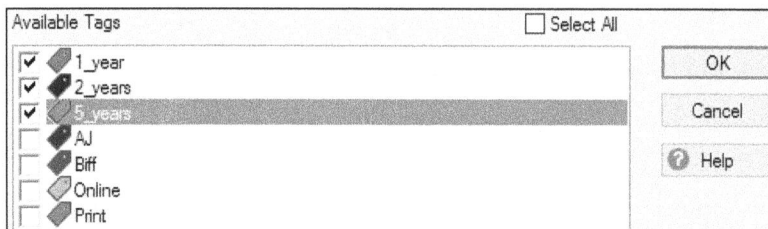

Available Tags	☐ Select All
☑ 1_year	OK
☑ 2_years	Cancel
☑ 5_years	❓ Help
☐ AJ	
☐ Biff	
☐ Online	
☐ Print	

   ❑ click the **OK** button

   The selected expressions appear in the Dynamic Content Filter dialog box.

   ❑ right-click the **1_year** expression and choose **Rename**
   ❑ type **1 Year** and press [**enter**]

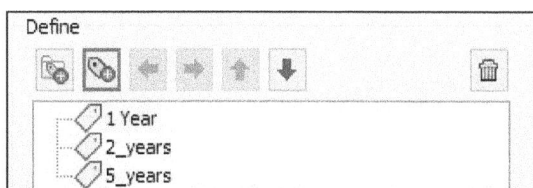

Define
🔗 🔗 ← → ↑ ↓   🗑
◇ 1 Year
◇ 2_years
◇ 5_years

The change you just made was subtle. Because the names you see in this dialog box will be seen by your user, you've made the text a bit easier to read.

❏ change the name of **2_years** to **2 Years**
❏ change the name of **5_years** to **5 Years**

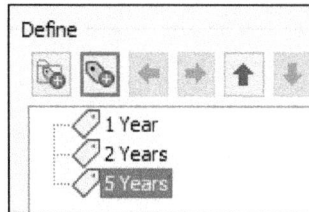

❏ from the bottom of the dialog box, deselect **Allow Multiple Selection in a Group**

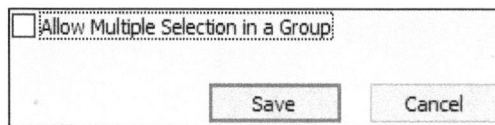

By deselecting **Allow Multiple Selection in a Group**, the user can apply only one filter at a time. If you had left this option selected, the user could apply the filters for 1 Year, 2 Years, and 5 Years simultaneously.

❏ click the **Save** button to close the Content Filter dialog box

3. View Dynamic Filters in output.

❏ with the Responsive HTML5 Settings dialog box still open, click the **Save and Generate** button
❏ when the layout is finished generating, click the **View Result** button
❏ from the TOC, open **General Office Information**
❏ open the **Unique Benefits** topic

Because no filter is applied, all of the benefits are visible in the Unique Benefits topic.

❏ from just above the TOC, click **Filter**

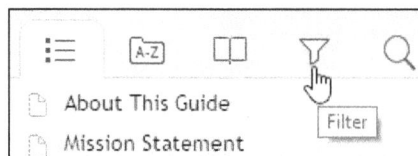

❏ on the Filter tab, select **1 Year**

The filter is applied and only the 1 Year benefits are shown.

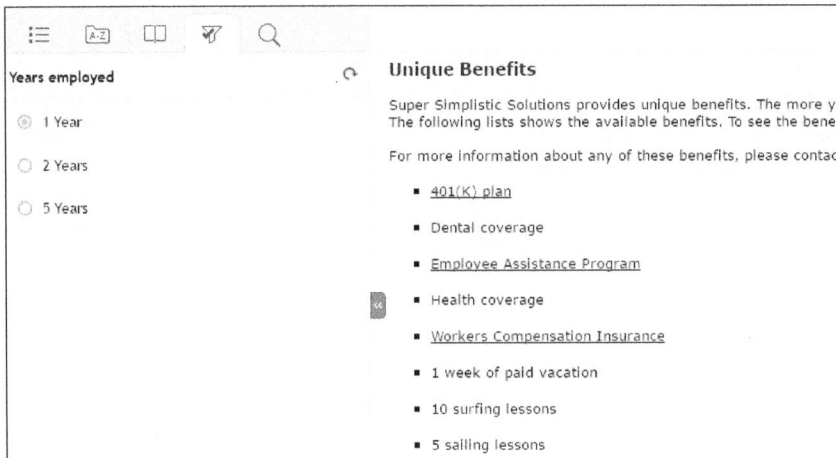

❏ on the Filter tab, select **2 Years**

The new filter is applied, and only the 2 Year benefits are shown.

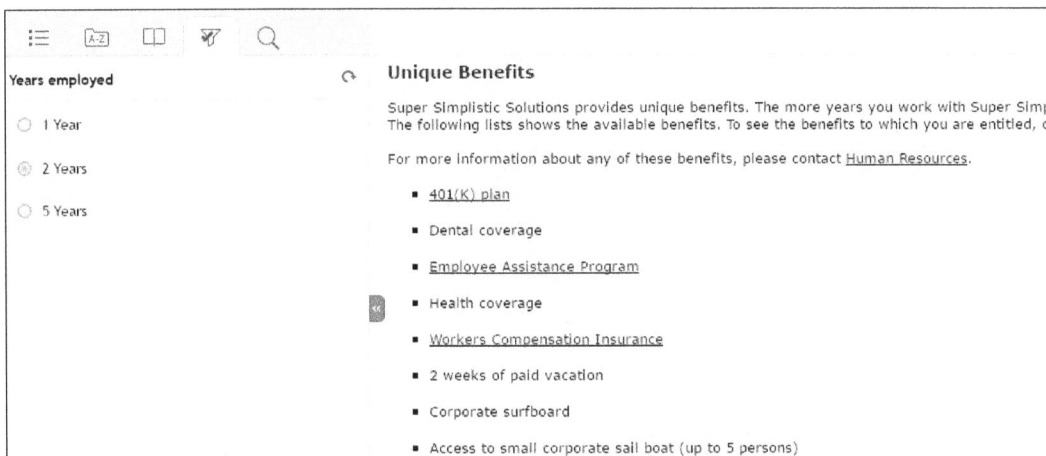

4. Close the browser window and return to the RoboHelp project.

Student Activity: Tag Selected Content for a Build Expression

1. Ensure that the **content_vars_snipps** project is still open.

2. Tag content for a Build Expression.

   ❐ in the **Unique Benefits** topic, select the three **surfing benefits**
   ❐ right-click the selected text and choose **Apply Conditional Build Tag > AJ**

3. Save your work.

4. Select a Conditional Build Expression to be output.

   ❐ on the **Outputs(SSL)** pod, double-click the **Responsive HTML5** layout

   The Responsive HTML5 Settings dialog box opens.

   ❐ from the list of categories at the left, select **Content**
   ❐ from the **Conditional Build Expression** drop-down menu, choose **SSSEast**

Conditional Build Expression		
SSSEast	⌄	Define...

   ❐ click the **Save and Generate** button
   ❐ when the layout is finished generating, click the **View Result** button
   ❐ open the **Unique Benefits** topic
   ❐ spend a few minutes applying Filters

   - 2 weeks of paid vacation
   - 3 weeks of paid vacation
   - 5 sailing lessons
   - Access to small corporate sail boat (up to 5 persons)
   - Access to large corporate sail boat (up to 25 persons)

   Regardless of the filter applied, the surfing benefits are hidden. Why? You selected the **SSSEast** Build Expression. Because employees working for SSSEast work in an area of the country where surf boards aren't necessary, the content is excluded from the output. If you exclude content with a Conditional Build Expression, the content will never be available for a filter.

5. Close the browser window and return to the RoboHelp project.

Dynamic Filters Confidence Check

1. Add a new Conditional Tag named **10_years**.

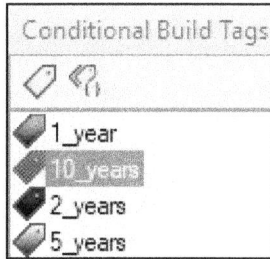

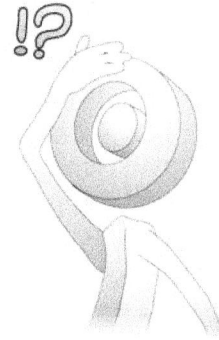

   Conditional Build Tags

   1_year
   10_years
   2_years
   5_years

2. In the **Unique Benefits** topic, add the following benefits to the topic and tag them as 10_years:

   4 weeks of paid vacation

   Family golf membership

   Any car below $45,000 as a company car

   Access to worldwide corporate vacation homes

3. Add the new **10_years** tag to the **Years employed** Dynamic Content Filter to the **Responsive HTML5** output and rename it **10 Years** (look for the **Customize** button in the Responsive HTML5 output).

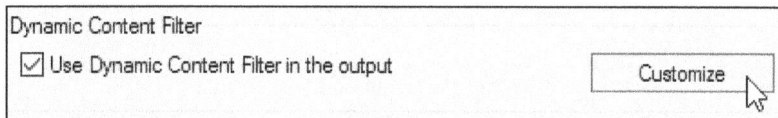

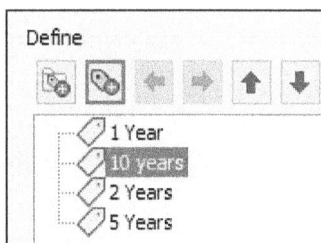

   Dynamic Content Filter

   ☑ Use Dynamic Content Filter in the output   Customize

   Define

   1 Year
   10 years
   2 Years
   5 Years

4. On the **Unique Benefits** topic, tag the sailing benefits as **Biff**.

5. Generate an output for Super Simplistic Solutions **SSSWest**.

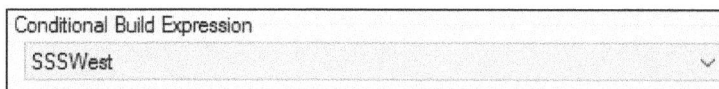

   Conditional Build Expression

   SSSWest

   Because you tagged the sailing benefits as Biff (SSSEast), SSSWest users will not see the sailing benefits in the SSSWest output.

User Defined Variables

Let's say you want to have your company name with a link to your website appear throughout the project. You could accomplish the task the old-fashioned way by typing the company name over and over again. Or you can create a Variable called CompanyName, whose definition is your actual company name. After creating the Variable, it's a simple matter of dragging the CompanyName Variable into any topic.

Now here's the cool part. Assume your company name now appears throughout your project, and now you want to change it. Without the Variable, you would have to use RoboHelp's Find and Replace in Files feature to update the company name (you learned how on page 70). Thanks to Variables, all you'll need to do is update the definition of the CompanyName Variable to change the displayed company name throughout the project.

Student Activity: Work With Variables

1. Ensure that the **content_vars_snipps** project is still open.

2. Show the User Defined Variables pod.

   ❏ click **Pods** and choose **User Defined Variables**

   By default, the User Defined Variables pod is empty.

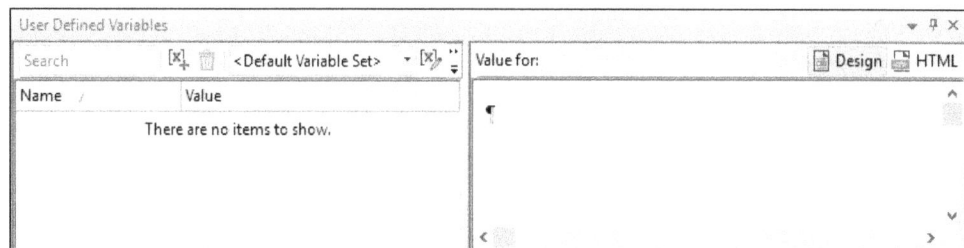

User Defined Variables					▾ 무 ✕
Search	[x] 🗑	<Default Variable Set> ▾ [x] ⁝	Value for:		Design HTML
Name /	Value		¶		^
	There are no items to show.				∨
			<	>	

3. Create a Variable that displays a topic modification date.

   ❏ at the top of the **User Defined Variables** pod, click the **Create a new User Defined Variable** tool [x]

   The New Variable dialog box opens.

   ❏ in the Variable Name field, type **SSSWebAddress**
   ❏ in the Variable value field, type **Super Simplistic Solutions**

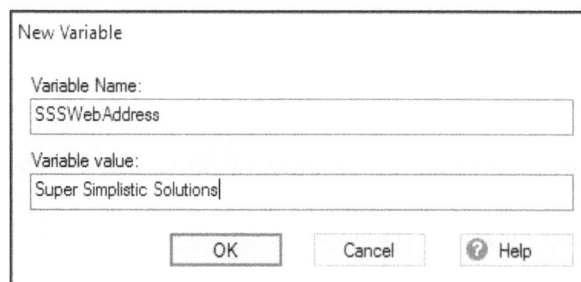

New Variable
Variable Name:
SSSWebAddress
Variable value:
Super Simplistic Solutions|
OK   Cancel   ❓ Help

   ❏ click the **OK** button

The Variable text appears in a panel to the right of the Variable list. You will add a hyperlink to the Variable value next.

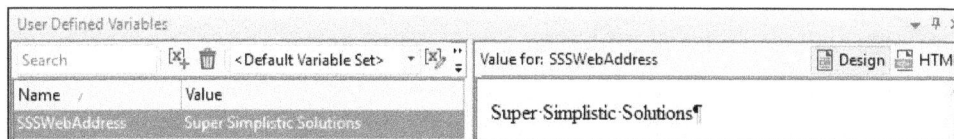

User Defined Variables			▼ ⊣ ×
Search	[x] 🗑 <Default Variable Set> ▾ [x] ⁝	Value for: SSSWebAddress	🖹 Design 🖹 HTML
Name	Value		
SSSWebAddress	Super Simplistic Solutions	Super·Simplistic·Solutions¶	

4. Add a hyperlink to a Variable value.

    ☐ highlight the Variable value (the words **Super Simplistic Solutions**) in the right side of the User Defined Variables pod
    ☐ right-click the selected text and choose **Insert Hyperlink**

    The Hyperlink dialog box opens.

    ☐ from the **Link to** drop-down menu, choose **Web Address**
    ☐ to the right of **http://**, type **www.sss.com**

Link to:	▾	http://www.sss.com

    This isn't a correct web address, but it's an intentional error.

    ☐ click the **OK** button

5. Save your work.

6. Insert a User Defined Variable value into a topic.

    ☐ open the **Nondiscrimination Policy** topic
    ☐ at the top of the topic, highlight the words **Super Simplistic Solutions** at the beginning of the first paragraph
    ☐ on the **Insert** tab, **Variables** group, choose **Variable**

    The Insert Under Defined Variables dialog box opens. The Variable you just created is the only Variable listed in the list of User Defined Variables.

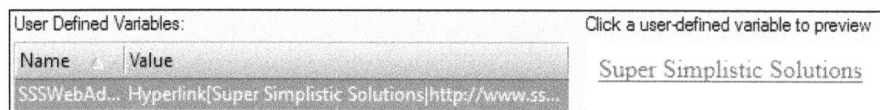

User Defined Variables:		Click a user-defined variable to preview
Name △	Value	
SSSWebAd...	Hyperlink[Super Simplistic Solutions|http://www.ss...	Super Simplistic Solutions

    ☐ click the **Insert** button one time
    ☐ click the **Close** button

    The Variable value appears in the topic in place of the selected text, and the text contains a hyperlink.

7. Replace more text with a Variable value.

    ☐ open the **Absentee Policy** topic
    ☐ in the first paragraph, highlight the words **Super Simplistic Solutions**
    ☐ on the **Insert** tab, **Variables** group, click **Variable**

The Insert Under Defined Variables dialog box reopens.

❏ click the **Insert** button one time and then click the **Close** button

The Variable value has been added to a second topic.

8. Save your work.

9. Edit a User Defined Variable value.

❏ at the right of the User Defined Variables pod, double-click the linked text **Super Simplistic Solutions**

The Hyperlink dialog box opens.

❏ replace www.sss.com with **www.supersimplisticsolutions.com**

Link to:	▼	www.supersimplisticsolutions.com

❏ click the **OK** button

10. Show Variables in topics.

❏ on the **Edit** tab, **View** group, click **Show/Hide > Variables**

Variables in topics are now displayed in green.

> **Note:** If you don't see the variables in green, you are experiencing a known refresh issue in RoboHelp. In that case, close all the topics, reopen them, and show the variables again.

Variables Confidence Check

1. If necessary, open the **Nondiscrimination Policy** topic.

2. Double-click the hyperlink in the topic and notice that the variable value has been updated to the correct web address.

Link to:	▼	http://www.supersimplisticsolutions.com

3. Open the **Absentee Policy** topic.

4. Double-click the hyperlink in the topic and notice that this variable value has also been updated to the correct web address.

5. Go from topic to topic and replace the phrase **Super Simplistic Solutions** with the **SSSWebAddress** variable as appropriate. (**Note:** Because the HolidaySchedule topic is a linked Word document, don't make any edits to the document. Also, there is no need to add the variable to any topic more than once, and not every topic will need the variable—use your best judgment.)

6. Save the project and then close all topics.

Snippets

You can add custom HTML code Snippets to a project and later insert them into a desired topic. When you modify a code Snippet shared by different topics, the changes to the code Snippet are reflected in all the associated topics.

HTML code Snippets are stored in a Snippet library as separate files with an HTS extension. You can view thumbnails of Snippets in the Snippet pod. You can select Snippets and drag and drop them to desired locations in a topic. You can also copy, duplicate, and delete Snippets after you have selected them.

Snippets are similar to variables but can contain multiple paragraphs of text (variable values can contain multiple lines, but not paragraphs), popups, tables, DHTML, and other higher-end code.

Student Activity: Work With Snippets

1. Ensure that the **content_vars_snipps** project is still open.

2. Show the Snippet pod.

   ❒ on the **Project** tab, click **Pods**, and choose **Snippet**

3. Create a new Snippet.

   ❒ at the top right of the Snippet pod, click the **Create New Snippet** tool

   The New Snippet dialog box opens.

   ❒ type **AbuseInfo** into the Name field

   ```
   General   ? Appearance

        Name: AbuseInfo

   File Name: AbuseInfo.hts

   Description:

   Category: Default                              ⌄
   ```

   ❒ select the **Appearance** tab
   ❒ from the Style Sheet list, select **policies.css**

   ```
   General   ? Appearance

   Style Sheet:

   (None)
   policies.css                                   📂
   Leave_and_Vacation\HolidaySchedule\HolidaySchedule.css
   default.css                                    Edit...
   ```

   ❒ click the **OK** button

   The Snippet opens in its own window, similar to creating a new topic.

❐ select all of the text in the window and replace it with **Super Simplistic Solutions recognizes that alcoholism and drug abuse are treatable illnesses, and encourages employees who may have alcohol or drug abuse problems to seek treatment for them. Any individual afflicted by alcoholism or drug dependency will have the same options that employees with other illnesses have to participate in prescribed treatment programs, including the use of paid leave and unpaid leave of absence.**

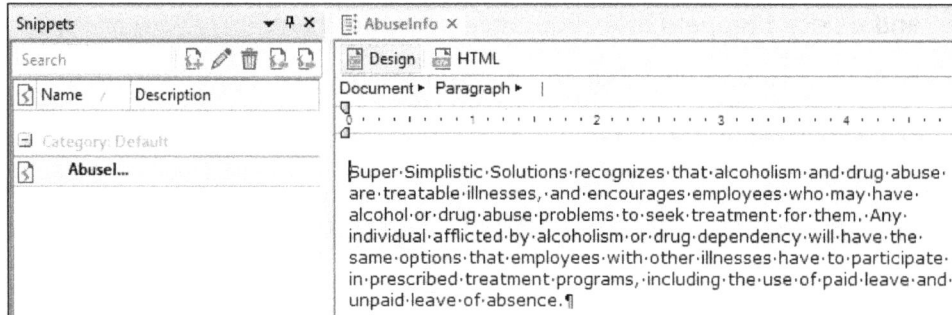

Snippets ▾ ⯐ ✕	▤ AbuseInfo ✕
Search ⯅ ✎ 🗑 ⯐ ⯐	▤ Design ▤ HTML
⟨⟩ Name ／ Description	Document ▸ Paragraph ▸	
⊟ Category: Default	
⟨⟩ **AbuseI...**	Super·Simplistic·Solutions·recognizes·that·alcoholism·and·drug·abuse· are·treatable·illnesses,·and·encourages·employees·who·may·have· alcohol·or·drug·abuse·problems·to·seek·treatment·for·them.··Any· individual·afflicted·by·alcoholism·or·drug·dependency·will·have·the· same·options·that·employees·with·other·illnesses·have·to·participate· in·prescribed·treatment·programs,·including·the·use·of·paid·leave·and· unpaid·leave·of·absence.¶

4. Save your work.

5. Add a Snippet to a topic.

   ❐ using the Topic List pod, open the **Alcohol Policy** topic

   ❐ from the Snippet pod, drag the AbuseInfo Snippet just to the left of the words "See also" at the end of the topic

   The text you typed into the Snippet appears within the topic.

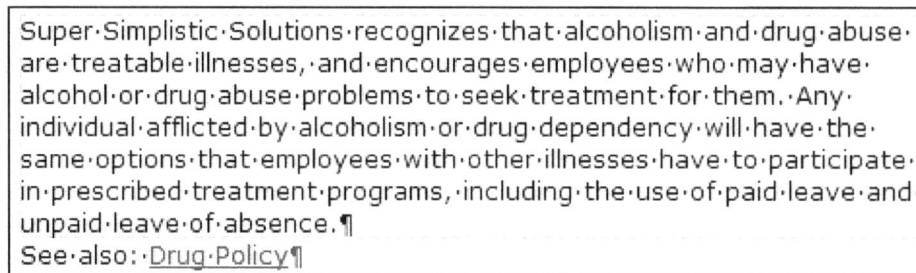

   > Super·Simplistic·Solutions·recognizes·that·alcoholism·and·drug·abuse·
   > are·treatable·illnesses,·and·encourages·employees·who·may·have·
   > alcohol·or·drug·abuse·problems·to·seek·treatment·for·them.·Any·
   > individual·afflicted·by·alcoholism·or·drug·dependency·will·have·the·
   > same·options·that·employees·with·other·illnesses·have·to·participate·
   > in·prescribed·treatment·programs,·including·the·use·of·paid·leave·and·
   > unpaid·leave·of·absence.¶
   > See·also:··Drug·Policy¶

Snippets Confidence Check

1. Add the **AbuseInfo** Snippet to the end of the Drug Policy topic.

2. Preview the two topics containing the Snippet.

3. After closing the preview, double-click the **AbuseInfo** Snippet on the Snippets pod.

4. From near the end of the Snippet text, remove the following text: **to participate in prescribed treatment programs**.

5. From the beginning of the Snippet text, replace the text **Super Simplistic Solutions** with the User Defined Variable **SSSWebAddress**.

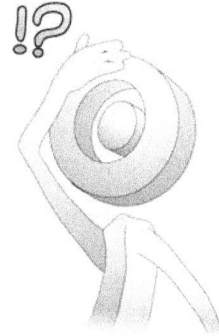

> Super·Simplistic·Solutions·recognizes·that·alcoholism·and·drug·abuse·
> are·treatable·illnesses,·and·encourages·employees·who·may·have·
> alcohol·or·drug·abuse·problems·to·seek·treatment·for·them.·Any·
> individual·afflicted·by·alcoholism·or·drug·dependency·will·have·the·
> same·options·that·employees·with·other·illnesses,·including·the·use·of·
> paid·leave·and·unpaid·leave·of·absence.¶

6. Save and close the Snippet.

7. Open both topics that are using the Snippet.

   Notice that the text has been updated in both topics.

   Note: Keep in mind that Snippets and Variables are similar. Unlike Variables, Snippets can contain multiple paragraphs, popups, tables, DHTML, and other higher-end code.

8. Save and then close the project.

Sharing Resources

RoboHelp's Resource Manager pod allows you to share resources among RoboHelp projects. One of the coolest ways to use the Resource Manager and share resources is via Dropbox, a free service that lets you store and share photos, documents, videos, and more over the Internet.

For the remainder of this module, Kevin describes how he used Dropbox to work with a fellow RoboHelp author (who happens to works in another state). Because you'll need to either team up with another RoboHelp author or create two Dropbox accounts to follow along with each of his steps below, review the following step and then try them on your own later.

Demonstration Only: Share Dropbox Resources

1. I visited Dropbox.com and created an account. I also created a folder in Dropbox called **SharedRoboHelpTopics** and shared it through Dropbox (both tasks, creating and sharing the folder took mere seconds).

2. Once the Dropbox account had been set up, I opened a RoboHelp project and chose **Project > Pods > Resource Manager**. (The pod opened at the right of my RoboHelp window.)

3. From the top of the Resource Manager pod, I clicked the **Add Shared Location** tool.

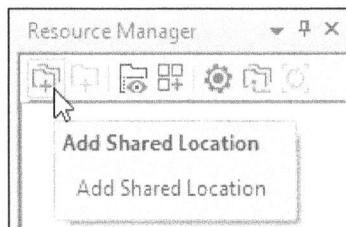

4. In the Add Shared Location dialog box, I clicked the **Location type** drop-down menu and selected **Dropbox**.

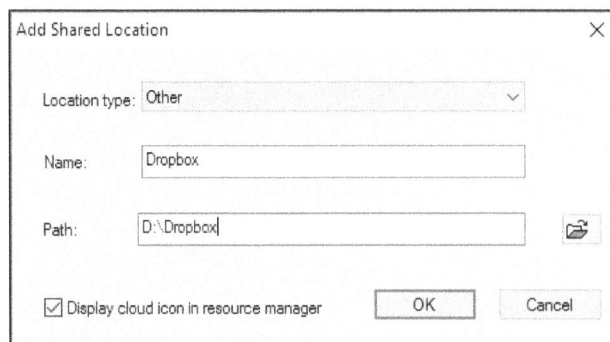

Note: Each time I performed this step, RoboHelp consistently loaded the Dropbox folder and Path. Alternatively, you can click the **Browse** button and manually locate your Dropbox folder.

5. I added content to the shared Dropbox folder on the RoboHelp Resource Manager.

   As mentioned earlier, my shared Dropbox folder is called **SharedRoboHelpTopics**. When I dragged a topic (**Alcohol_Policy**) to the shared folder, I was delighted to see that in addition to the topic, the Cascading Style Sheet being used by the topic (policies.css) and the Snippet (AbuseInfo) were also added to the shared folder.

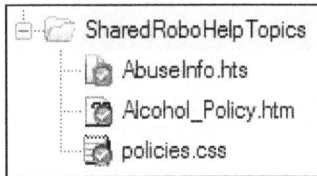

   ```
   ⊟ 📁 SharedRoboHelpTopics
        📄 AbuseInfo.hts
        📄 Alcohol_Policy.htm
        📄 policies.css
   ```

   A team member, who is located in another state, was working on his own RoboHelp project and needed to use some of my content. Although we don't share a network connection, we each have Dropbox accounts.

6. I accessed my Dropbox account and sent the team member an invite to the **SharedRoboHelpTopics** folder.

7. He checked his email and followed the instructions in the email to add my SharedRoboHelpTopics folder to his Dropbox account.

8. He used RoboHelp's Resource Manager pod to add his Dropbox as a Shared Location.

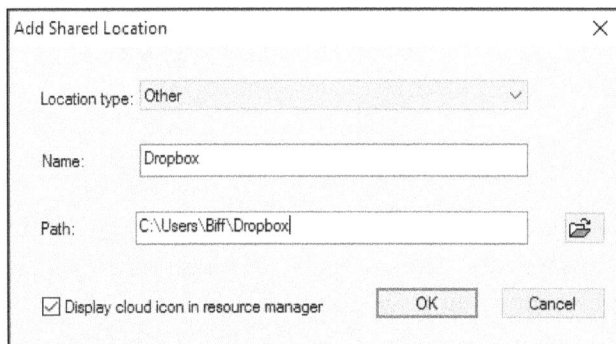

   ```
   Add Shared Location                                    ✕

   Location type: Other                              ⌄

   Name:      Dropbox

   Path:      C:\Users\Biff\Dropbox              📂

   ☑ Display cloud icon in resource manager    [ OK ]   [ Cancel ]
   ```

   Because my team member's Dropbox included my shared folder, his Resource Manager immediately displayed the shared resources.

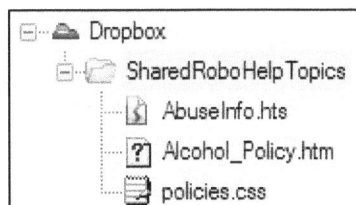

   ```
   ⊟ ☁ Dropbox
        ⊟ 📁 SharedRoboHelpTopics
             📄 AbuseInfo.hts
             📄 Alcohol_Policy.htm
             📄 policies.css
   ```

9. To add the shared content to his RoboHelp project, he right-clicked the Alcohol_Policy topic on the Resource Manager pod and chose **Add to Project**.

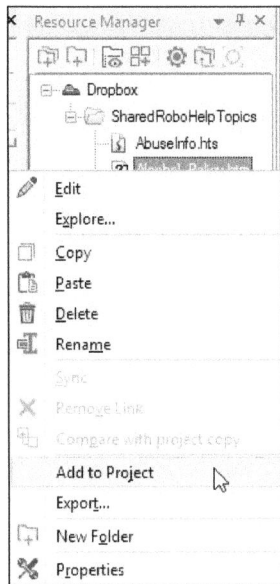

Like magic, RoboHelp content was now being used in two projects in two different locations. What do you think? Cool?

At some point, a shared topic was edited in my RoboHelp project. The Resource Manager showed an alert that the shared assets weren't synchronized (via the red icon shown in the image below). When content isn't synchronized, it's likely that team members aren't using the same content.

10. Because I wanted to ensure that everyone was working with the same assets, I right-clicked the topic on the Resources Manager and selected **Sync**.

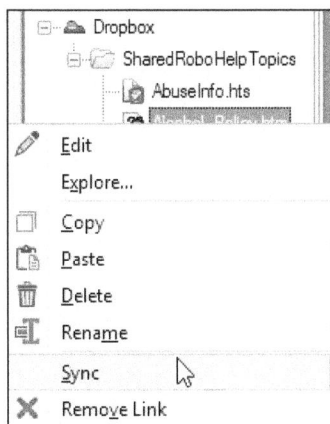

Green check marks indicated that all was well between the content in my RoboHelp project and the assets in the Dropbox.

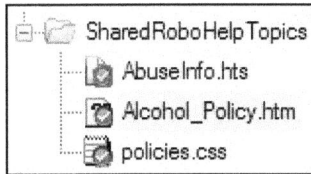

```
SharedRoboHelpTopics
    AbuseInfo.hts
    Alcohol_Policy.htm
    policies.css
```

I was curious to learn if my team member actually got the updated content in his project. And if so, what was his experience? Was it painful?

It turns out that his experience was almost, well, routine. He told me that when he opened his project with RoboHelp later that day, he was greeted with the **Linked Resource Notification** dialog box shown below.

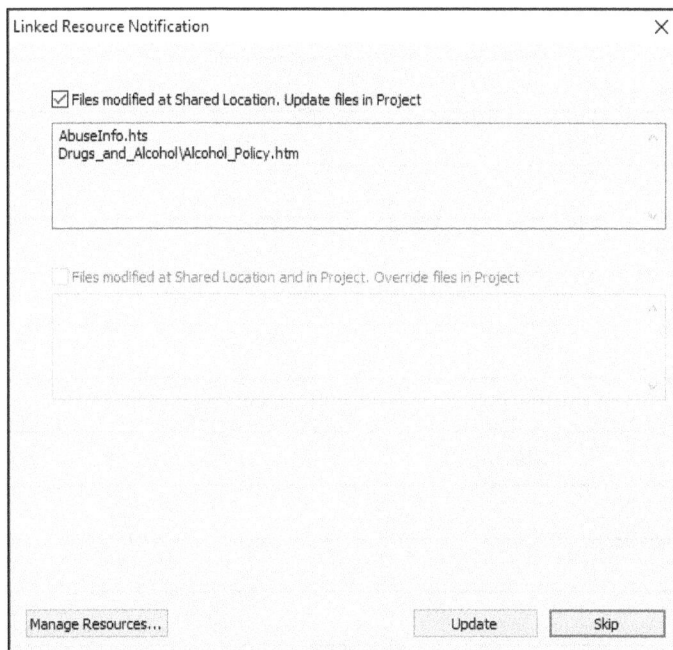

```
Linked Resource Notification                              ×

  ☑ Files modified at Shared Location. Update files in Project

  ┌─────────────────────────────────────────────────────┐
  │ AbuseInfo.hts                                       △│
  │ Drugs_and_Alcohol\Alcohol_Policy.htm                │
  │                                                     ▽│
  └─────────────────────────────────────────────────────┘

  ☐ Files modified at Shared Location and in Project. Override files in Project

  ┌─────────────────────────────────────────────────────┐
  │                                                     △│
  │                                                      │
  │                                                     ▽│
  └─────────────────────────────────────────────────────┘




  ┌──────────────────┐              ┌────────┐ ┌────────┐
  │ Manage Resources…│              │ Update │ │  Skip  │
  └──────────────────┘              └────────┘ └────────┘
```

11. All he had to do was click the **Update** button, and his content was automatically synchronized with mine. In a word, that's awesome!

Notes

Module 8: Tables and Lists

In This Module You Will Learn About:

- Working With Tables, page 164
- Lines, Symbols, and Lists, page 175
- Global Formatting, page 185

And You Will Learn To:

- Insert a Table, page 164
- Insert a Table Row, page 167
- Work With Table Styles, page 168
- Change Table Properties, page 171
- Add a Horizontal Line, page 175
- Insert a Symbol, page 177
- Add a Bulleted List, page 178
- Create a List Style, page 181
- Edit a List Style, page 183
- Set Global Formatting, page 185

Working With Tables

Tables, which are made up of **cells** (a rectangle that can contain data), **columns** (a vertical collection of cells) and **rows** (a horizontal collection of cells) allow you to organize data in an easy-to-read format. During the activities that follow, you will learn how to insert and edit tables—and how to work with Table Styles that will make Table formatting a breeze.

Student Activity: Insert a Table

1. Open the **tables** RoboHelp project file.

2. Insert a table into the Vacation Policy topic.

   ❑ open the **Vacation Policy** topic
   ❑ click after the topic text **10,001 + 20 days** and press [**enter**] to create a new paragraph
   ❑ on the **Insert** tab, click **Table** and insert a table with **4 rows** and **2 columns**

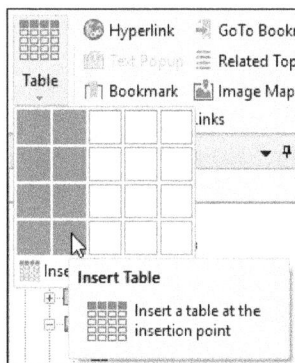

   There is now an empty table just above the last paragraph in the topic.

3. Select a Table Template.

   ❑ click within the table and then, from the **Table Format** tab, **Table** group, click **Style**

   The **Select Table Style** dialog box opens.

   ❑ from the **Table Templates** list, scroll down and select **SimpleGridBlue**

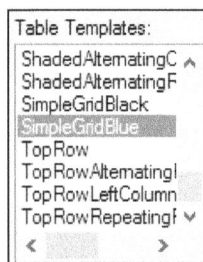

   ❑ click the **OK** button

   The table now has a blue border.

4. Drag existing topic text into the table.

☐ from above the table, highlight the phrase **Hours Worked**

☐ drag the text into the **first** cell in the **first** row

Hours Worked·Days·Allowed·per·Year¶

0·–·6000·10·days¶

6001·–·10,000·15·days¶

10,001·+·20·days¶

¶	¶
¶	¶
¶	¶
¶	¶

·Days·Allowed·per·Year¶

0·–·6000·10·days¶

6001·–·10,000·15·days¶

10,001·+·20·days¶

Hours Worked¶	¶
¶	¶

5. Save your work.

Tables Confidence Check

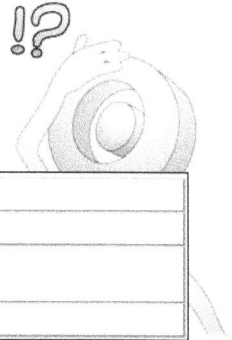

1. Continue dragging topic content (the hours worked and the days allowed per year) into the table until your table looks like the picture below.

Hours·Worked¶	Days·Allowed·per·Year¶
0·—·6000¶	10·days¶
6001·-·10,000¶	¶ 15·days¶
10,001·+¶	20·days¶

2. Delete the white space between the table and the text above it.

3. Delete any extra space beneath the table.

   Your table and topic should look like the picture below.

Vacation·Policy¶

Annual·vacation·leave·is·based·on·the·following·schedule·related·to·years·of·employment·with·Super·Simplistic·Solutions:¶

Hours·Worked¶	Days·Allowed·per·Year¶
0·—·6000¶	10·days¶
6001·-·10,000¶	¶ 15·days¶
10,001·+¶	20·days¶

You·are·eligible·to·take·vacation·days·earned·after·you·have·been·paid·for·1000·hours.·Each·employee·will·be·allowed·to·carry·over·into·the·next·calendar·year·120·hours·of·vacation.·Any·unused·vacation·in·excess·of·120·hours·will·be·forfeited.·Leave·may·be·taken·only·after·it·is·earned;·no·advance·leave·will·be·approved.·Use·of·vacation·time·is·subject·to·management·approval,·and·requests·should·be·made·at·least·2·weeks·in·advance.·Only·persons·who·remain·employed·are·eligible·for·vacation.·Upon·voluntary·resignation,·employees·may·be·paid·for·accrued·vacation·hours·to·a·maximum·of·120·hours.·Leave·hours·of·any·kind·will·not·be·accrued·on·any·overtime·hours.¶

4. Save the project.

Student Activity: Insert a Table Row

1. Ensure that the **tables** project is still open.

2. Insert a table row.

   ❏ click in first table cell **(Hours Worked)**
   ❏ on the **Table Format** tab, **Insert** group, click **Row**

   A new row is inserted above the first row.

   ❏ click in the first cell of the new row
   ❏ type **Super Simplistic Solutions' Annual Vacation Schedule**

Super·Simplistic·Solutions'·Annual·Vacation·Schedule¶	¶
Hours·Worked¶	Days·Allowed·per·Year¶
0·–·6000¶	10·days¶
6001·–·10,000¶	15·days¶
10,001·+¶	20·days¶

3. Use the Tag List to select a row.

   ❏ on the **Edit** tab, **View** group, click **Show/Hide** and choose **Tag List**

   A list of tags appears just above the topic. (If the Tag List does not appear, it's possible that it was already open, and you have just hidden it. In that case, repeat this step.)

   ❏ click anywhere in the first row ("Super Simplistic Solutions' Annual Vacation Schedule")
   ❏ on the **Tag List**, click **Row**

   The entire row should now be selected.

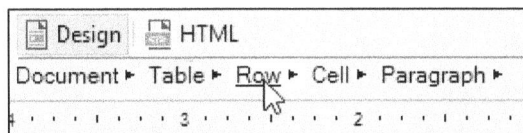

🖼 Design	🖼 HTML
Document ▸ Table ▸ Row ▸ Cell ▸ Paragraph ▸	

4. Merge cells.

   ❏ on the **Table Format** tab, **Merge** group, click **Merge**

   The two individual cells in the first row are now one long cell.

Super·Simplistic·Solutions'··Annual·Vacation·Schedule¶	
Hours·Worked¶	Days·Allowed·per·Year¶
0·–·6000¶	10·days¶
6001·–·10,000¶	15·days¶

Student Activity: Work With Table Styles

1. Ensure that the **tables** project is still open.

2. Create a Table Style to use on all project tables.

   ❐ on the **Project Manager** pod, open the Project Files folder
   ❐ double-click **policies.css** to open the style sheet for editing
   ❐ click the plus sign to the left of the **Table** group to expand the group

   There is one Table Style listed—SimpleGridBlue.

   ❐ right-click **SimpleGridBlue** and choose **Duplicate**
   ❐ name the new style **SSS_Tables** and press [**enter**]

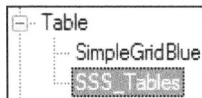

   ```
   ⊟ Table
       SimpleGridBlue
       SSS_Tables
   ```

3. Change the font and font size used in the table's odd rows.

   ❐ ensure the **SSS_Tables** style is selected
   ❐ from the **Apply Formatting to** drop-down menu, choose **Odd Rows**

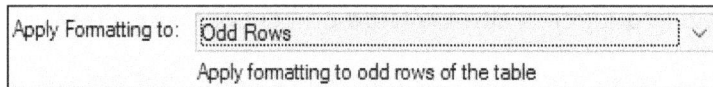

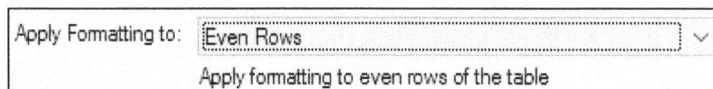

   Apply Formatting to: | Odd Rows | ⌄
   Apply formatting to odd rows of the table

   ❐ change the Font to **Verdana**
   ❐ change the Font size to **10pt**

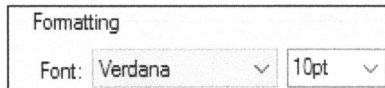

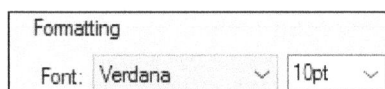

   Formatting
   Font: Verdana ⌄ 10pt ⌄

4. Change the font and font size used in the table's even rows.

   ❐ from the **Apply Formatting to** drop-down menu, choose **Even Rows**

   Apply Formatting to: | Even Rows | ⌄
   Apply formatting to even rows of the table

   ❐ change the Font to **Verdana**
   ❐ change the Font size to **10pt**

   Formatting
   Font: Verdana ⌄ 10pt ⌄

5. Change the font used in the First Row.

☐ from the **Apply Formatting to** drop-down menu, choose **First Row**

Apply Formatting to:	First Row	⌄
	Apply formatting to the first row of the table	

☐ change the **Font** to **Verdana**
☐ change the **Font Size** to **11pt**
☐ change the **Type Style** to **Bold**
☐ from the **Align** drop-down menu, choose **Center**

Formatting

Font:	Verdana	⌄	11pt	⌄	**A**	✎	**T**	*I*	**T**
Border:	Solid	⌄	1px	⌄	Top-Left Corner	⌄	✎	🪣
Align:	Left	⌄				Cell Properties	

In the Table Preview, notice that the right side of the border is white. You will change the border formatting next.

ABCD	**1234**	**ABCD**	**1234**	**ABCD**
✻ ✻ ✻	✻ ✻ ✻	✻ ✻ ✻	✻ ✻ ✻	✻ ✻ ✻
✻ ✻ ✻ ✻	✻ ✻ ✻ ✻	✻ ✻ ✻ ✻	✻ ✻ ✻ ✻	✻ ✻ ✻ ✻
✻ ✻ ✻	✻ ✻ ✻	✻ ✻ ✻	✻ ✻ ✻	✻ ✻ ✻
✻ ✻ ✻ ✻	✻ ✻ ✻ ✻	✻ ✻ ✻ ✻	✻ ✻ ✻ ✻	✻ ✻ ✻ ✻

6. Change the Borders used for the First Row.

☐ from the **Border Position** drop-down menu, choose **Bottom-Right Corner**

Bottom-Right Corn ⌄	✎	🪣
	Cell Properties	

☐ click the **OK** button

Because you have not yet applied the Table Style to the table in the topic, the appearance of the existing table does not look any different.

7. Apply a Table Style to a table.

   ❒ click within the Vacation Policy topic
   ❒ on the **Edit** tab, click **Style Pod**

   The Styles and Formatting pod appears at the right of the workspace.

   ❒ from the drop-down menu at the top of the **Styles and Formatting** pod, choose **Table Style**
   ❒ click within the table in the **Vacation Policy** topic
   ❒ on the **Styles and Formatting** panel, right-click **SSS_Tables** and choose **Apply**

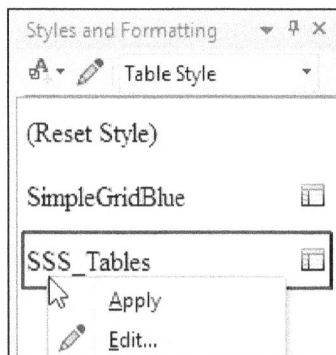

   The table takes on the formatting specified in the SSS_Tables style.

8. Edit the Table Style so that all even rows are shaded.

   ❒ on the **Styles and Formatting** panel, right-click **SSS_Tables** and choose **Edit**

   The Styles dialog box opens.

   ❒ from the **Apply Formatting to** drop-down menu, choose **Even Rows**

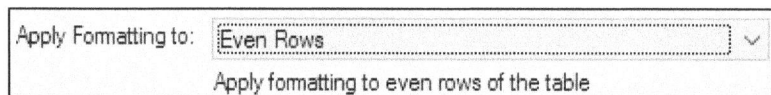

   ❒ click the **Change the fill color of selection** tool
   ❒ select any color you like and then click the **OK** button

   The table's even rows should now have the fill color you specified.

9. Edit the Table Style again.

   ❒ on the Styles and Formatting panel, right-click **SSS_Tables** and choose **Edit**
   ❒ from the **Apply Formatting to** drop-down menu, choose **First Row**
   ❒ change the Font Size to **10pt**
   ❒ click the **Change the fill color of selection** tool and select **Maroon** from the list of colors
   ❒ click the **Change font color** tool and choose **White**
   ❒ click the **OK** button

Student Activity: Change Table Properties

1. Ensure that the **tables** project is still open.

2. Change the table's width.

   ❏ click anywhere within the table in the **Vacation Policy** topic
   ❏ on the **Table Format** tab, **Table** group, click **Properties**

   The Table dialog box opens.

   ❏ on the Table tab, ensure **Preferred width** is selected from the Size area and then type **75%** into the Preferred width area

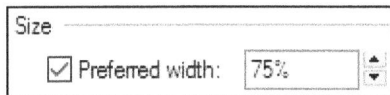

3. Change the table's horizontal alignment.

   ❏ from the Alignment area, select **Center**

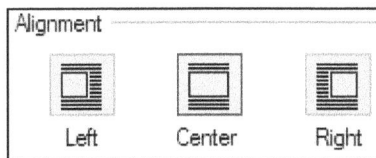

4. Add a Table caption.

   ❏ from the Table caption area, select **Below**

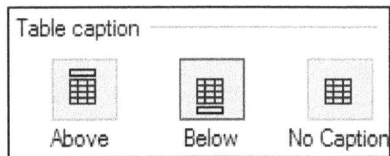

   ❏ click the **OK** button

   The table is now centered horizontally in the topic and is resized to 75% of the width of the topic window. In addition, there is a space beneath the table (the Table caption).

   Vacation·Policy¶

   Annual·vacation·leave·is·based·on·the·following·schedule·related·to·years·of·employment·with·Super·Simplistic·Solutions:¶

Super·Simplistic·Solutions'·Annual·Vacation·Schedule¶	
Hours·Worked¶	Days·Allowed·per·Year¶
0·–·6000¶	10·days¶
6001·–·10,000¶	15·days¶
10,001·+¶	20·days¶

   You·are·eligible·to·take·vacation·days·earned·after·you·have·been·paid·for·1000·hours.·Each·employee·will·be·allowed·to·carry·over·into·the·next·calendar·year·120·hours·of·vacation.·Any·

Another Tables Confidence Check

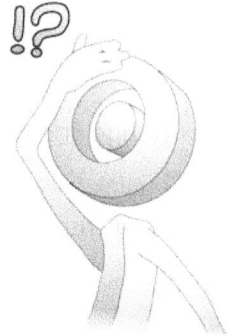

1. In the caption area beneath the table, type **Note: Days allowed subject to change without notice.**

Super·Simplistic·Solutions'·Annual·Vacation·Schedule¶	
Hours·Worked¶	Days·Allowed·per·Year¶
0·-·6000¶	10·days¶
6001·-·10,000¶	15·days¶
10,001·+¶	20·days¶
Note:·Days·allowed·subject·to·change·without·notice.¶	

2. Select the text you just entered.

3. Using the **Character** group on the **Edit** tab, change the Font to **Verdana** and the Font Size to **8pt**.

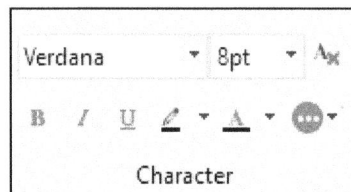

4. Ensure that the caption text you just formatted is still selected and then click the word **CAPTION** (in the Style group).

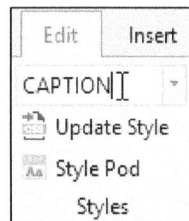

5. Press [**enter**] on your keyboard.

   You will be prompted to add a New Paragraph style named CAPTION.

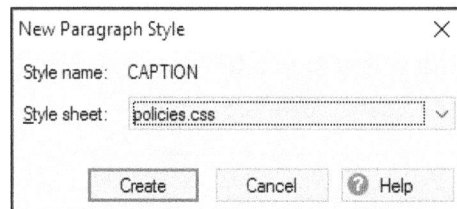

6. Click the **Create** button.

7. Preview the topic. (A fast way to preview is to press [**ctrl**] [**w**].)

8. Resize the Preview window and notice that, depending on the width of the window, the table changes size and the text wraps as needed.

   In the next few steps, you will assign a fixed size to the table and add color to the table.

9. Close the preview.

10. Click anywhere in the table and on the **Table Format** tab, **Table** group, click **Properties**.

11. From the **Size** area of the Table tab, change the Preferred width to **400px** (not 400%)

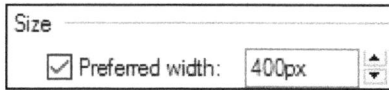

```
Size
  ☑ Preferred width:  400px  ▲▼
```

12. Click the **OK** button.

13. Preview the topic and resize the window.

   As you resize the window, the table should always be centered horizontally, but should NOT change size. By changing the Table Size to a set value (400 pixels) instead of a percentage (100%), the table stays a constant size as you resize the window.

   Note: If you have more than one browser on your computer, you can see how your topic displays in an alternate browser by clicking the **View with** button and selecting a different browser.

```
        View with...
      Google Chrome
      Internet Explorer
      Mozilla Firefox
```

14. Close the Preview window.

15. Create a new topic called **Table Test**.

```
🖥 General  ✓ Status  ? Appearance  ☰ Index

Topic Title:   Table Test
Variables:    <Select a Variable to Insert in Topic Title>
File Name:    Table_Test.htm
```

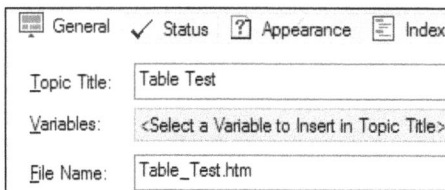

16. If necessary, apply the **policies.css** style sheet to the new topic.

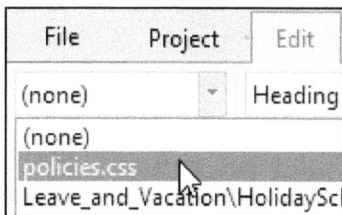

```
 File      Project     Edit

(none)        ▾    Heading

(none)
policies.css
Leave_and_Vacation\HolidaySc
```

17. Insert a new 3-row, 3-column table that uses the **SSS_Tables** style.

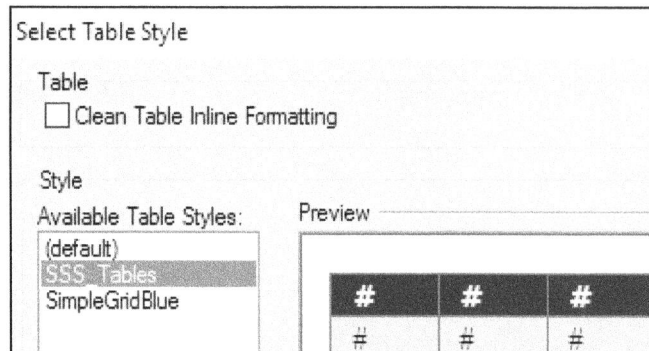

Select Table Style

Table
☐ Clean Table Inline Formatting

Style
Available Table Styles: Preview
(default)
SSS_Tables
SimpleGridBlue

#	#	#
#	#	#

18. Fill the new table with data similar to the image below (merge the cells in the first row).

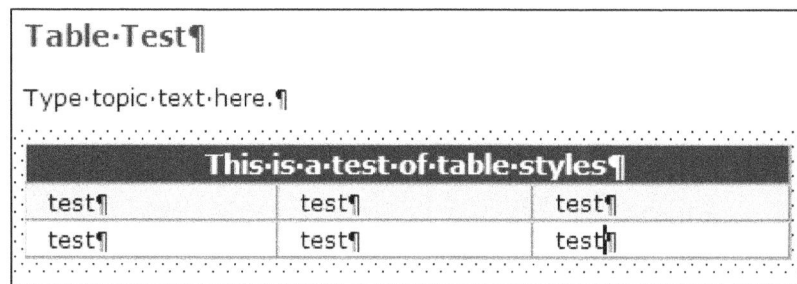

Table·Test¶

Type·topic·text·here.¶

This·is·a·test·of·table·styles¶		
test¶	test¶	test¶
test¶	test¶	test¶

19. Edit the SSS_Tables style (via the Styles and Formatting panel) and change the shading color of the **even rows** to any color you like.

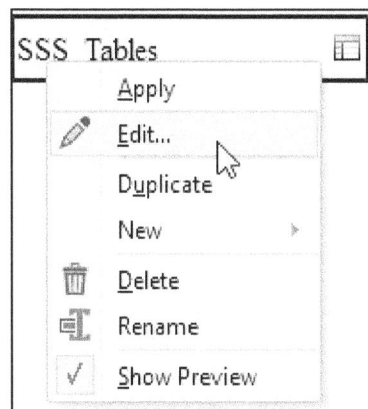

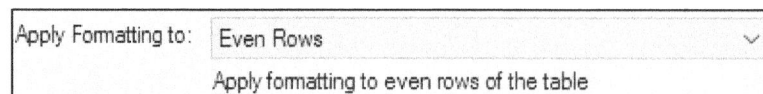

SSS_Tables

- Apply
- ✐ Edit...
- Duplicate
- New ▸
- 🗑 Delete
- ⬛ Rename
- ✓ Show Preview

Apply Formatting to: Even Rows   ⌄
                        Apply formatting to even rows of the table

After closing the Styles dialog box, notice that the shading color for both tables in the project have changed (there is a table in the Table Test topic and the Vacation Policy topic).

20. Save and close all topics.

21. Delete the Table Test topic.

Lines, Symbols, and Lists

During the next few activities, you will add horizontal rules, symbols, bullets, and numbers to select paragraphs.

Student Activity: Add a Horizontal Line

1. Ensure that the **tables** project is still open.

2. Insert a Horizontal line within the topic.

   ☐ open the **Pets in the Office Policy** topic

   ☐ scroll down and click in front of the paragraph **Banned From the Office!**

   ☐ on the **Insert** tab, **HTML** group, click the drop-down menu to the right of **Text Box** and choose **Horizontal Line**

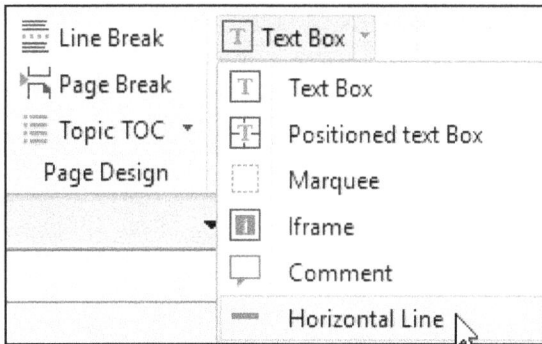

☰ Line Break	T Text Box ▾
⊓ Page Break	T Text Box
☰ Topic TOC ▾	▦ Positioned text Box
Page Design	⬚ Marquee
▾	🄘 Iframe
	⬚ Comment
	— Horizontal Line ↖

   A thin horizontal line is inserted.

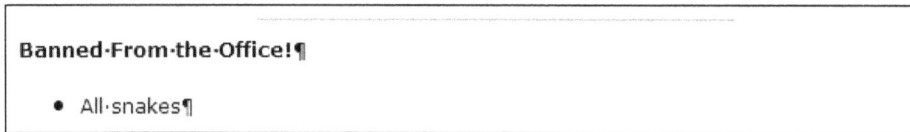

   Banned·From·the·Office!¶

   - All·snakes¶

3. Resize the horizontal line.

   ☐ double-click the **horizontal line** you just inserted

   The Horizontal Line dialog box opens.

   ☐ change the Size Width to **60%** and the Size Height to **3px**

   Horizontal Line

   Size

   Width: `60%`   Height: `3px`

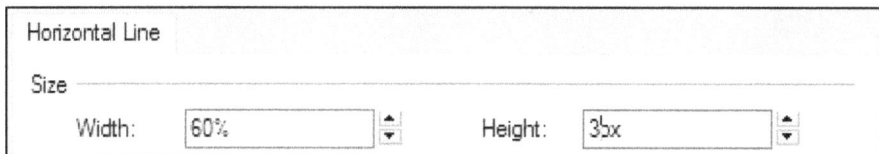

   ☐ from the Appearance area, click **Custom**

❏ select any **Fill color** you like

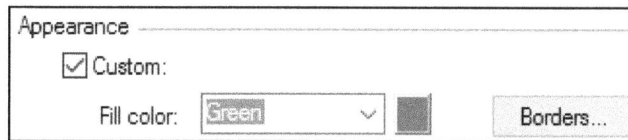

```
┌ Appearance ─────────────────────────────────────┐
│     ☑ Custom:                                     │
│                                                   │
│     Fill color:  [Green          ▼]  ▣   [Borders...] │
└───────────────────────────────────────────────────┘
```

❏ click the **OK** button twice to close both dialog boxes

The line is thicker and has a different color. In addition, it will always be 60% of the window's width.

Student Activity: Insert a Symbol

1. Ensure that the **tables** project is still open.

2. Open the **About This Guide** topic

3. Add a registered mark.

   ❒ in the first paragraph, after the words **Super Simplistic Solutions**
   ❒ on the **Insert** tab, **Media** group, click **Symbol**

   The Symbol dialog box opens.

   ❒ scroll down and select **Registered**

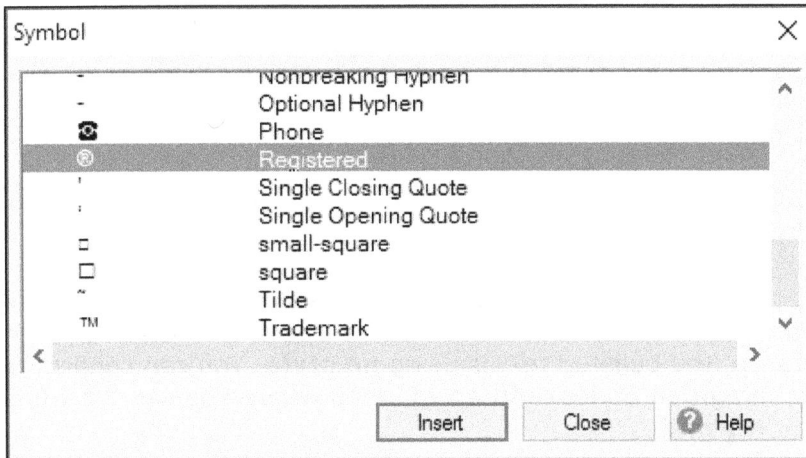

Symbol	✕
	Nonbreaking Hyphen
-	Optional Hyphen
☎	Phone
®	**Registered**
'	Single Closing Quote
'	Single Opening Quote
▫	small-square
☐	square
~	Tilde
™	Trademark

   [Insert] [Close] [? Help]

   ❒ click the **Insert** button
   ❒ click the **Close** button

   A registered mark should now be at the end of the text.

   About·This·Guide¶

   This·guide·has·been·prepared·to·assist·Super·Simplistic·Solutions®·staff·employees·in·
   understanding·the·general·operation·of·Super·Simplistic·Solutions·and·its·present·policies·
   and·procedures.¶

   ---

4. Save and close all open topics.

Student Activity: Add a Bulleted List

1. Ensure that the **tables** project is still open.

2. Add bullets to selected text.

   ❏ open the **Leave Policy** topic
   ❏ scroll down and highlight the text **to care for the employee's child...** through **...perform the employee's job.**
   ❏ on the Edit tab, click the **Create a Bulleted List** tool

Each of the selected paragraphs should now be formatted with a standard bullet.

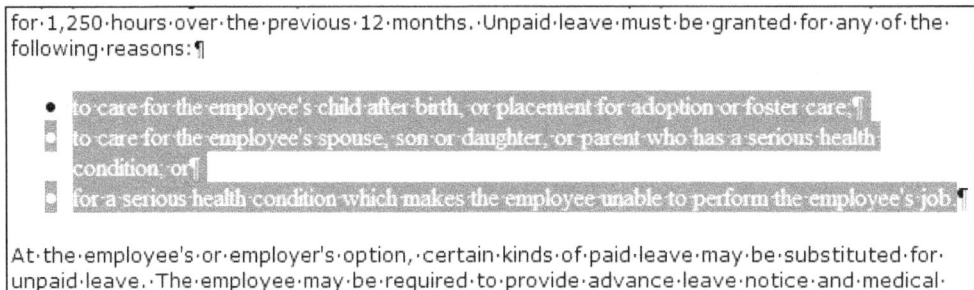

for·1,250·hours·over·the·previous·12·months.··Unpaid·leave·must·be·granted·for·any·of·the· following·reasons:¶

- to·care·for·the·employee's·child·after·birth,·or·placement·for·adoption·or·foster·care;¶
- to·care·for·the·employee's·spouse,·son·or·daughter,·or·parent·who·has·a·serious·health· condition;·or¶
- for·a·serious·health·condition·which·makes·the·employee·unable·to·perform·the·employee's·job.¶

At·the·employee's·or·employer's·option,·certain·kinds·of·paid·leave·may·be·substituted·for· unpaid·leave.··The·employee·may·be·required·to·provide·advance·leave·notice·and·medical·

Notice, however, that the text is no longer using the same font used by the rest of the text. When you apply bullets to selected text, the text loses touch with its style. In this instance, the bulleted text is using **no style**. You can confirm this by looking at the Paragraph Styles drop-down menu where you see the word **(none)** instead of **Normal**.

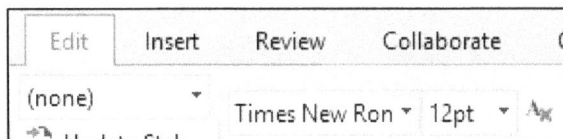

Edit	Insert	Review	Collaborate	C

(none) ▾   Times New Ron ▾ 12pt ▾ A꜀

3. Apply the Normal style to the bulleted text.

   ❏ ensure the bulleted text is still selected
   ❏ from the **Apply Style** drop-down menu, choose **Normal**

Normal ▾

4. Apply squares instead of standard bullets to the bulleted text.

   ❏ ensure the **Tag List** is open (**Edit > Show/Hide > Tag List**)
   ❏ click anywhere within the bulleted text
   ❏ on the **Tag List**, right-click the word **List** and choose **Bullets and Numbering**

Two things occur: the Bullets and Numbering dialog box opens, and behind the box, the bulleted text is selected.

❒ select the last type of bullet in the first row (the squares)

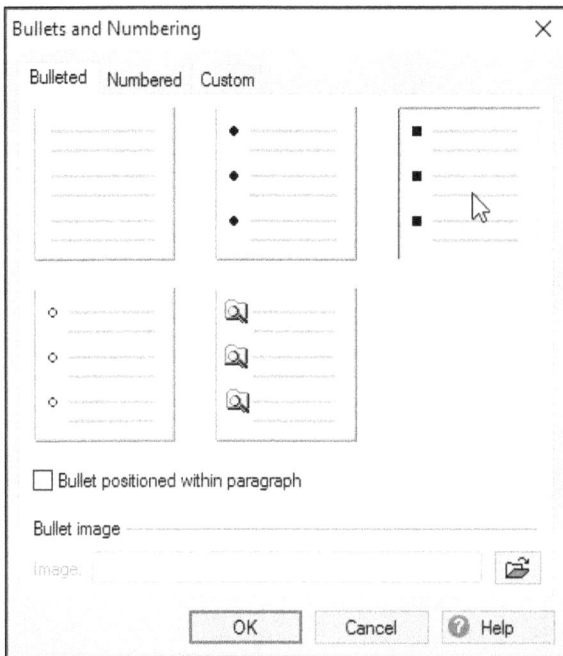

❒ click the **OK** button

The bulleted text should now be reformatted using squares instead of standard bullets.

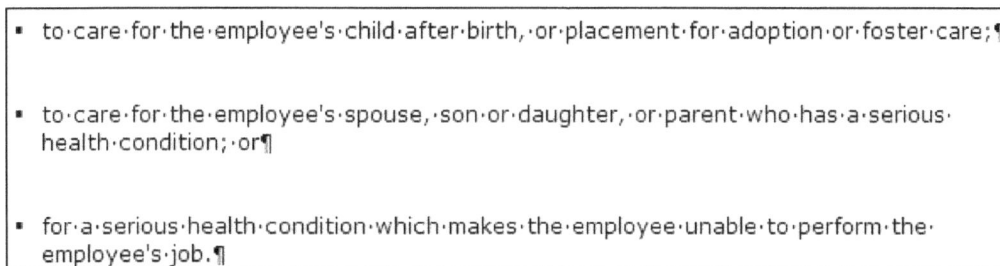

- to·care·for·the·employee's·child·after·birth,·or·placement·for·adoption·or·foster·care;¶

- to·care·for·the·employee's·spouse,·son·or·daughter,·or·parent·who·has·a·serious· health·condition;·or¶

- for·a·serious·health·condition·which·makes·the·employee·unable·to·perform·the· employee's·job.¶

5. Save the project.

Bullets Confidence Check

1. Right-click the word **List** on the Tag List again and choose **Bullets and Numbering**.

2. At the bottom of the dialog box (Bullet image Image area), click the yellow folder to open the **Image** dialog box.

3. On the Gallery tab, select the **bullets** category.

4. Select any Gallery file name you like.

Image	✕
Image Gallery	

Gallery category:

Preview

```
arrows
backgrounds
bars
Books_and_Pages
bullets
buttons
headers
Skin_Toolbar
```

Gallery file name:

```
bgblue.jpg
bgbluebevel.gif
bgbluebevel.jpg
bgbrown.gif
bgbrown.jpg
bgbrownbevel.gif
bgbrownbevel.jpg
bggray.gif
bggray.jpg
bggraybevel.gif
bggraybevel.jpg
bggreen.gif
bggreen.jpg
bggreenbevel.gif
bggreenbevel.jpg
bglime.gif
bglime.jpg
bglimebevel.gif
bglimebevel.jpg
```

[OK] [Cancel] [Apply] [? Help]

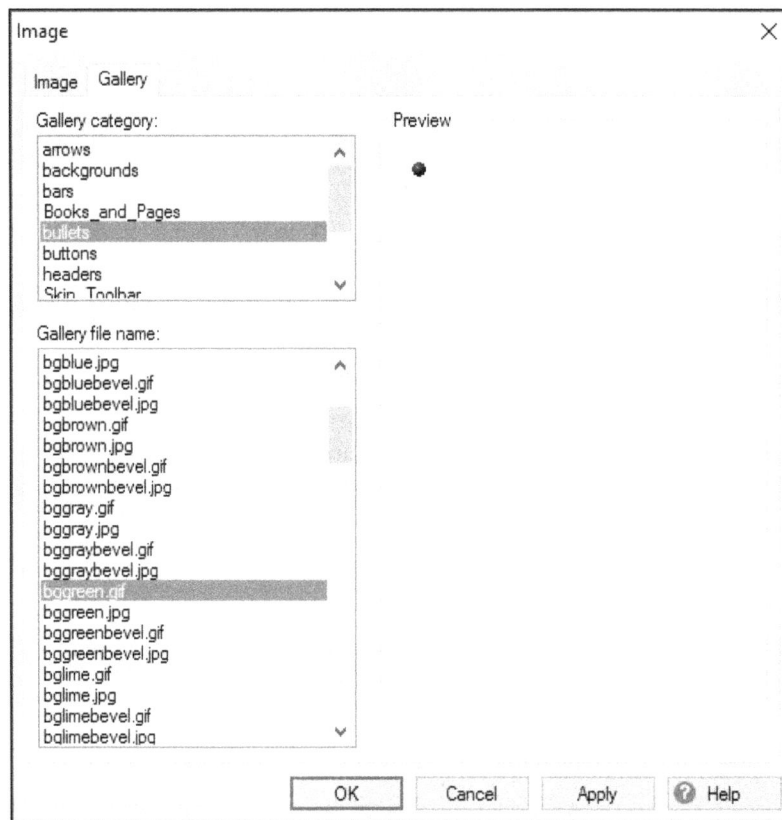

5. Click the **OK** button twice (to close both the Image dialog box and the Bullets and Numbering dialog box).

   Your bulleted list should include an image for the bullet.

6. Save and close the topic.

Student Activity: Create a List Style

1. Ensure that the **tables** project is still open.

2. Open the **Termination Policy** topic.

3. Add numbers to selected text.

   ❑ scroll down and highlight the paragraphs **First Notice. The first notice is normally an oral notification of unsatisfactory performance** through the next three paragraphs

   Note: Don't highlight the paragraph beginning "The supervisor recommends..."

   ❑ on the Edit tab, click the **Create a Numbered List** tool ▤

   By default, the list includes a hanging indent and standard numbers. However, the list isn't formatted properly (there is no vertical paragraph spacing, and it's using the wrong font) because it isn't following a style, just like the bulleted list you created earlier. It would be great if you didn't have to manually apply a style to a list each time you use the Bulleted or Numbered List tools. You'll take care of that next as you create a List Style. Once the style has been created, it can be used in any topic that is using the CSS containing the List Style.

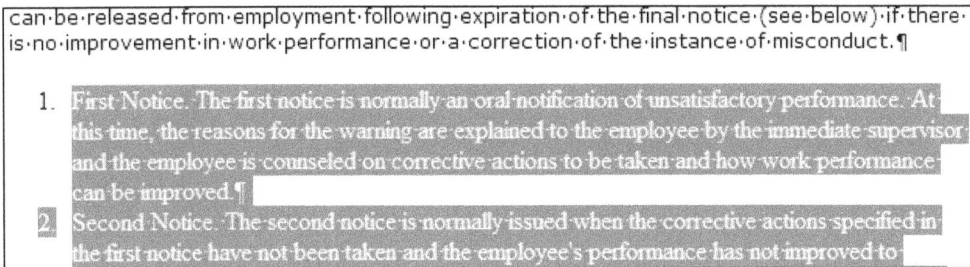

   > can·be·released·from·employment·following·expiration·of·the·final·notice·(see·below)·if·there·is·no·improvement·in·work·performance·or·a·correction·of·the·instance·of·misconduct.¶
   >
   > 1. First·Notice.·The·first·notice·is·normally·an·oral·notification·of·unsatisfactory·performance.·At·this·time,·the·reasons·for·the·warning·are·explained·to·the·employee·by·the·immediate·supervisor·and·the·employee·is·counseled·on·corrective·actions·to·be·taken·and·how·work·performance·can·be·improved.¶
   > 2. Second·Notice.·The·second·notice·is·normally·issued·when·the·corrective·actions·specified·in·the·first·notice·have·not·been·taken·and·the·employee's·performance·has·not·improved·to·

4. Create a List Style.

   ❑ with the numbered list still selected, right-click the **List** tag on the Tag List and choose **List Style**

   The Select List Style dialog box opens.

   ❑ from the List Templates at the bottom left of the dialog box, choose **BasicNumber**

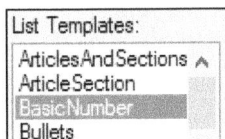

   > List Templates:
   > ArticlesAndSections ⌃
   > ArticleSection
   > BasicNumber
   > Bullets

   ❑ click the **OK** button

The BasicNumber List Style has been applied to the list. There is now white space between the list items (because, by default, the new style is using the Normal style).

> 1) First·Notice.··The·first·notice·is·normally·an·oral·notification·of·unsatisfactory· performance.··At·this·time,··the·reasons·for·the·warning·are·explained·to·the·employee·by·the· immediate·supervisor·and·the·employee·is·counseled·on·corrective·actions·to·be·taken·and· how·work·performance·can·be·improved.¶
>
> 2) Second·Notice.··The·second·notice·is·normally·issued·when·the·corrective·actions· specified·in·the·first·notice·have·not·been·taken·and·the·employee's·performance·has·not·

Next you will change the color of the numbers and indent the list.

5. Save the project.

Student Activity: Edit a List Style

1. Ensure that the **tables** project is still open.

2. Change the font and font color used by the BasicNumber style.

   ☐ on the Project Manager pod, double-click **policies.css** to open the style sheet file for editing

   ☐ from the **Multilevel List** group, select **BasicNumber**

   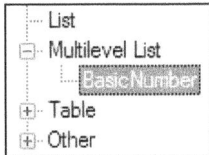

   ☐ from the Formatting area, change the Font to **Verdana**

   ☐ change the Size to **10pt** and then change the Font Color to **Maroon**

   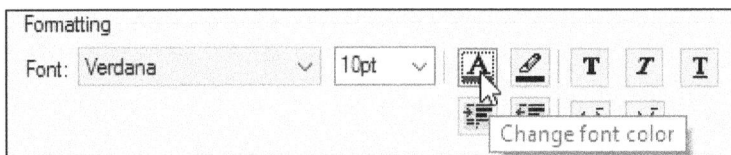

   ☐ click the **OK** button

   The numbers in the list are now formatted to match the font specifications of the BasicNumber style.

3. Change the punctuation used after the numbers in the list.

   ☐ on the **Project Manager** pod, double-click **policies.css** to open the style sheet file for editing again

   ☐ from the **Multilevel List** group, select **BasicNumber**

   ☐ in the **Edit Style** field, change **<x>)** to **<x>.**

   Edit Style: ⟨x⟩.

   ☐ click the **OK** button

   The numbers in the list should now each end with a period.

   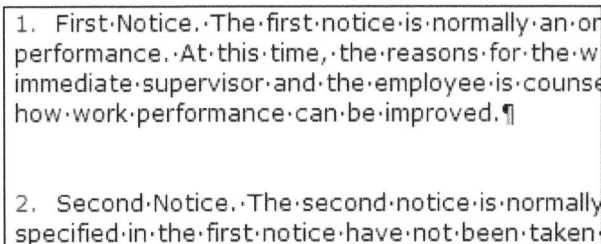

4. Create a hanging indent style to be used by the list style.

☐ on the **Project Manager** pod, double-click **policies.css** to open the style sheet file for editing again

☐ from the **Multilevel List** group, select **BasicNumber**

☐ click the **Increase space between List prefix and paragraph** tool ⬚ twice so the List Preview shows the correct hanging indent.

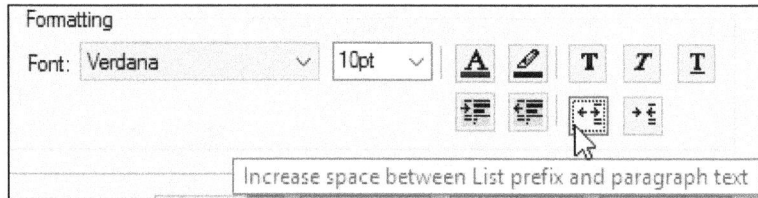

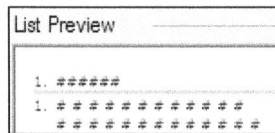

Formatting

Font: Verdana   10pt   A ✎ T *I* T̲

📑 📑 📑 📑

Increase space between List prefix and paragraph text

List Preview

1. ######
1. # # # # # # # # # #
    # # # # # # # # # # # #

☐ click the **OK** button

Check out your list in the Termination Policy topic. The numbers are now indented with a hanging indent.

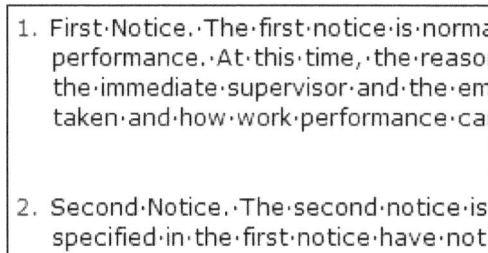

1. First·Notice.··The·first·notice·is·norma
   performance.··At·this·time,··the·reaso
   the·immediate·supervisor·and·the·em
   taken·and·how·work·performance·ca

2. Second·Notice.··The·second·notice·is
   specified·in·the·first·notice·have·not

Note: You can apply the new style to any text from this point forward using the **Styles and Formatting** panel (the Multilevel List Styles group).

5. Save the project.

Global Formatting

As you have learned while working through this book, styles are an awesome way to ensure formatting consistency across topics. You'll also likely agree that styles save you a significant amount of manual formatting work. However, you still need to spend time formatting text every time you insert a table or create a list. By setting a global format, you can eliminate some of your repetitive work permanently.

Student Activity: Set Global Formatting

1. Ensure that the **tables** project is still open.

2. Create a bulleted list.

   ❏ open the **Overtime Policy** topic

   ❏ select the last four paragraphs of the topic, starting with **Accrued compensatory time**

   ❏ click the **Bulleted List** tool

   department·manager·will·determine,·based·on·overtime·worked,·the·appropriate·and·
   applicable·amount·of·compensatory·time.¶

   - Accrued·compensatory·time·must·be·taken·within·two·pay·periods·after·accruing·it·or·it·will·be·
     forfeited.¶
   - An·"Authorization·for·Employee's·Earned·Compensatory·Time"·request·must·be·completed·and·
     signed·prior·to·taking·compensatory·time·in·excess·of·8·hours.·Request·forms·are·available·in·
     Human·Resources.¶
   - Vacation·hours,·administrative·leave·hours,·and·holidays·are·not·considered·when·computing·
     overtime.¶
   - Leave·hours·of·any·kind·will·not·be·accrued·on·any·overtime·hours.¶

   See·also:··Payroll·Policy¶

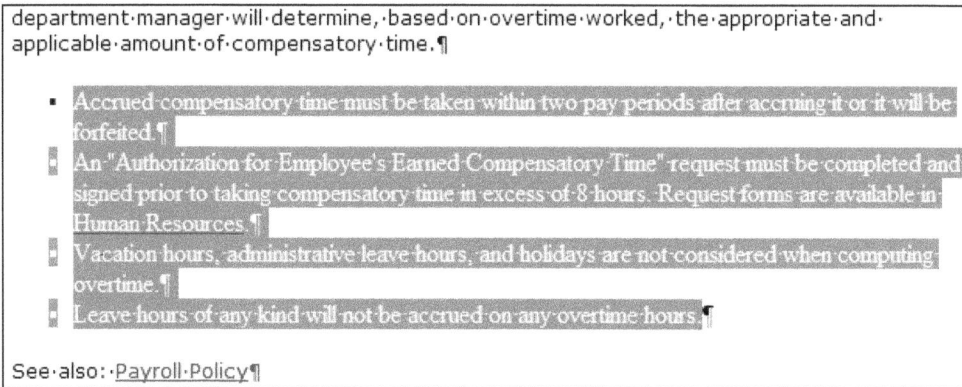

   Notice that the font is not set Verdana, 10 points (which is the preferred formatting for this Help System).

3. Set the global font.

   ❏ on the **Project Manager** pod, double-click **policies.css** to open the style sheet file for editing

   ❏ from the **Other** group, select **Background +Text (BODY)**

   ⊟··Other
   ····Background + Text (BODY)
   ····CAPTION

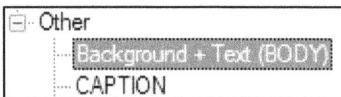

   ❏ change the **Formatting** to **Verdana, 10pt**

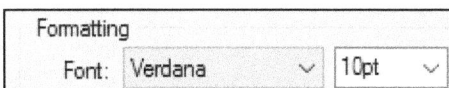

   Formatting
   Font: Verdana ⌄ 10pt ⌄

   ❏ click **OK**

   Everything that is applied to **Background + Text (BODY)** is inherited by all content on the page. So after setting the font, you will never have to specify the

correct font again in a style. And when you create a list or add a table, the font will always be correct.

department·manager·will·determine,·based·on·overtime·worked,·the·appropriate·and·
applicable·amount·of·compensatory·time.¶

- Accrued·compensatory·time·must·be·taken·within·two·pay·periods·after·accruing·it·or·
it·will·be·forfeited.¶
- An·"Authorization·for·Employee's·Earned·Compensatory·Time"·request·must·be·
completed·and·signed·prior·to·taking·compensatory·time·in·excess·of·8·hours.·Request·
forms·are·available·in·Human·Resources.¶
- Vacation·hours,·administrative·leave·hours,·and·holidays·are·not·considered·when·
computing·overtime.¶
- Leave·hours·of·any·kind·will·not·be·accrued·on·any·overtime·hours.¶

See·also:·Payroll·Policy¶

4. Save your work and close the project.

iCONLOGiC

"Skills and Drills" Learning

Module 9: Indexes, Search and Glossaries

In This Module You Will Learn About:

And You Will Learn To:

Indexes

You learned how to create a Table of Contents (TOC) on page 44. Although a TOC is easy to create, not everyone is going to find your TOC easy to navigate. And while the TOC structure you set up might make sense to you, it's possible it won't make sense to your users. If the TOC is cluttered, most of your users will forgo the TOC and rely on the Index and Search capabilities of your Help System.

An index is a list of keywords associated with project topics. Although often overlooked by novice Help authors, the index is the second most commonly used feature of a Help System (behind the Search feature).

The fastest way to create an index is to have RoboHelp do the work for you. RoboHelp features the **Smart Index Wizard**—a tool that takes much of the work out of creating an index. You will learn how to use the Smart Index Wizard and how to control it. You can also create indexes on the Index pod, and you can convert index entries from imported Word documents as you import the document into your project.

If you are not happy with the entries added to your index by the Smart Index Wizard, you can remove them and add your own. You can either add index entries in the topic properties area for any existing topic or add keywords by dragging words from a list of keywords to any topic (or topics) into the Index pane. And you can add the keywords to topics directly from the Index pane or while in the Design window, you can right-click selected words and add them to the index.

> **Note:** Creating a good index is an art form. It needs to be well planned. There are professional organizations that specialize in creating indexes, and there are many resources available for you on the web (such as **http://www.indexres.com**).

Student Activity: Run the Smart Index Wizard

1. Open the **indeglo.xpj** RoboHelp project file.

2. Generate and View the WebHelp (Primary Output). (You first learned how to generate a project on page 17.)

3. Review the current index.

   ❏ click the **Index** tab

   While there is an Index tab, the current project does not have any Index keywords so the Index is empty. You will put an Index together during the activities that follow.

4. Close the web browser and return to the RoboHelp project.

5. Open the default Index.

   ❏ on the **Project Manager** pod, open the **Index** folder
   ❏ double-click **policies (Default)** to open the Default Index

   By default, a project's Index is always empty (unless you import a Word or FrameMaker book that already includes an Index).

6. Start the Smart Index Wizard.

    ❑ on the **Tools** tab, **Index** group, click **Smart Index Wizard**

    The Smart Index Wizard dialog box opens.

7. Customize the Smart Index Wizard.

    ❑ select **Use custom search settings**
    ❑ click the **Settings** button

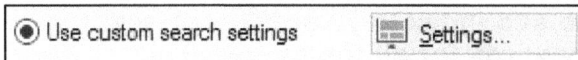

    ⦿ Use custom search settings   🖳 Settings...

    The Smart Index Settings dialog box opens. You can change the options RoboHelp uses when it creates the index.

    ❑ select **Words with punctuation (e-mail)**
       (if necessary, turn the option on)

    The remaining options should match the picture below. Most of the options will make sense to you. If you would like information about a specific option, click the **Help** button in the lower right of the dialog box.

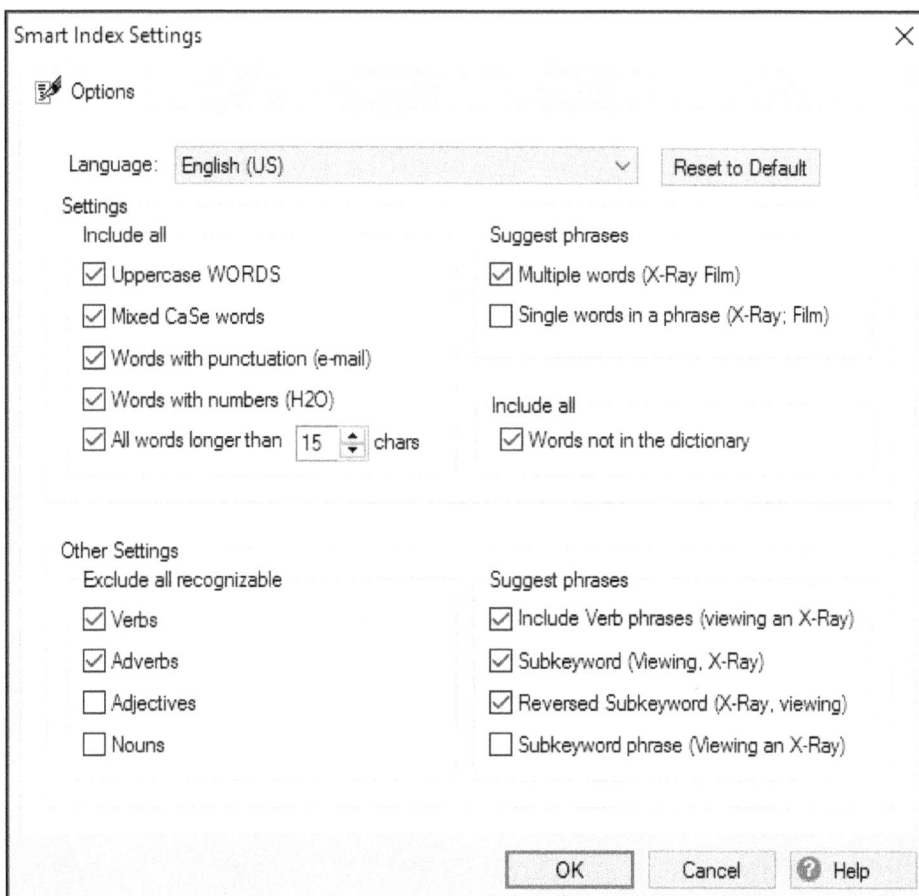

    Smart Index Settings   ✕

    📝 Options

    Language: English (US)   ∨   Reset to Default

    Settings
      Include all   Suggest phrases
      ☑ Uppercase WORDS   ☑ Multiple words (X-Ray Film)
      ☑ Mixed CaSe words   ☐ Single words in a phrase (X-Ray; Film)
      ☑ Words with punctuation (e-mail)
      ☑ Words with numbers (H2O)   Include all
      ☑ All words longer than 15 ⬍ chars ☑ Words not in the dictionary

    Other Settings
      Exclude all recognizable   Suggest phrases
      ☑ Verbs   ☑ Include Verb phrases (viewing an X-Ray)
      ☑ Adverbs   ☑ Subkeyword (Viewing, X-Ray)
      ☐ Adjectives   ☑ Reversed Subkeyword (X-Ray, viewing)
      ☐ Nouns   ☐ Subkeyword phrase (Viewing an X-Ray)

                        OK   Cancel   ❓ Help

    ❑ click the **OK** button

    You should be back within the Smart Index Wizard.

❏ from the **Search for index keywords in** area, ensure **Topic title and topic text** is selected

> Search for index keywords in:
> ● Topic title and topic text
> ○ Topic title only
> ☐ Include hotspot text

❏ click the **Next** button

❏ from the **How do you want to add index keywords?** area, select **Automatically add index keywords for all topics**

> How do you want to add index keywords?
> ○ Confirm adding index keywords for each topic
> ● Automatically add index keywords for all topics

❏ click the **Finish** button

Clicking the Finish button allows RoboHelp to create the index. Once the process is complete, a Results dialog box opens. More than 140 keywords have been added to the default index.

> Results
>
> The Smart Index Wizard has completed indexing your topic(s). To see the keywords you added to your inde
> Topics Reviewed: 21
> Topics Updated: 21
> Topic Keywords Added: 144
>
> [Close]   ❓ Help

❏ click the **Close** button

On the Index pod, notice that the Index now sports many entries.

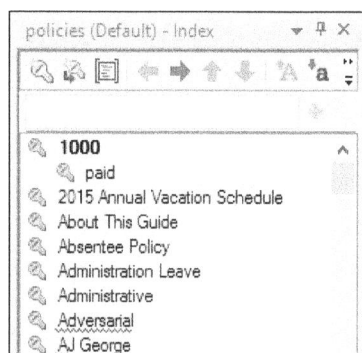

> policies (Default) - Index
>
> 🔍 1000
>   🔍 paid
> 🔍 2015 Annual Vacation Schedule
> 🔍 About This Guide
> 🔍 Absentee Policy
> 🔍 Administration Leave
> 🔍 Administrative
> 🔍 Adversarial
> 🔍 AJ George

8. Generate and View the WebHelp (Primary Output).

9. Click the **Index** tab.

   The index is complete and ready to use. Notice that although many of the index entries are fine, some entries should be removed (you will learn how next).

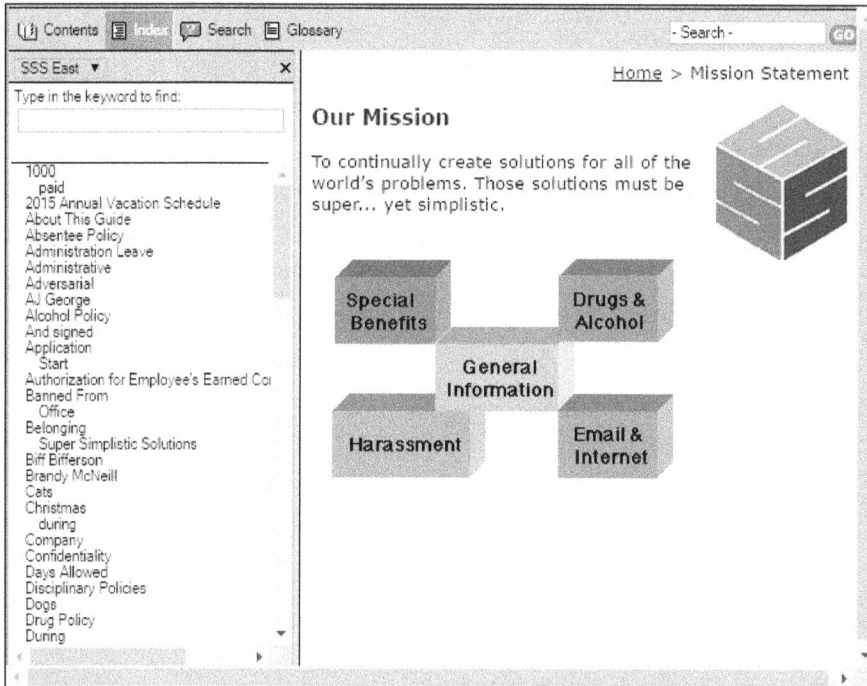

10. Spend a moment or two clicking some of the index entries (the topic they are linked to shows up in the right side of the Help window).

11. When finished, close the browser and return to the RoboHelp project.

Student Activity: Remove and Add Index Entries

1. Ensure that the **indeglo** project is still open.

2. Remove an index entry.

   ❑ from the top of the Index Entries list, select the **1000** keyword
   ❑ right-click the keyword and choose **Delete**

   The unwanted keyword (and thus the index entry) is removed from the index.

3. Remove more index entries.

   ❑ select the **And signed** keyword
   ❑ right-click the keyword and choose **Delete**

4. Manually add index keywords.

   ❑ using the Topic List pod, open the **Special Benefits** topic
   ❑ highlight any word(s) in the topic
   ❑ **right-click** the selection and choose **Add to > Index Keyword > policies (Default)** from the shortcut menu

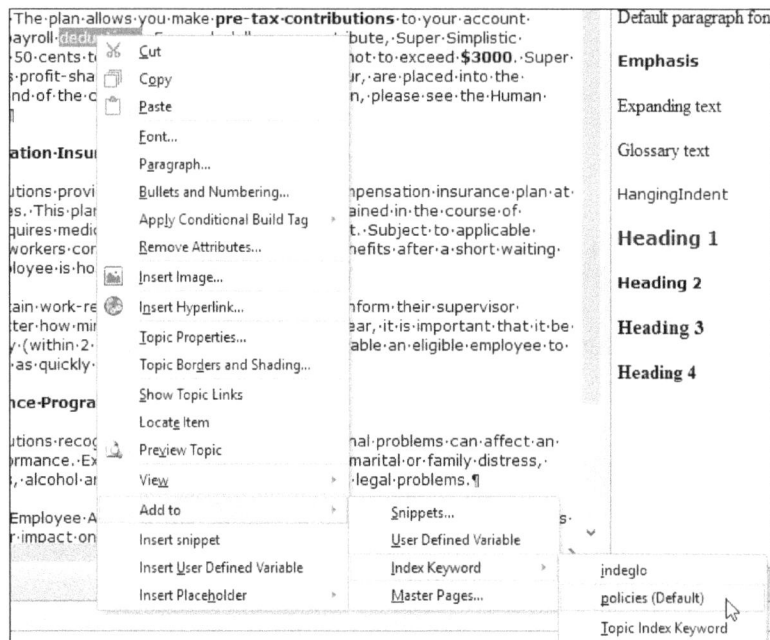

Using this technique, you can add a keyword to a topic only one time. If you select a word that is already in the index, you will get a message telling you the word is already in the index for this topic.

Index Confidence Check

1. Spend the next few moments adding topic text to the **policies** index using the right-click technique that you just learned.

2. Go through the policies index and remove any entries that you think do not need to be within the index.

3. Save the project.

4. Close all open topics.

Student Activity: Add Keywords via Topic Properties

1. Ensure that the **indeglo** project is still open.

2. Show the properties of a topic.

   ☐ on the Topic List pod, select the **Leave Policy** topic
   ☐ on the **Project** tab, **File** group, click **Properties**

3. Remove index entries using the topic properties.

   ☐ select the **Index** tab

   This is a handy screen for reviewing, adding, and deleting index entries on a topic-by-topic basis.

   ☐ select **Family** from the list of entries
   ☐ click the **Delete** button

4. Add an index entry using the topic properties.

   ☐ in the **Index Keywords** area, type **Bereavement Leave**

Index Keywords		
Select Index: policies (Default)	⌄	
Bereavement Leave		Add
🔍 Administration Leave	⌃	Add Existing...
🔍 Christmas		

   ☐ click the **Add** button
   ☐ click the **OK** button

5. Save the project.

Another Index Confidence Check

1. Show the Properties for the **Alcohol Policy** topic.

2. Use the **Index Tab** to add the following keywords (one at a time) to the topic:

   Alcohol

   Disciplinary Action

   Overindulgence

   Alcoholic Beverages

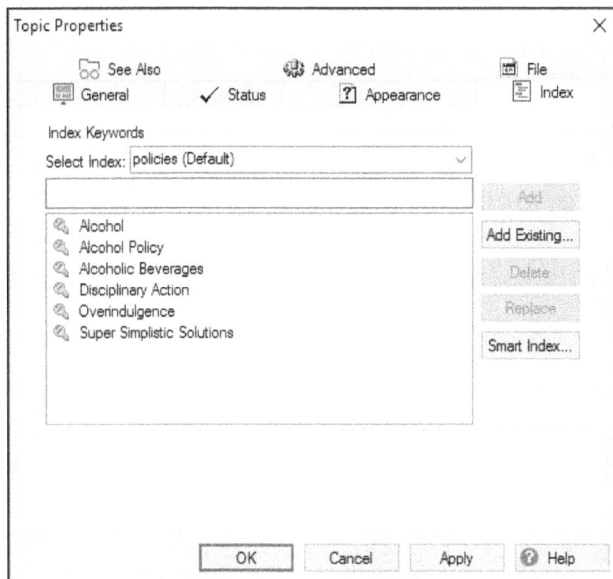

3. Show the Properties for the **Drug Policy** topic.

4. Use the **Index Tab** to add the following keywords (one at a time) to the topic:

   Illegal

   Contraband

   Controlled Dangerous Substances

   Rehabilitation

5. Save the project.

6. Generate and View the Primary Output.

7. On the Index tab, Index area, type **controlled**.

8. Click the **Controlled Dangerous Substances** keyword phrase.

   The **Drug Policy** topic should open.

9. Close the web browser and return to RoboHelp.

Cross-reference Index Keywords

An index typically contains many different variants of a keyword allowing users an opportunity to find a topic even though they don't know the name of the tool or subject they might be trying to find. As an alternative to creating variants for index keywords, you can create Cross-reference keywords—synonym keywords that are related to other keywords.

Student Activity: Create a Cross-reference Keyword

1. Ensure that the **indeglo** project is still open.

2. Add a new keyword to the index.

   ☐ if necessary, open the **policies (Default)** Index
   ☐ from the top of the **policies** pod, click the **New Index Keyword** tool 🔍
   ☐ type **Ideology** and then press [**enter**]

   > 🔍 Human Resources Manager
   > 🔍 Ideology
   > 🔍 Information Services Director

   ☐ right-click the **Ideology** keyword and choose **Properties**
   ☐ select **Cross-reference** (put a check in the box)
   ☐ select the **Philosophy** keyword from the drop-down menu

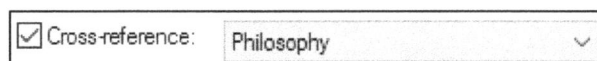

   > ☑ Cross-reference: Philosophy   ⌄

   ☐ click the **OK** button

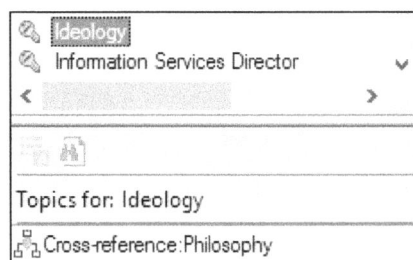

   > 🔍 Ideology
   > 🔍 Information Services Director   ⌄
   > ‹   ›
   > ▦ 🔍
   > Topics for: Ideology
   > 🔗 Cross-reference:Philosophy

   The Ideology topic now has a cross-reference to the Philosophy keyword. All topics indexed with the Philosophy keyword can also be found using the Ideology keyword.

Subkeywords

You can add more flexibility to your index if you set up certain keywords as a multilevel index. Simply put, if you want one keyword to be associated with several others, you add subkeywords to first-level keywords.

Student Activity: Add Subkeywords to the Index

1. Ensure that the **indeglo** project is still open.

2. Add a keyword to the Index pod.

   ☐ if necessary, open the **policies (Default)** Index
   ☐ near the top of the Index, click in the **text field** and type **Discrimination**

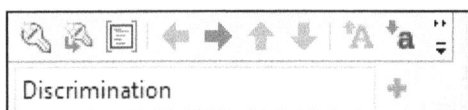

   ☐ press [**enter**]

   The word appears in your index list. Notice that the word appears in **bold**. Bold keywords are keywords that are not associated with any topic.

3. Add a subkeyword to the discrimination keyword.

   ☐ select the **Discrimination** keyword
   ☐ at the top of the Index pod, click the **New Index Subkeyword** tool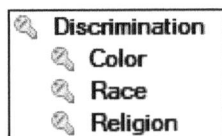
   ☐ type **Race** and press [**enter**]
   ☐ select the **Discrimination** keyword
   ☐ click the **New Index Subkeyword** tool
   ☐ type **Color** and press [**enter**]
   ☐ select the **Discrimination** keyword
   ☐ click the **New Index Subkeyword** tool
   ☐ type **Religion** and press [**enter**]

4. Associate topics with index keywords.

❑ on the Index pod, select **Discrimination** from the list of keywords

❑ from the Topic List pod, drag the **Nondiscrimination Policy** topic from the list of topics to the **Topics for: Discrimination** area of the Index

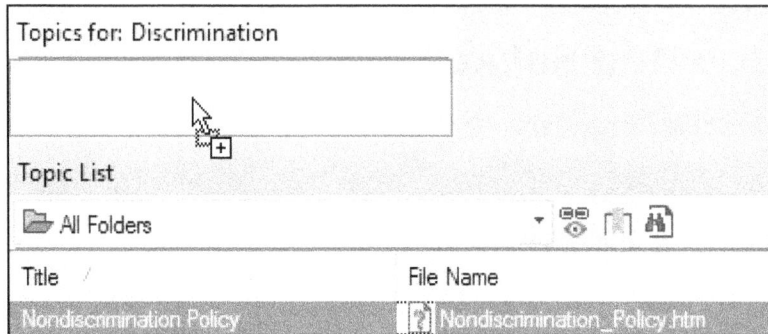

Topics for: Discrimination

Topic List

📂 All Folders

Title	File Name
Nondiscrimination Policy	Nondiscrimination_Policy.htm

You have just associated the keyword Discrimination with the Nondiscrimination Policy topic. You may need to resize the **Topics for** area to see the Nondiscrimination Policy in the area.

❑ select the subkeyword **Color**

❑ drag the **Nondiscrimination Policy** topic from the list of topics to the **Topics for: Color** area of the Index pane

Subkeywords Confidence Check

1. Associate the subkeyword **Race** with the **Nondiscrimination Policy** topic.

2. Associate the keyword **Religion** with **Nondiscrimination Policy**.

3. Add the following subkeyword to Discrimination: **Sex**.

4. Associate the new keyword with the **Nondiscrimination Policy**.

5. Save the project.

Relating Topics

You have now learned about index entries and how to create them. Every index entry that you associate with a topic appears on the Index pane of the generated project. But there is a second type of keyword known as See Also. See Also keywords allow you to place related topics into one common group. See Also keywords do not appear on the Index when you generate the project. Instead, See Also keywords remain hidden and appear only when told to. One popular way to get a See Also to appear is to use Link Controls (a button that links to topics or See Also keywords).

In the next activity, you will create a See Also keyword and associate some topics with it. Then you will create a Link Control in a topic that tells the See Also to appear if the control is clicked by a user.

Student Activity: Create a See Also Keyword

1. Ensure that the **indeglo** project is still open.

2. Open the See Also pod.

    ❏ on the **Project Manager** pod, double-click **See Also**

3. Create a See Also keyword.

    ❏ near the top of the **See Also** pod, click in the **white text field**
    ❏ type **Managers** and then press [**enter**]

4. Associate topics with the new See Also keyword.

    ❏ on the **Topic List** pod, show the **Company_Officers** folder

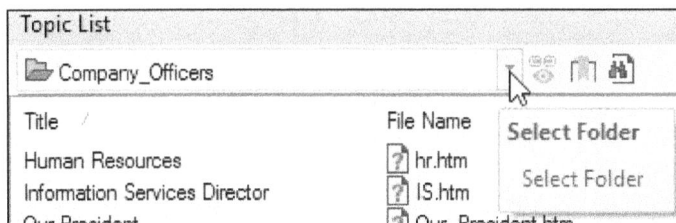

    ❏ drag all four of the topics in the Company_Officers folder into the **Topics for: Managers** area

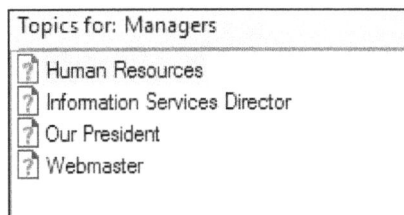

Student Activity: Insert a Link Control

1. Ensure that the **indeglo** project is still open.

2. Open the **Our President** topic.

3. Insert a Link Control.

   ❏ click at the end of the text and press [**enter**] to create a new paragraph

   ❏ on the **Insert** tab, **Links** group, click the drop-down menu next to **Related Topics** and choose **See Also**

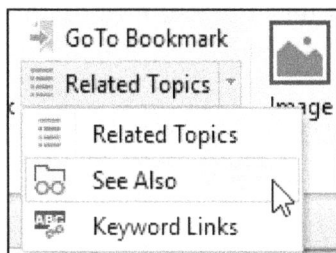

The **See Also Wizard - Link Options** dialog box opens.

   ❏ in the **Label** area, type **Our Managers**

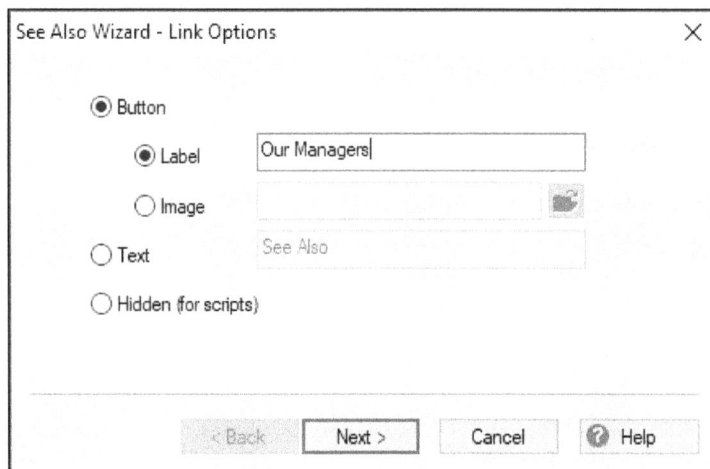

   ❏ click the **Next** button

The **See Also Wizard - See Also Keywords Selection** screen appears. The Managers See Also keyword you created is the only keyword available to Add.

   ❏ click the **Add** button to move the Manager keyword to the **See Also keywords in control** column

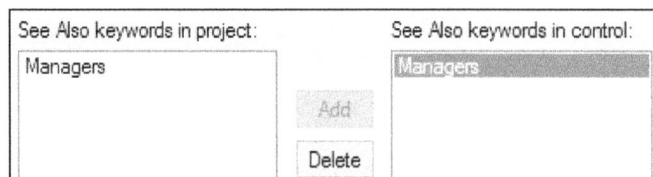

   ❏ click the **Next** button

❏ from the **Choose topic from** area, select **Popup menu**

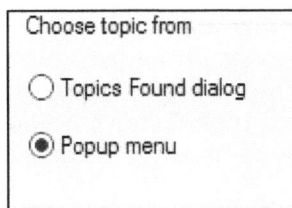

```
Choose topic from

○ Topics Found dialog

◉ Popup menu
```

❏ click the **Next** button

The Font Options dialog box opens.

❏ change the Font to **Verdana**

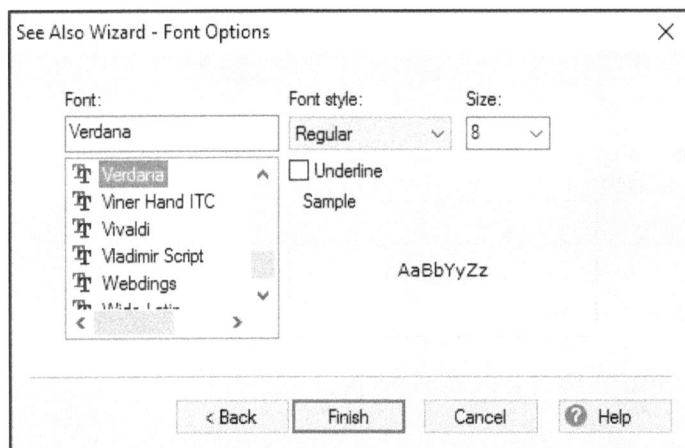

```
See Also Wizard - Font Options                                    ✕

  Font:                  Font style:        Size:
  Verdana                Regular       ⌄    8      ⌄

  𝕋𝕋 Verdana        ∧    ☐ Underline
  𝕋𝕋 Viner Hand ITC      Sample
  𝕋𝕋 Vivaldi
  𝕋𝕋 Vladimir Script
  𝕋𝕋 Webdings                      AaBbYyZz
  𝕋𝕋 Wide Latin     ∨
  <           >

              < Back    Finish      Cancel    ❓ Help
```

❏ click the **Finish** button

There is an **Our Managers** button (control) at the bottom of the topic. Next you will test the control.

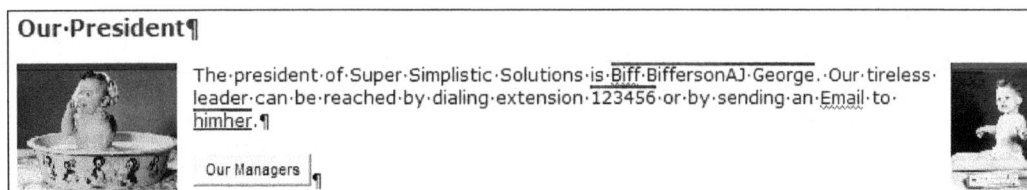

Our·President¶

The·president·of·Super·Simplistic·Solutions·is·Biff·BiffersonAJ·George.··Our·tireless·leader·can·be·reached·by·dialing·extension·123456·or·by·sending·an·Email·to·himher.¶

Our Managers ¶

4. Save, Generate, and View the Primary Output.

5. Select the **Search** tab.

6. In the **Type in the word(s) to search for:** field type **president** and press [**enter**].

   The Help System is searched and topics containing the word "president" display in the results area (the results are ranked in order of relevance).

7. Click the first result (**Our President**) to open the Our President topic.

8. Click the **Our Managers** button.

   A drop-down menu appears listing the other three company managers. Notice that the current topic, Our President, does not appear in the list, even though Our President is part of the control. Nice! And if you were to copy and paste the control into the other three manager topics and then Generate and View the Help System, you would see that the control dynamically changes the results shown in the drop-down menu.

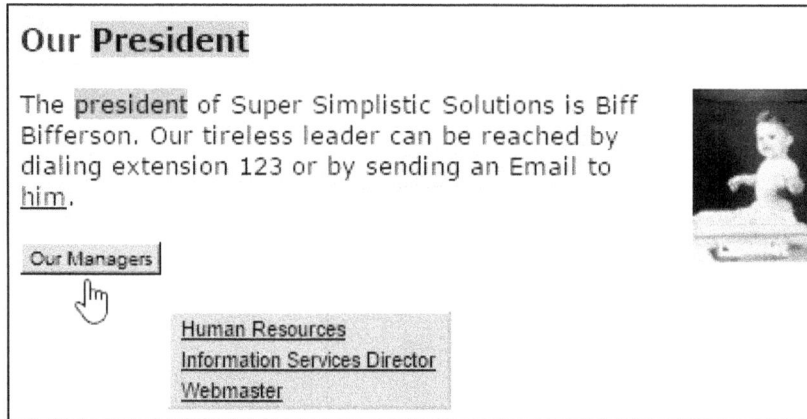

9. Select any of the topics in the menu.

10. Close the browser and return to the RoboHelp project.

See Also Confidence Check

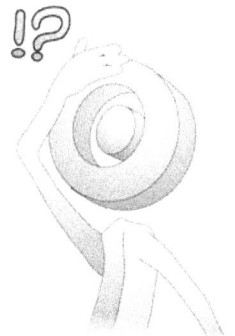

1. Copy the Link Control (the Our Managers button) in the Our President topic to the clipboard.

2. Open the **Human Resources** topic and paste the Link Control at the end of the topic.

3. Paste the Link Control at the end of the other two manager topics (**Information Services Director** and **Webmaster**).

4. Generate and View the output.

5. Use the Search tab to search for **webmaster**.

6. In the Webmaster topic, test the Link Control.

7. Close the browser and return to the RoboHelp project.

8. Save the project and close all open topics.

Search

During the last activity you used the Search feature to find a topic. You may have noticed that the Search results were ranked based on their relevance. If a word being searched appears in the title of a topic, its rank is higher than the word appearing in the body of a topic. In addition, a topic with the word appearing in a paragraph using a Heading 1 style ranks higher than the same word appearing in a paragraph using a Heading 2 style.

During the following activity, you will learn how to add search terms to a topic when those terms do not actually appear in the topic. Topics with custom search terms will appear higher in the search results than topics without these search terms set.

Student Activity: Add Custom Search Terms

1. Ensure that the **indeglo** project is still open.

2. Open the **Human Resources** topic.

   There isn't much text in the topic, in fact, just 10 words (12 if you count the heading). Anyone searching for Brandy, McNeill, Human Resources, or Human would correctly find the topic. However, if someone searches for a word that is not physically in the topic, such as **conflict**, they won't find anything. Let's test that.

3. Generate and View the output.

4. Use the Search tab to search for **conflict**.

   You should be presented with the unfortunate message: "No topics found."

   > Type in the word(s) to search for:
   >
   > | conflict| **GO**
   >
   > ☑ Highlight search results
   >
   > Search results per page | 10 |
   >
   > No topics found

5. Close the web browser and return to the RoboHelp project.

6. Add a custom Search term to a topic's Properties.

   ❏ right-click within the open Human Resources topic and choose **Topic Properties**
   ❏ on the General tab, type **conflict** into the Keywords field

Keywords:	conflict|
	e.g. SearchKeywordOne, SearchKeywordTwo

   ❏ click the **OK** button

7. Generate and View the output.

8. Use the Search tab to search for **conflict**.

   This time the Human Resources topic is found even though the word "conflict" is not actually within the topic.

   > **Note:** If you want to exclude a topic from appearing on the Search tab, you can right-click and choose Topic Properties. On the General tab, select **Exclude this topic from Search**.

   ☑ Exclude this topic from Search

9. Close the browser and return to the RoboHelp project.

Student Activity: Add a Search Synonym

1. Ensure that the **indeglo** project is still open.

2. Open the **Alcohol Policy** topic.

   This topic contains the text "Alcohol" in the heading. When searching for "alcohol" a reader is sure to find this topic. A common misspelling of "alcohol" is "alchohol." If someone searches for "alchohol" they won't find topics. By adding a search synonym, you take misspelled search terms into account.

3. Create a search synonym.

   ❏ on the **Output** tab, **Search** group, click **Synonyms**

   The Advanced Settings for Localization dialog box opens.

   ❏ click **New**
   ❏ in the **Word** column, type **alcohol**
   ❏ in the **Synonym** column, type **alchohol**

   ❏ click the **OK** button

4. Save the project.

5. Generate and View the output.

6. Use the Search tab to search for **alchohol**.

   All topics with the text "alcohol" will be found.

7. Close the browser, return to the RoboHelp project and close all open topics.

External Content Search

One of the limitations of the Search feature has always been the inability to hook specific URLs to Search terms. We're happy to say that the External Content Search feature puts that issue to rest.

Using External Content Search, you can display content from specific URLs based on terms that users are likely to search. You are going to set the Help System so that when users search for the word **super**, they'll be presented with a link that takes them to a web page displaying the word **super** as it relates to **simplistic solutions**.

Student Activity: Create External Search

1. Ensure that the **indeglo** project is still open.

2. Create an Advanced Search on Google.

   ❑ using your web browser, go to **www.google.com/advanced_search**
   ❑ in the **all these words** field, type **super**
   ❑ in the **this exact word or phrase** field, type **simplistic solutions**

Find pages with...	
all these words:	super
this exact word or phrase:	simplistic solutions

   ❑ from the **language** drop-down menu, choose **English**
   ❑ scroll down and then click the **Advanced Search** button

   Only web pages that contain the word **super** and the wording **simplistic solutions** are listed on the resulting Search page. The top links all deal with Super Simplistic Solutions.

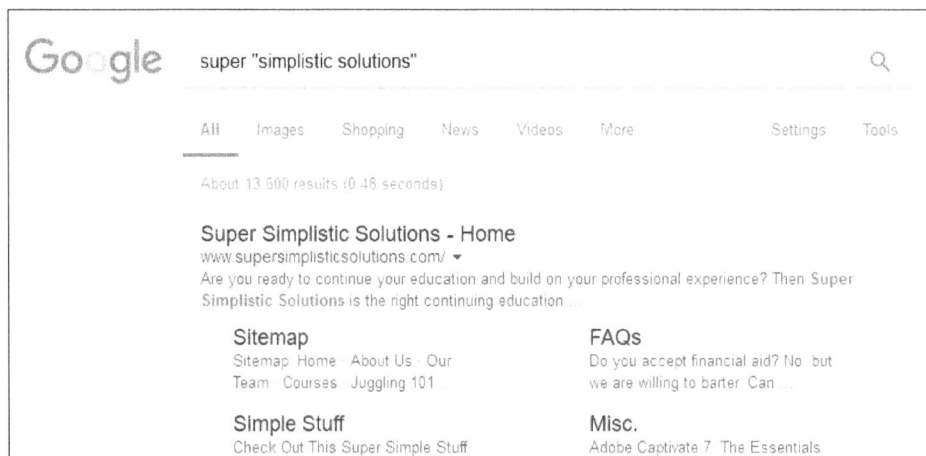

   Google   super "simplistic solutions"

   All   Images   Shopping   News   Videos   More   Settings   Tools

   About 13,600 results (0.48 seconds)

   Super Simplistic Solutions - Home
   www.supersimplisticsolutions.com/ ▾
   Are you ready to continue your education and build on your professional experience? Then Super Simplistic Solutions is the right continuing education ...

   Sitemap
   Sitemap Home About Us Our
   Team Courses Juggling 101 ...

   FAQs
   Do you accept financial aid? No but
   we are willing to barter Can ...

   Simple Stuff
   Check Out This Super Simple Stuff

   Misc.
   Adobe Captivate 7 The Essentials

3. Select and copy the **URL** in the browser's address bar.

4. Close the browser window and return to RoboHelp.

5. Add External Content Search.

☐ on the **Project** tab, click **Pods** and choose **External Content Search** (you may need to fully expand the Pod menu to see External Content Search)

The External Content Search pod appears like a topic in the center of the RoboHelp window.

☐ right-click within the pod and choose **Add**

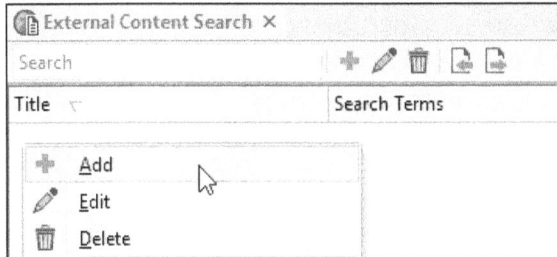

The Add dialog box opens.

☐ change the Title to **super**
☐ in the Search Terms field, type **super**
☐ in the URL field, delete the current entry and **paste** the URL that you copied from the Google Advanced Search
☐ in the Description field, type **Search the web for the term super as it relates to Super Simplistic Solutions.**

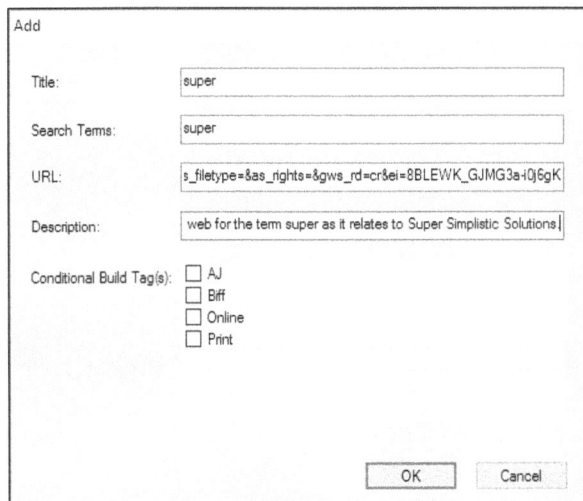

☐ click the **OK** button

The new item appears on the External Content Search pod.

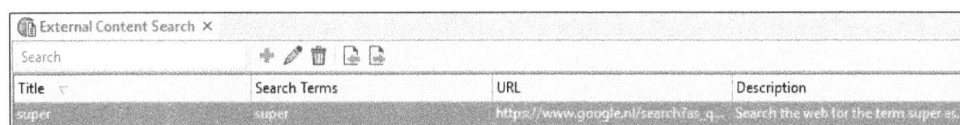

6. Enable External Content Search and test the results.

❏ on the Outputs(SSL) pod, double-click **WebHelp (Primary Output)**

❏ select the **Search** group

❏ ensure that **Enable External Content Search** is selected

☑ Enable External Content Search

☑ Show Context in Search Results

☐ Hide Rank Column in Search Results

❏ click the **Save and Generate** button and then View the results

❏ on the Search tab, type **super** and press [**enter**]

❏ locate **super** (you will find it around the 10th position)

❏ right-click the word **super** and choose **Open link in new window**

The thing that we find cool about RoboHelp's External Content Search, especially using a URL like the one you copied from Google, is that the results automatically update for your users when Google's search algorithms get updated (which is frequently).

7. Close the browser windows and return to the RoboHelp project.

8. Save the project.

Glossaries

A glossary gives your users a list of words and their definitions related to content presented in your Help System. Most users rely heavily on both the Index and Search features. Because access to the Glossary is conveniently located next to both of those tools, it's a good bet that it will see plenty of use.

Student Activity: Add Glossary Terms

1. Ensure that the **indeglo** project is still open.

2. View the Glossary pod.

   ☐ on the Project Manager pod, open the **Glossary** folder
   ☐ double-click **policies (Default)** to open the default Glossary

   There are no glossary terms. You add glossary entries similarly to how you added index keywords earlier.

3. Add a Glossary Term.

   ☐ at the top of the Glossary pod, click in the **Term** field
   ☐ type **SSS** and then press [**enter**]

   You now have one Glossary Term with no definition.

4. Add a definition to a Glossary Term.

   ☐ click in the **Definition for: SSS** area at the bottom of the Glossary pod
   ☐ type **Super Simplistic Solutions**

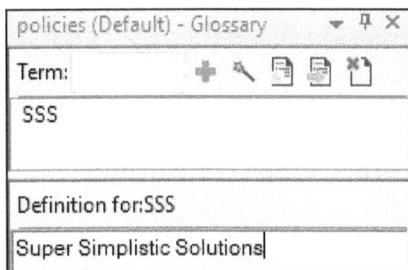

5. Save the project.

Glossary Confidence Check

1. Add the following Glossary terms and definitions to the Glossary pod.

   EAP

   Employee Assistance Program

   SWF

   Small Web File

2. Generate and View the output.

   Notice that there is now a **Glossary** tab.

3. Click the **Glossary** tab and spend a moment clicking on the Glossary Terms and reviewing the definitions at the bottom of the window.

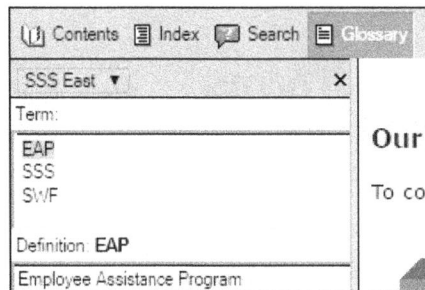

Contents Index Search Glossary
SSS East ▼   ×
Term: Our
EAP   To co
SSS
SWF
Definition: EAP
Employee Assistance Program

4. When finished, close the Help window and return to the RoboHelp project.

5. Add **Family and Medical Leave Act** as a new Term to the Glossary.

   Note: Check your spelling *carefully*. If the term you typed is off by even one character, step 8 below *(a very cool* step) will NOT work.

6. Add the following definition for your newest Glossary entry: **The text of the Act as passed by Congress and signed into law in 1993.**

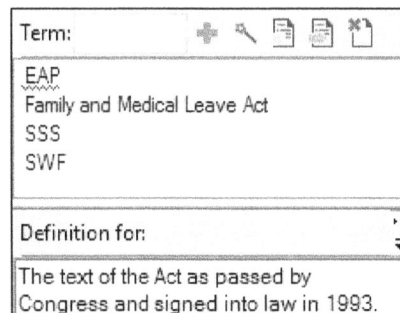

Term: ✚ ⚲ ▤ ▤ ✖
EAP
Family and Medical Leave Act
SSS
SWF
Definition for:
The text of the Act as passed by Congress and signed into law in 1993.

7. From the top of the Glossary pod, click the **Start Glossary Hotspot Wizard** tool ⚲

   The Glossary Hotspot Wizard can automatically add expanding hotspots to any topics containing an identical phrase found in the glossary.

   Note: The Glossary Hotspot Wizard works correctly only with the default glossary. If you have more than one glossary, use the wizard only for the default glossary.

8. Select **Automatically mark Terms for all topics**.

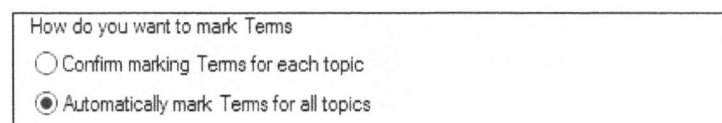

How do you want to mark Terms
○ Confirm marking Terms for each topic
● Automatically mark Terms for all topics

9. Click the **Finish** button.

   The Results screen should indicate that a few terms were marked.

10. Click the **Close** button.

11. Open the **Leave Policy** topic and scroll down to the Family and Medical Leave Act heading.

    Because the exact words **Family and Medical Leave Act** were in this topic's body text, the Glossary term you added has automatically been formatted as an expanding hotspot text by the Wizard.

12. Preview the topic.

13. Click the words **Family and Medical Leave Act** in the paragraph to see the expanding text.

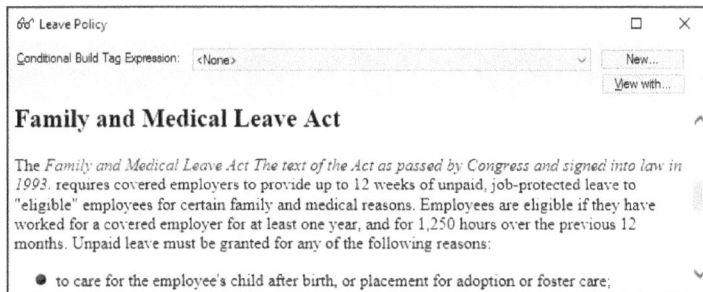

14. Close the preview.

15. Save and close all open topics.

    Note: We've been using the Glossary Hotspot Wizard for years without issue. However, in RoboHelp 10 and later, we've found that after the wizard runs, the formatting the topics gets fouled up. For whatever reason, the CSS file (policies.css) gets trashed, and the text in all of the topics becomes Times New Roman. If this happened to you (and it probably did unless Adobe released a patch that fixed the issue), there is a workaround for you. Select all of the topics on the Topic List pod. Right-click any of the selected topics and choose **Properties**. On the **Appearance** tab, click the browse button (the yellow folder at the top right). From the **RoboHelp2017Data** folder, open **policies.css**. Replace the existing CSS file in the project when prompted.

16. Save and close the project.

Notes

Module 10: Skins and Master Pages

In This Module You Will Learn About:

And You Will Learn To:

Responsive Layouts

When you are finished with your project, the final step for most Help authors is to generate the output. For most outputs from RoboHelp, you can style your output to adhere to your company's style guide. RoboHelp Responsive HTML5 uses so called Screen Layouts for the look and feel.

Student Activity: Create a Screen Layout

1. Open the **skins_masterpages.xpj** RoboHelp project file.

2. Open the **Output Setup** pod.

3. Create a Responsive HTML5 Screen Layout

   ❐ on the **Output Setup** pod, right-click **Screen Layouts** and choose **New Responsive Layout**

   The New Screen Layout dialog box opens.

   ❐ select **Azure_Blue** from the Gallery

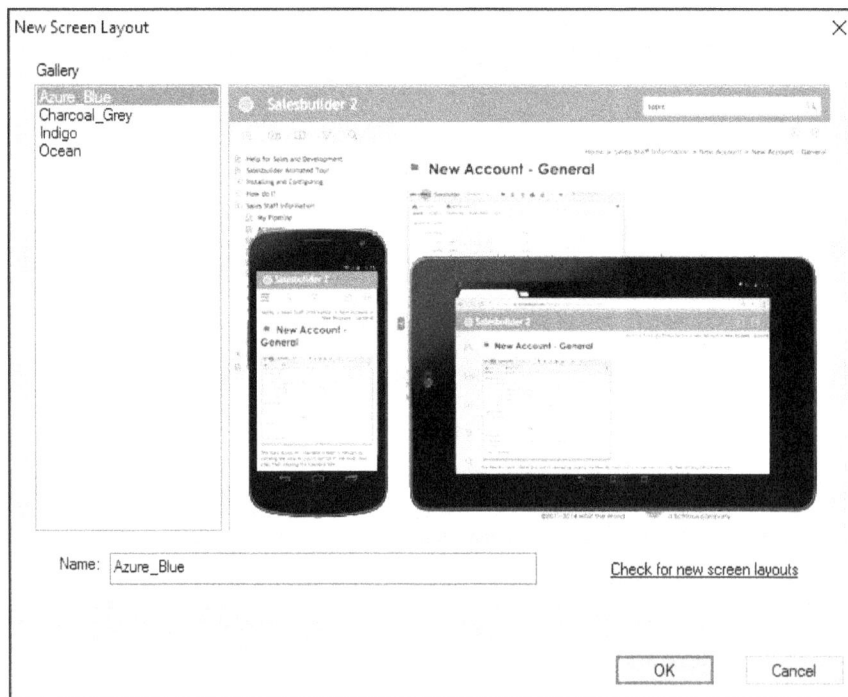

   ❐ click the **OK** button

   The new Screen Layout is added to the Output Setup pod.

4. Change the logo.

   ❑ on the **Output Setup** pod, right-click the **Azure_Blue** Screen Layout and choose **Edit**

   ❑ from the left of the dialog box, select **Header**

   ❑ from the right of the dialog box, select **Logo**

Properties	Reset component	Reset property
Show header on phones	false	
Title text color	☐ FFFFFF	
Logo	logo.png	...
Background color	▨ 509DE6	

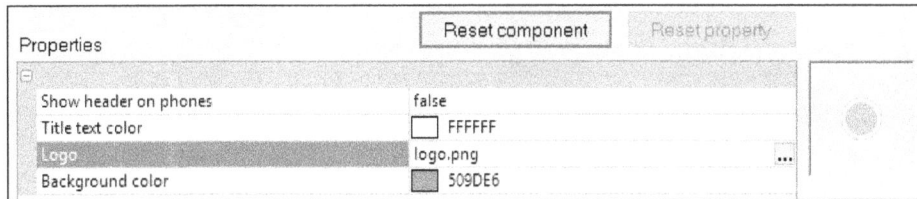

A Browse button appears at the right.

   ❑ click the **Browse** button [...]

   ❑ from the **RoboHelp2017Data** folder, open the **images** folder

   ❑ open **Responsive_Logo.png**

   ❑ click the **Save and Preview** button

The preview opens. To get the most reliable results, open the preview in a browser.

   ❑ click the **View with** button and choose any browser

   ❑ resize the browser window to see how the layout might look on different screen sizes

   ❑ close the browser and the preview to return to the Layout Customization dialog box

5. Show the header on phones.

   ❑ from the left of the dialog box, select **Header**

   ❑ change **Show header on phones** to **true** and then click **Save and Preview**

The Header is shown circled below.

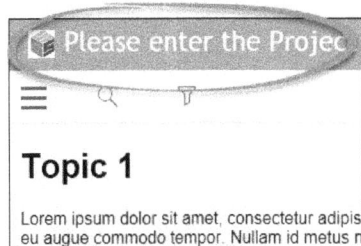

   ❑ close the preview, and click the **Close** button to close the Layout dialog box

Student Activity: Generate Responsive HTML5

1. Ensure that the **skins_masterpages** RoboHelp project file is still open.

2. Create a Responsive HTML5 output.

   ❏ on the **Outputs(SSL)** pod, click the **Create Output** tool

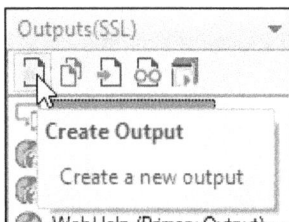

   The New Output dialog box opens.

   ❏ from the **Output Type** drop-down menu, choose **Responsive HTML5**

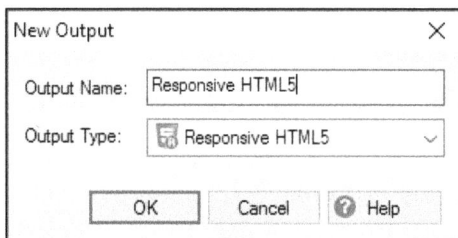

   ❏ click the **OK** button

   The Responsive HTML5 Settings dialog box opens.

3. Add a Title Bar to the output.

   ❏ if necessary, select the **General** group
   ❏ in the **Title Bar** field, type **Policies & Procedures**

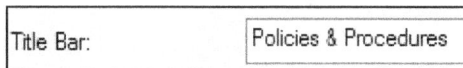

Title Bar:	Policies & Procedures

4. Select a Screen Layout.

   ❏ in the **Manage Layout** section, ensure that the **Azure_Blue** layout is selected

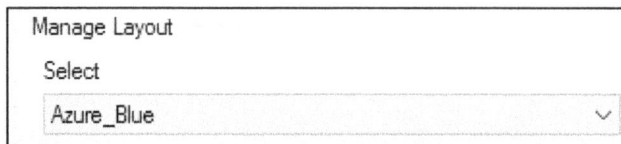

   Manage Layout
   Select
   Azure_Blue

5. Set optimization for mobile devices.

   ❑ from the left of the dialog box, select **Optimization**

   ❑ select **Convert auto-sizing and custom-sized popups to hyperlinks**

   ☑ Convert auto-sizing and custom-sized popups to hyperlinks
   ☐ Convert text-only popups to hyperlinks

   This option converts all pop-ups in your output to regular links. Popups are not very good on mobile devices. The smaller the screen size, the more the popups obscure the content. Always enable this option if you target mobile devices.

   ❑ ensure that **Convert absolute image size to relative image size** is selected

   ❑ ensure that **Convert absolute table size to relative table size** is selected

   ☑ Convert absolute image size to relative image size
   ☑ Convert absolute table size to relative table size

   These options change tables and images with a size in pixels to relative sizes to scale them to the available space of the mobile device.

   ❑ ensure **Use Adobe Captivate HTML5 output** selected

   ☑ Use Adobe Captivate HTML5 output

   During "eLearning Integration" on page 118 you integrated both SWF and HTML5 Captivate output to the project. When **Use Adobe Captivate HTML5 output** is selected, RoboHelp uses the HTML5 Captivate output. If this option is deselected, the SWF output is used. Always check this option to ensure mobile devices are able to use your eLearning content.

6. Click the **Save and Generate** button and View the results when prompted.

7. Close the browser window and return to the RoboHelp project.

Responsive Confidence Check

1. Open the **Layout Customization** screen for the **Azure_Blue** layout by double clicking the layout in the Output Setup pod.

2. Change the text color of the title to **black**.

3. Set the search results position of the desktop to display in the right pane. To do this, set the option **Search results in sidebar** to **false**. This option is in the **Search (All)** component.

4. Spend a few moments selecting other Layout Components from the Layout Components area at the left and making changes to the Properties as you see fit.

   Note: If you'd like to see your changes in action, you can get a quick preview of the layout by clicking the **Save and Preview** button.

5. When finished, click the **Save** button and then click the **Close** button.

6. Open the Responsive HTML5 Settings dialog box, click the **Save and Generate** button, and **View the result** when prompted.

7. Resize the browser window to simulate different screen displays. In the images below, you can see how the screen components change window position dependent upon the size of my window.

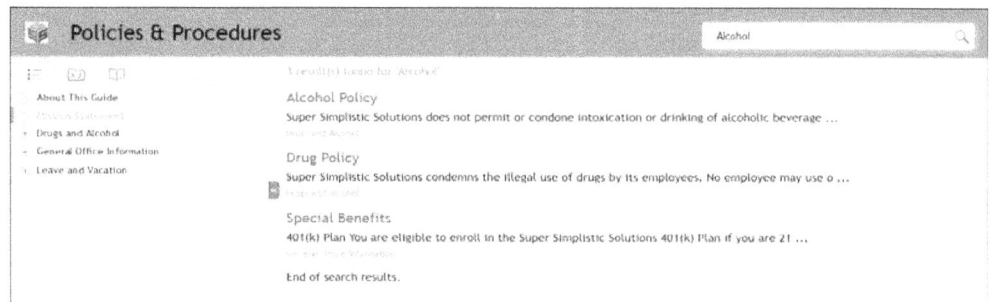

The image above shows how the Responsive HTML5 layout looks when viewed on a typical desktop. Notice that the navigation area is visible at the left of the window.

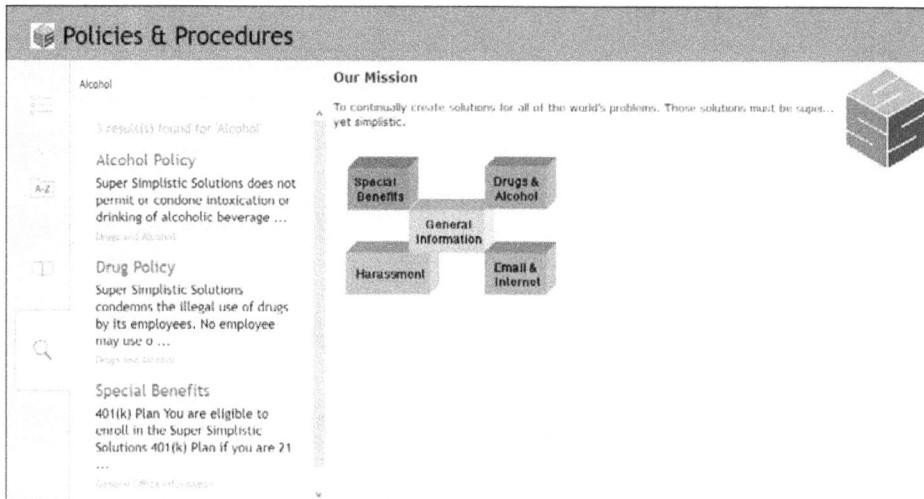

The image above shows how the Responsive HTML5 layout could look when viewed on a tablet. Notice that the navigation area has its icons on the left.

The image above shows how the Responsive HTML5 layout could look when viewed on a phone. The navigation area is hidden and becomes visible only after the user clicks the menu button.

8. When finished exploring the different window sizes, close the browser window.

9. Save the RoboHelp project.

WebHelp Skins

If you are planning to create WebHelp, you can apply an editable "skin" that can change the appearance of the navigation area and top toolbar.

You can apply a skin that controls (1) the colors and images used in the navigation area; (2) the appearance of the text on the TOC, Index, and Search areas; (3) the icons used for the TOC, Index, and Search areas; and (4) the icons used for the Book and Page images on the TOC. You can select a skin from the **WebHelp Gallery** or customize skins via the Skins Editor. If you have customized a skin, you can export it and allow other RoboHelp authors to use it, or you can import a skin from another author or the web.

Student Activity: Create a New WebHelp Skin

1. Ensure that the **skins_masterpages** project is still open.

2. Open the Output Setup pod.

   ❏ on the **Project** tab, click **Pods** and choose **Output Setup**

3. Preview the Default WebHelp skin.

   ❏ on the **Output Setup** pod, open the **Skins** folder

   Notice there are two skins in the Skins folder: one is used by FlashHelp (Beautiful Vista Flash); the other, by WebHelp (Default).

   ❏ right-click the **Default** skin and choose **View**

   A preview opens. Notice the color across the top of the window and the images used for Contents, Index, Search, and Glossary. Although there is nothing wrong with using the Default skin, let's see if another output might add a bit more excitement to the generated WebHelp output.

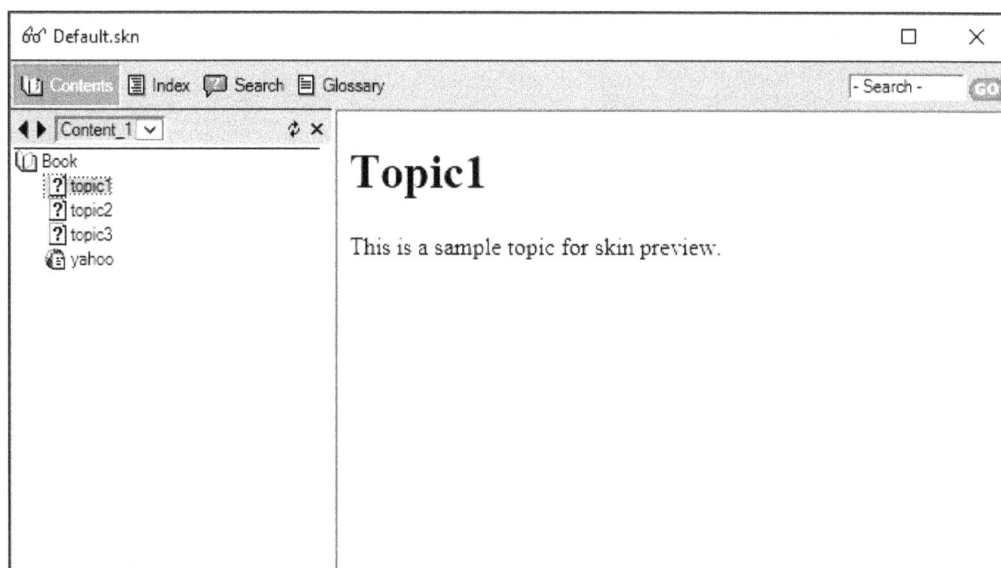

   ❏ close the preview

4. Create a New Skin from the gallery.

    ❏ on the **Output Setup** pod, right-click the **Skins** folder and choose **New Skin**

    The New Skin Options dialog box opens.

    ❏ select **Create skin from gallery**
    ❏ click the **OK** button

    The Skin Gallery dialog box opens.

    ❏ select **Fiesta** from the list of WebHelp skins

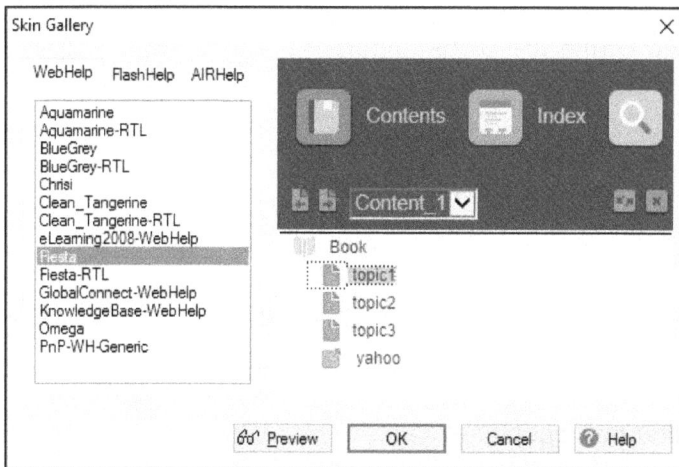

    ❏ click the **OK** button

    The WebHelp Skin Editor opens. This is where you can customize just about every aspect of the skin. For now, you will leave the skin as it is.

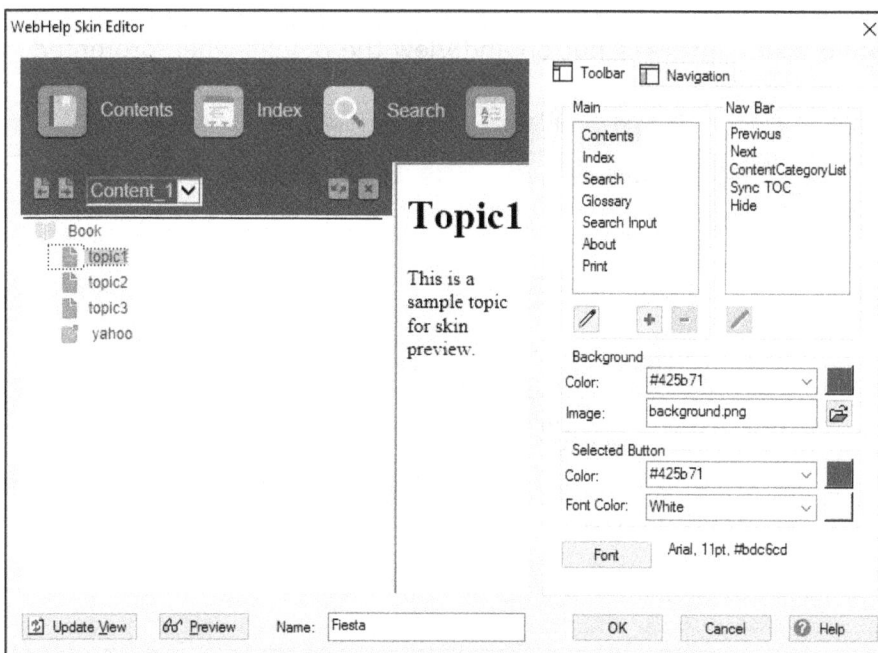

    ❏ click the **OK** button

The Save As dialog box opens. You could rename the skin, but the suggested name (**Fiesta**) will suffice.

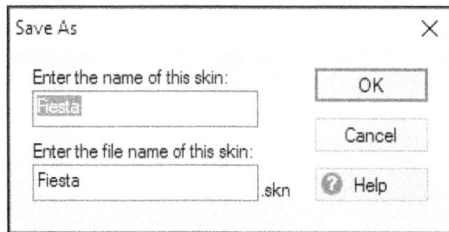

Save As	X
Enter the name of this skin:	OK
Fiesta	
Enter the file name of this skin:	Cancel
Fiesta .skn	? Help

❑ click the **OK** button

The Fiesta skin is now listed within the Skins folder.

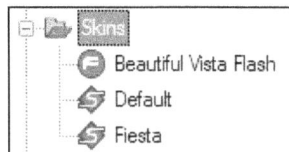

- Skins
  - Beautiful Vista Flash
  - Default
  - Fiesta

5. Attach the Fiesta skin to the WebHelp output.

   ❑ on the **Outputs(SSL)** pod, double-click WebHelp (Primary Output)

   The WebHelp Settings dialog box opens.

   ❑ from the left of the dialog box, select the **Navigation** category
   ❑ from the **Skin Selection** drop-down menu, choose **Fiesta**

Skin Selection:	Fiesta	∨	Gallery...

6. Click the **Save and Generate** button and View the results when prompted.

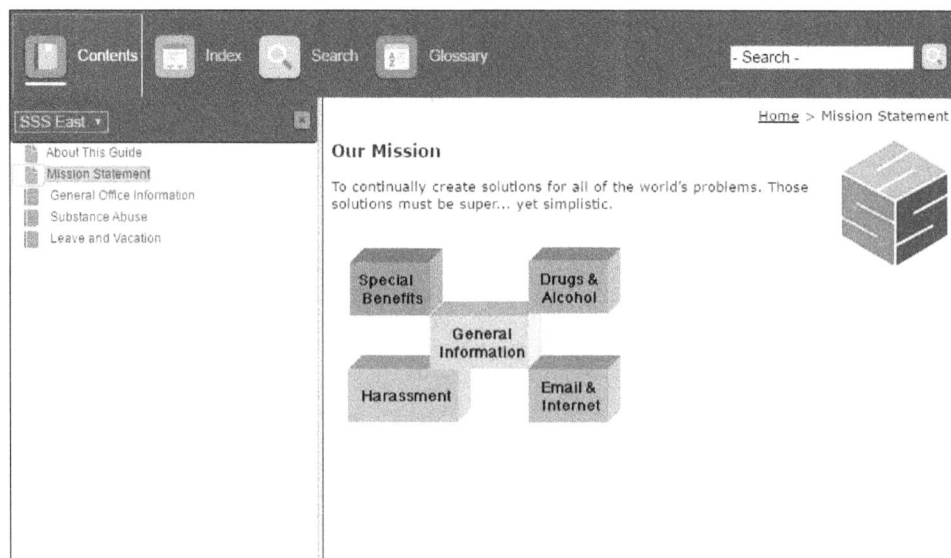

Contents	Index	Search	Glossary	- Search -

   SSS East ▾

   Home > Mission Statement

   - About This Guide
   - Mission Statement
   - General Office Information
   - Substance Abuse
   - Leave and Vacation

   Our Mission

   To continually create solutions for all of the world's problems. Those solutions must be super... yet simplistic.

   - Special Benefits
   - Drugs & Alcohol
   - General Information
   - Harassment
   - Email & Internet

7. Close the browser window and return to the RoboHelp project.

Student Activity: Customize a WebHelp Skin

1. Ensure that the **skins_masterpages** project is still open.

2. Change the font used on the Navigation pane.

   ❏ on the **Output Setup** pod, right-click the **Fiesta** skin and choose **Edit**

   The Skin Editor opens.

   ❏ at the right of the dialog box, select the **Navigation** tab
   ❏ at the bottom of the dialog box, click the **Font** button

   The Font dialog box opens.

   ❏ change the Font to **Verdana** and the Size to **8pt**
   ❏ click the **OK** button to close the Font dialog box

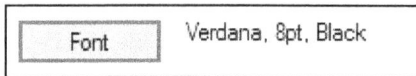

Font	Verdana, 8pt, Black

   ❏ click the **OK** button to close the WebHelp Skin Editor dialog box

3. Save and Generate the output and then View the results.

   The WebHelp output is now using your customized Skin—the font used on the navigation panel at the left is now Verdana, 8pt.

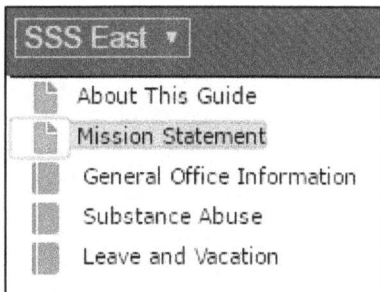

   SSS East ▾
   📄 About This Guide
   📄 Mission Statement
   📄 General Office Information
   📄 Substance Abuse
   📄 Leave and Vacation

4. Close the web browser and return to the RoboHelp project.

Student Activity: Customize the Search Highlight Color

1. Ensure that the **skins_masterpages** project is still open.

2. View the Primary Output without generating.

   ☐ on the Outputs(SSL) pod, right-click **WebHelp (Primary Output)** and choose **View**

   Note: Because you haven't made any changes to project content, it isn't necessary to Generate the output prior to viewing the results.

3. Search for a topic.

   ☐ click the **Search** tab

   ☐ type **bifferson** into the Search field and then press [**enter**]

   One topic is found and listed in the results area.

   ☐ select **Our President** from the results area to open the topic

   The word **bifferson** is highlighted; the current highlight color is gray.

4. Close the browser and return to the RoboHelp project.

5. Customize the Highlight color.

   ☐ on the Outputs(SSL) pod, double-click **WebHelp (Primary Output)** to open the WebHelp Settings dialog box
   ☐ from the left of the dialog box, select the **Search** category
   ☐ ensure **Enable Highlighting in Search Results** is selected
   ☐ to the right of **Enable Highlighting in Search Results**, select any color you like from the color drop-down menu

   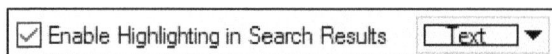

6. Save and Generate the output and then click View the results.

7. Use the Search button to once again search for **bifferson**.

   This time, the highlight color should reflect the change you made during the previous step.

8. Close the browser and return to the RoboHelp project.

Master Pages

You learned how to create and use style sheets earlier in this book (page 49). Style sheets control the appearance of many topic components, such as font formatting, page color, and link color. So what are Master Pages? A Master Page is a background that can be used on a topic. Master Pages can contain style sheets and page elements such as headers and footers (style sheets cannot contain a Master Page or page elements such as headers and footers).

If you need to display information, such as a copyright notice at the top or bottom of a topic, headers and footers offer just the ticket. Among the many things you can add to headers and footers are text, graphics, animation, and time stamps. You can control the margins, shading, background color, borders, and background image used in the headers and footers. And headers and footers can be used in one topic or many. You can create a Master Page with headers and footers and apply the Master Page topics quickly. When you make changes to the headers and footers in the Master Page, any topics using the Master Page are updated. Using this concept, you can make a change on a Master Page and update thousands of topics in seconds.

Student Activity: Create a Master Page

1. Ensure that the **skins_masterpages** project is still open.

2. Create a new Master Page

   ❐ on the **Output Setup** pod, right-click the **Master Pages** folder and choose **New Master Page**

   The New Master Page dialog box opens.

   ❐ on the **General** tab, change the **Name** to **Copyright Notice in Footer**

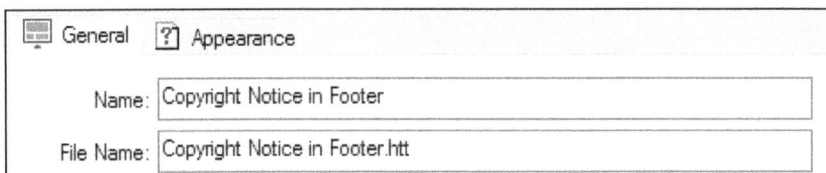

🖥 General	？ Appearance
Name:	Copyright Notice in Footer
File Name:	Copyright Notice in Footer.htt

   The file name of the Master Page is the same name except it has an **HTT** extension.

   ❐ click the **Appearance** tab
   ❐ from the list of Style Sheets, select **policies.css**

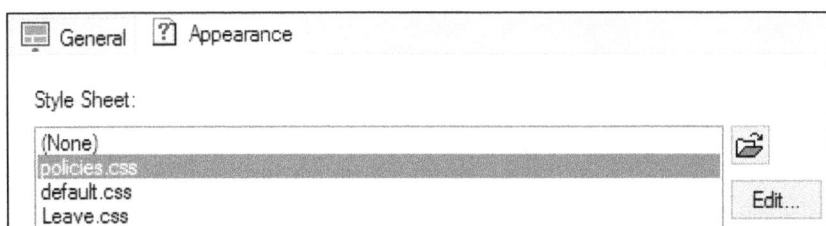

🖥 General	？ Appearance

   Style Sheet:

(None)
policies.css
default.css
Leave.css

   Edit...

   ❐ click the **OK** button

The new Master Page appears in the Master Pages folder and automatically opens for editing within the Design Window.

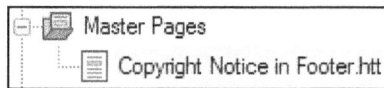

```
Master Pages
    Copyright Notice in Footer.htt
```

3. Add content to the Master Page footer.

   ❏ at the right top of the master page, click the **Edit Footer** tool

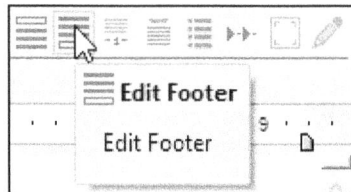

   Edit Footer

   Edit Footer

   The footer appears at the bottom of the Master Page.

4. Insert a copyright symbol.

   ❏ on **Insert** tab, **Media** group, click **Symbol**
   ❏ select the **Copyright** symbol

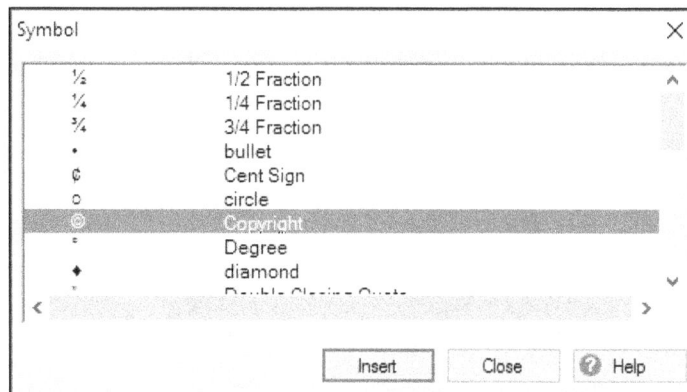

Symbol	✕
½	1/2 Fraction
¼	1/4 Fraction
¾	3/4 Fraction
•	bullet
¢	Cent Sign
°	circle
©	Copyright
°	Degree
♦	diamond

   [Insert] [Close] [? Help]

   ❏ click the **Insert** button
   ❏ click the **Close** button
   ❏ press [**spacebar**] and type **2017 Super Simplistic Solutions**
   ❏ on **Edit** tab, **Paragraph** group, click the **Align Center** tool

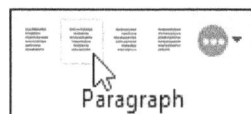

   Paragraph

   The footer should look like this:

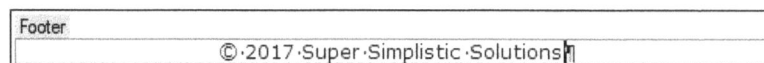

   ```
   Footer
                    © ·2017·Super·Simplistic·Solutions¶
   ```

5. Save and close the Copyright Notice in Footer master page.

6. Apply a Master Page to a topic.

    ☐ open the **Special Benefits** topic
    ☐ right-click within the topic and choose **Topic Properties**
    ☐ select the **General** tab
    ☐ from the **Master Page** drop-down menu, choose **Copyright Notice in Footer**

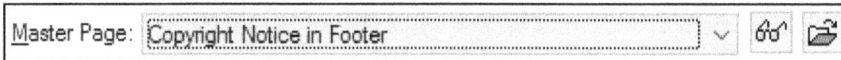

Master Page:	Copyright Notice in Footer	⌄	6ó	🖆

    ☐ click the **OK** button

7. Scroll down and notice that the footer you set up in the Master Page appears at the bottom of the topic.

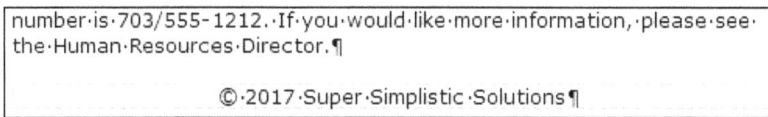

    > number·is·703/555-1212.·If·you·would·like·more·information,·please·see·
    > the·Human·Resources·Director.¶
    >
    >   ©·2017·Super·Simplistic·Solutions¶

8. Apply the Master Page to more topics.

    ☐ on the Topic List pod, select the **Drugs_and_Alcohol** folder

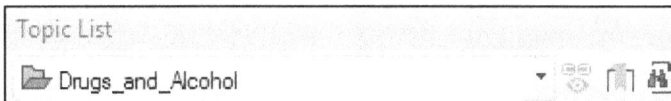

    Topic List

    📂 Drugs_and_Alcohol   ▾ ⑤ 🏛 🗗

    ☐ select both of the topics in the topics list
    ☐ on the **Project** tab, **File** group, **Properties**

    The Topic Properties dialog box opens.

    ☐ on the **General** tab, **Master Page** drop-down menu, choose the **Copyright Notice in Footer**
    ☐ click the **OK** button

    Both topics are now using the Copyright Notice in Footer Master Page (when you open them, you see the footer at the bottom of both topics).

9. Save the project.

10. Close all open topics.

Student Activity: Edit a Master Page

1. Ensure that the **skins_masterpages** project is still open.

2. Edit the footer on the Master Page.

   ☐ on the **Output Setup** pod, double-click the **Copyright Notice in Footer** Master Page (to open the Master Page for editing)
   ☐ at the right top of the master page, click the **Edit Footer** tool ▤
   ☐ click after the word "Solutions" and type **, Inc.**

   > Simplistic ·Solutions **· Inc.**¶

3. Save and close the Master Page.

4. Open the **Alcohol Policy** topic.

   The topic displays the updated footer. In fact, any topics in your project that are using the Copyright Notice in Footer Master Page now have the updated footer.

   > · leave·of·absence.¶
   >
   > © ·2017·Super·Simplistic·Solutions, ·Inc.¶

Master Page Confidence Check

1. Apply the Copyright Notice in Footer Master Page to all of the topics in the following two folders: **General Office Information** and **Leave and Vacation**.

2. Remove the Copyright Notice in Footer Master Page from the **Mission Statement** topic. (Show the topic's Properties and set the Master Page to **None**.)

3. Save the project.

4. Generate and View your project.

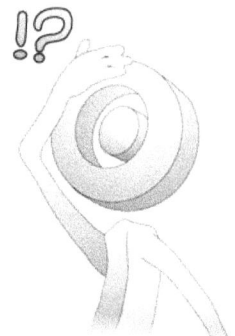

   All of the Help System topics, except Mission Statement, should now contain footers, and those footers should contain the corporate copyright notice.

5. When finished, close the browser and return to the RoboHelp project.

Breadcrumbs

Breadcrumbs provide an enhanced navigational aid to your Help System by adding links within the topics. These links display the user's position within the Help System as it relates to the table of contents. You can set up Breadcrumbs on a Master Page, or via the Properties of some Outputs(SSL).

Student Activity: Add Breadcrumbs to a Master Page

1. Ensure that the **skins_masterpages** project is still open.

2. Open the **Copyright Notice in Footer** Master Page.

3. Add a Breadcrumb Placeholder.

   ❏ click in the **white space** above the body placeholder
   ❏ on the **Insert** tab, **Page Design** group, click the drop-down menu to the right of **Topic TOC** and choose **Breadcrumbs**

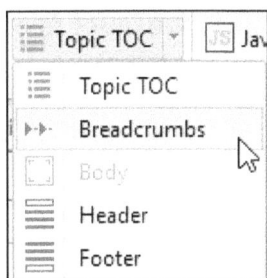

   ```
   ☰ Topic TOC  ▾   JS Ja
   ☰   Topic TOC
   ▸▸   Breadcrumbs
   ⬚   Body
   ☰   Header
   ☰   Footer
   ```

   The Breadcrumb Options dialog box opens.

   ❏ in the **Separator** field, type [**spacebar**] > [**spacebar**]

   Separator: [> ⌄]

   ❏ in the **Format** area, change the Font to **Verdana**
   ❏ change the Font Size to **10pt**

   Font: [Verdana ⌄] [10pt ⌄]

   ❏ click the **OK** button

   The breadcrumbs appear at the top of the master page.

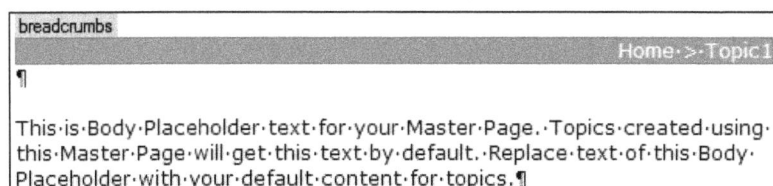

   ```
   breadcrumbs
                                        Home·>·Topic1
   ¶

   This·is·Body·Placeholder·text·for·your·Master·Page.·Topics·created·using·
   this·Master·Page·will·get·this·text·by·default.·Replace·text·of·this·Body·
   Placeholder·with·your·default·content·for·topics.¶
   ```

4. Save and close the Master Page.

5. Generate and View the Primary Output.

   Two sets of Breadcrumbs appear. One of the Breadcrumbs is from the Copyright Notice Master Page you just added and the other is from the WebHelp output. Breadcrumbs can be added either by a Master Page or by the output. Because you don't need both Breadcrumbs, you will disable the Breadcrumbs option in the WebHelp output.

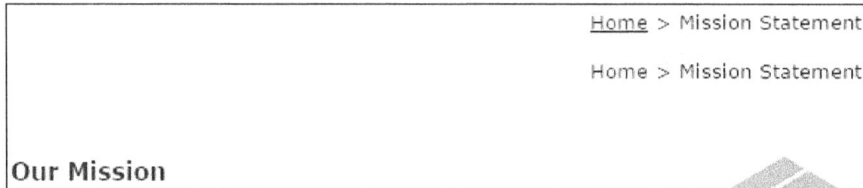

Home > Mission Statement
Home > Mission Statement
Our Mission

6. Close the browser and return to the RoboHelp project.

7. Remove the Breadcrumbs from an output.

   ❑ on the Outputs(SSL) pod, double-click **WebHelp (Primary Output)** to open the WebHelp Settings dialog box
   ❑ from the **Navigation** category, remove the check mark from **Add Breadcrumbs Links**

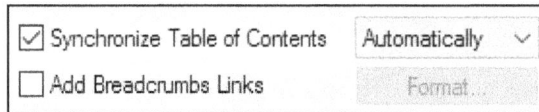

☑ Synchronize Table of Contents	Automatically ⌄
☐ Add Breadcrumbs Links	Format...

8. Save and Generate the output and then View the results.

   There should now be only one set of Breadcrumbs in any topic and only for those topics that follow the **Copyright Notice in Footer** Master Page.

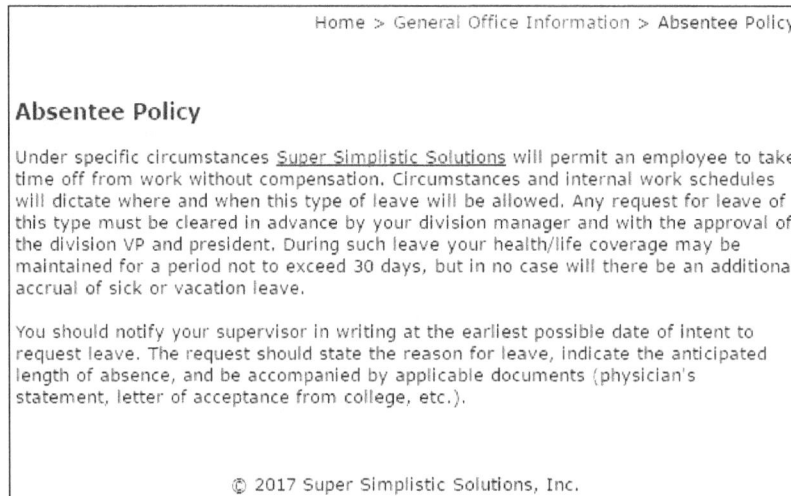

Home > General Office Information > Absentee Policy
Absentee Policy
Under specific circumstances Super Simplistic Solutions will permit an employee to take time off from work without compensation. Circumstances and internal work schedules will dictate where and when this type of leave will be allowed. Any request for leave of this type must be cleared in advance by your division manager and with the approval of the division VP and president. During such leave your health/life coverage may be maintained for a period not to exceed 30 days, but in no case will there be an additional accrual of sick or vacation leave.
You should notify your supervisor in writing at the earliest possible date of intent to request leave. The request should state the reason for leave, indicate the anticipated length of absence, and be accompanied by applicable documents (physician's statement, letter of acceptance from college, etc.).
© 2017 Super Simplistic Solutions, Inc.

9. Close the browser window and return to the RoboHelp project.

iCONLOGiC

"Skills and Drills" Learning

Module 11: Windows, Browsing, and CSH

In This Module You Will Learn About:

And You Will Learn To:

Custom Windows

You learned about WebHelp skins on page 220. Using a skin, you can customize the look and feel of the WebHelp window. Microsoft HTML Help (see page 14) isn't viewed via a web browser. Instead, the Help window using a program called the Help Viewer, opens in a specific location on the user's display and is set to a specific size and width. These weren't features you were asked to notice when you generated HTML Help earlier in this book, so it's likely you didn't. Nevertheless, you can control several HTML Help window features by creating a custom window and then attaching the window to the output prior to generating. In addition to controlling the placement and size of the window, you can add a search tab, browse sequence, and custom buttons to the Help window.

Student Activity: Create a Custom Window

1. Open the **custom_app.xpj** RoboHelp project file.

2. Change the default output to Microsoft HTML Help.

   ❑ on the Outputs(SSL) pod, right-click **Microsoft HTML Help** and choose **Set as Primary Output**

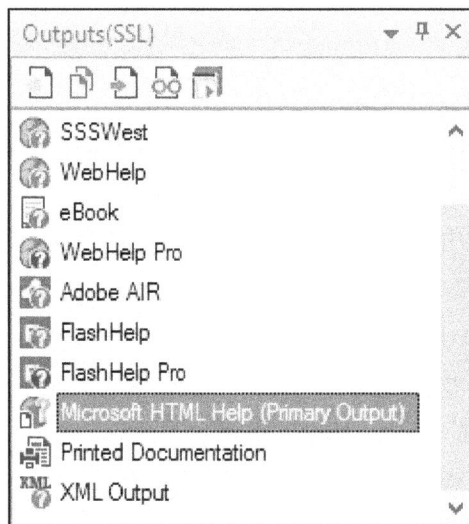

   By setting an output Primary, you can use the [**ctrl**] [**m**] keyboard shortcut to quickly generate the output.

3. Open the Output Setup pod.

4. Create a new window.

   ❑ on the **Output Setup** pod, right-click the **Windows** folder
   ❑ choose **New Window > Microsoft HTML Help** from the shortcut menu

   The Window Properties dialog box opens.

❑ in the **Window Name** field, type **Super Simplistic Solutions**

❑ in the **Window Caption** field, type **Super Simplistic Solutions: Policies**
(the Window Caption is the text that appears on the window's title bar)

Window Name:
Super Simplistic Solutions ∨
Window Caption:
Super Simplistic Solutions: Policies

5. Change the Width and Height of the new window.

❑ from the **Placement** area in the lower right of the window, change the **Top** Placement to **25**

❑ change the **Left** to **25**

❑ change the **Height** to **580**

❑ change the **Width** to **970**

Placement			
Top:	25	Height:	580
Left:	25	Width:	970

6. Set the Tri-pane Tabs and Windows options.

❑ from the **Tri-pane Tabs and Windows** area at the left, ensure that **TOC & Index** is selected

❑ ensure that **Glossary** is selected

You learned how to create a Glossary on page 209. The Glossary option ensures that the Glossary appears in the generated CHM file.

❑ ensure that **Search Tab** is selected

❑ ensure that **Browse Sequences** is selected

You will learn how to create a Browse Sequence soon. By selecting this option, the finished Browse Sequence appears in the Help window.

❑ ensure that the **Default Tab** is **Contents**

❑ ensure that the **Tab Position** is **Top**

Tri-pane Tabs and Windows			
☑ TOC & Index	☑ Search Tab	Default Tab:	Contents ∨
☐ Favorites	☐ Adv. Search	Tab Position:	Top ∨
☑ Glossary	☑ Browse Sequences		

❑ from the **Tri-pane Options** area at the bottom left of the window, ensure **Auto-synchronize TOC** is selected

The Auto-synchronize TOC option synchronizes the left and right panes of your generated Help System so that selected books or pages on the TOC and topics match as the Help System is used.

☐ select **Remember Window Size and Position**

> Tri-pane Options
> ☐ Hide Nav Pane on Startup   ☐ Auto-show/hide Nav Pane
> ☑ Auto-synchronize TOC   Nav Pane Width: [0   ⬍]
> ☑ Remember Window Size and Position

You are controlling the exact size and display position of the Help window. If users move or resize the window after it opens on their display, **Remember Window Size and Position** ensures that the Help window remembers the users' settings and puts the window in the same place the next time they open the Help System.

7. Add a Stop button.

☐ from the **Buttons** area on the right side of the dialog box, select **Stop** (turn the option on)

> Buttons
> ☑ Hide/Show   ☐ Refresh   ☐ Locate
> ☑ Back   ☐ Home   ☐ Button 1
> ☐ Forward   ☑ Options   ☐ Button 2
> ☑ Stop   ☑ Print

This option adds a Stop button to the Help window that instantly stops a web page from loading into the Help System, much like a web browser would do.

8. Add a custom button, set a target URL for a button, and set it to take users to the Super Simplistic Solutions website.

☐ from the **Buttons** area, select **Button 1**

> ☑ Button 1
> ☐ Button 2

☐ from the bottom right of the dialog box, click the **Advanced Properties** button

> Advanced Properties...
> OK   Cancel   ❓ Help

The Advanced Window Properties dialog box opens.

☐ on the **Destinations** tab, **Button 1 Label** field, type **Home**
☐ in the **Custom Button 1 URL** field, type **http://www.supersimplisticsolutions.com**

> Button 1 Label: Custom Button 1 URL:
> [Home]   [http://www.supersimplisticsolutions.com]

- ❏ click the **OK** button to close the Advanced Window Properties dialog box
- ❏ click the **OK** button again to close the Window Properties dialog box

Your new window appears in the Windows folder. Next you will tell RoboHelp to use the Super Simplistic Solutions window when you generate the project.

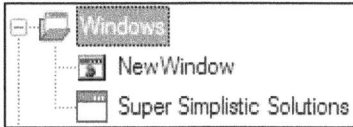

9. Edit the HTML Help output so that it uses the new window.

- ❏ on the **Outputs(SSL)** pod, double-click **Microsoft HTML Help (Primary Output)** to open the **HTML Help Options**
- ❏ from the Default Window drop-down menu in the middle of the dialog box, select **Super Simplistic Solutions**

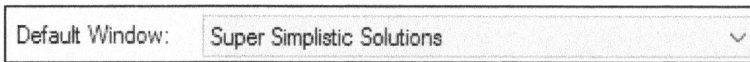

- ❏ click the **Save and Generate** button and **View** the results

The Help window should be quite large and positioned one-half inch from the upper left of your display. There is a Home button at the top of the window. This is a result of the Button 1 settings you applied. When clicked, the button takes you to the Super Simplistic Solutions home page. There is also a Stop button that stops the web page from loading.

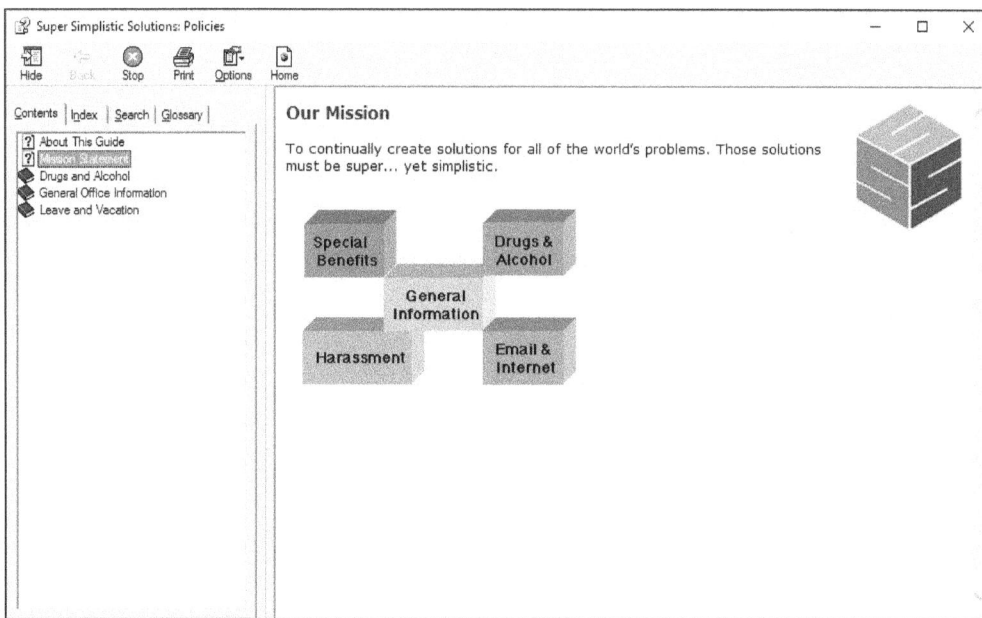

10. Close the Help window and return to the RoboHelp project.

Window Confidence Check

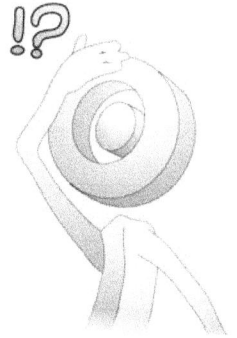

1. On the Output Setup pod, double-click the **Super Simplistic Solutions** window to open its Window Properties.

2. Change the **Top** and **Left** Placement to **36**.

3. Change the Window **Height** to **480**.

4. Change the Window **Width** to **640**.

Placement			
Top:	36	Height:	480
Left:	36	Width:	640

5. Deselect **Remember Window Size and Position**.

6. Close the Window Properties dialog box.

7. Press [**ctrl**] [**m**] on your keyboard to **Generate** the Primary Output and View the Results when prompted.

   The resulting Help window should be much smaller than before.

   Note: If you hadn't deselected **Remember Window Size and Position**, the size of your Help window would not have changed because you already viewed the window at the larger size.

8. Close the Help window and return to the RoboHelp project.

Browse Sequences

You can create a browse sequence for Responsive HTML5, HTML Help and WebHelp. A browse sequence gives your users the freedom to move forward and backward through your topics in an order you create. The browse order can be based on anything you think might improve the usability of your project.

In this lesson, you will learn how to use the Browse Sequence Editor to create a browse sequence. Keep in mind that only topics and bookmarks included in your project can be used and although you will be creating only one browse sequence in this activity, you can have multiple browse sequences.

Student Activity: Create a Browse Sequence

1. Start the Browse Sequence Editor.

   ❏ ensure that you are still working in the **custom_app** project
   ❏ on the **Project** tab, **Navigation** group, click **Browse Sequences**

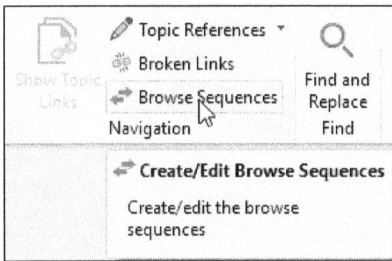

   The Browse Sequence Editor dialog box opens.

2. Create a new browse sequence.

   ❏ from the right side of the dialog box, click the **New** button

   The new sequence is created and is ready for a name.

   ❏ type **Managers**
   ❏ press [**enter**]

3. Add a topic to the browse sequence.

   ❏ from the **Available Topics** drop-down menu at the left, choose the **Company_Officers** folder
   ❏ double-click the **Our President** topic to move the topic into the new Browse Sequence

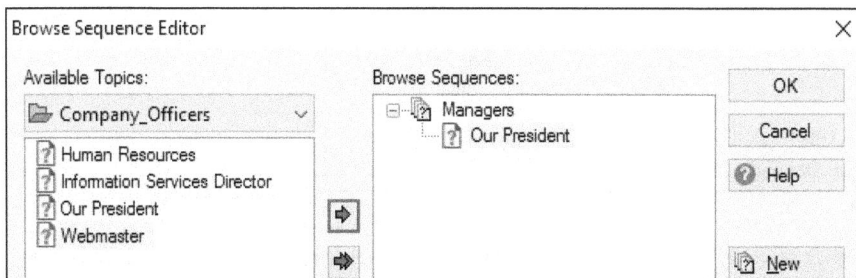

4. Using the image below as your guide, add more topics to the Managers browse sequence.

   As you add topics, keep the following in mind: (1) If you want to change the order of the browse sequence, use the arrows at the bottom right of the window to move the topics up or down; (2) If you want to remove a topic from the sequence, select the topic and click the **Remove** button.

5. When finished, click the **OK** button to close the Browse Sequence Editor.

6. Enable Browse Sequences for an Output

   ☐ on the Outputs(SSL) pod, double-click **WebHelp** to open the WebHelp Settings dialog box

   ☐ open the **Content Categories** group and select **SSSEast<Default>**

   ☐ select the **Managers** browse sequence

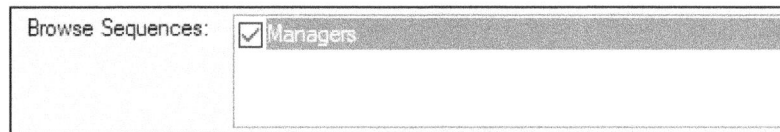

   ☐ from the left of the dialog box, select the **Navigation** category

   ☐ ensure **Enable Browse Sequence** is selected

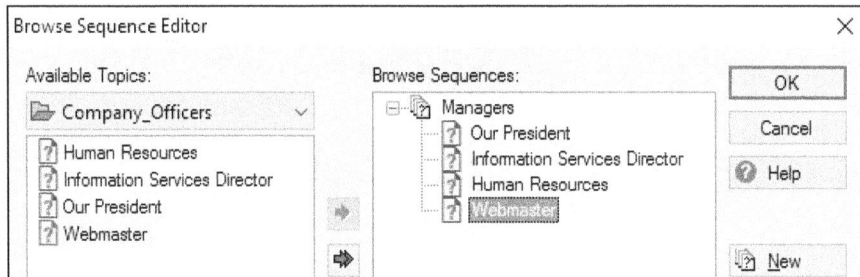

   ☐ click **Save and Generate** and view the result when prompted.

7. Use the Browse Sequence.

   ☐ find and open the **Our President** topic using search

   ☐ use the buttons over the search results to go through the browse sequence

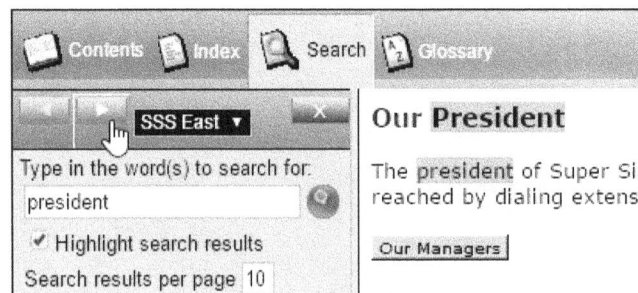

8. Close the browser and return to the RoboHelp project.

Application Help

Up until now, your generated outputs have been Standalone Help Systems, meaning that anyone can double-click the generated CHM file (if you generated HTML Help) or the Start Page (if you generated WebHelp or Responsive HTML5), and the Help System opens on his or her computer. **Application Help** simply means that your generated output is intended to work from within a program. There isn't much you have to do to go from Standalone Help to Application Help, except hand the generated output to your application developer. From there, the application developer programs the application to open your Help System when the user clicks a Help link or icon.

To demonstrate Application Help, a simple web application is included within the **webapp** folder called **SimpleWebApplication**. The application is looking for the polices and procedures Help System that you created during the previous modules in this book. When one application attempts to communicate with another, the interaction is called an Application Programming Interface (API) call.

> **Note:** When testing help locally, use Google Chrome or Mozilla Firefox. Microsoft Edge and Internet Explorer do not work well. After you have uploaded the Help System to a web server, any browser can be used.

Student Activity: Test an API Call for Help

1. Minimize RoboHelp.

2. Review the folder containing the published Help System files.

   ❏ open the **RoboHelp2017Data** folder
   ❏ open the **webapp** folder

   There's not much within the webapp folder. There are a few folders and a web page (named SimpleWebApplication.htm) that we created using basic HTML tags. The web page is communicating with the other assets within the webapp folder. The most important folder, from your perspective, is the **helpsystem** folder.

   ```
   helpsystem
   images
   policies.css
   RoboHelp_CSH.js
   SimpleWebApplication.htm
   ```

3. Open a web application and test the link to the Help System.

   ❏ double-click **SimpleWebApplication.htm** to open the application in your default web browser

   We added a link on the web page that is looking for a Help System similar to the one you've been building throughout this book. Because the generated output files have not been **published** into the **helpsystem** folder, the link to the Help

System on the web page fails when clicked. You'll see that problem next when you attempt to get help from within the web application.

4. Attempt to get help from within the web application.

   ❑ in the **second paragraph**, click the link (the word **here**)

   > If you click here, you will start the Help sy
   > window thank to the **target=_blank** tag.

   The Help System does not open because... yikes... you haven't yet published the RoboHelp output into the **helpsystem** folder.

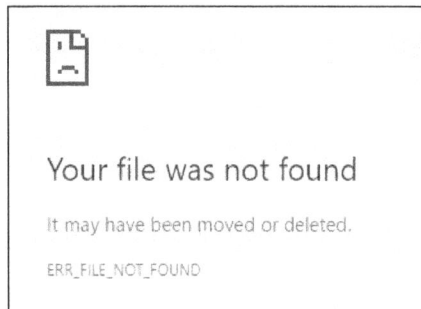

   > 🙁
   >
   > Your file was not found
   >
   > It may have been moved or deleted.
   >
   > ERR_FILE_NOT_FOUND

   ❑ close the File not found window and return to the **SimpleWebApplication** page

5. View an application's source code.

   ❑ using your mouse, point to (but don't click) the **link** in the **second paragraph** (the word **here**)

   In the status bar at the bottom of the browser window, the code that links the web application to the Help System appears.

   > file:///C:/RoboHelp2017Data/webapp/helpsystem/index.htm

   You do not have to be an HTML expert to get a feel for the code. The link is looking within the web application's **helpsystem** folder for a specific file named **index.htm**. Index.htm is the Start Page for the entire Help System, not a topic that you created. The Start Page is automatically created each time you generate the WebHelp output.

   Once the Help System has been published to the **helpsystem** folder (you will learn how to publish during the next activity), the Help System opens when the word **here** is clicked.

6. Close the browser window.

7. Open the **helpsystem** folder.

   The folder is empty, which explains the reason the call from the web page for index.htm failed. Let's publish all of the required assets to the helpsystem folder.

8. Close the **helpsystem** folder and then return to RoboHelp.

Publishing

You've generated your Help System multiple times during the activities in this book. When you generate an output, the generated files go into a folder within your project folder (by default, the **!SSL!** folder).

To make the generated files available to your users, you need to copy the files to a web server. Assuming users know the URL of the Help System's Start Page (the Start page is typically named index.htm and is created every time you generate), your job would be done. The problem with copying and pasting the output files to the server is that you need to replace all of the files each time you update the Help System—even if you make a minor change within a single topic.

The most efficient way to get your finished content to a web server is to have RoboHelp **Publish** the generated files to the server for you. Once the files are published, you can elect to republish the entire output each time you make a change **or** republish *only the files that changed*. In a word, the Publish feature, which is often overlooked, is awesome. It saves you tons of time waiting for file after file to copy to the server. Simply make a change to a topic, generate the output, and **Publish**—you are done in seconds.

Student Activity: Publish an Output

1. Ensure that the **custom_app** project is still open.

2. Change the default output to WebHelp.

   ❏ on the **Outputs(SSL)** pod, right-click **WebHelp** and choose **Set as Primary Output**

3. Set up a Publish destination.

   ❏ from the **Outputs(SSL)** pod, double-click **WebHelp (Primary Output)** to open the WebHelp Settings dialog box
   ❏ from the Category list at the left, select **Publish**

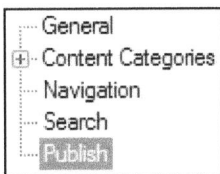

Use this screen to set up a destination to publish the generated output files.

   ❏ at the right of the dialog box, click the **New** button
   ❏ in the **Descriptive Name** area, type **Publish to WebApp**

Please provide a descriptive name for your web server/folder. This name will be used in selecting a destination when publishing files.

Descriptive Name:

Publish to WebApp

You can choose from among the following Connection Protocols: FTP, HTTP, File System, and SharePoint.

FTP: File Transfer Protocol uses a TCP/IP network that allows a user to *quickly* transfer large files from one computer to another over the Internet. You will likely need a password for access.

HTTP: Hypertext Transfer Protocol is similar to FTP, but is not as fast.

File System: This is a great option if you want to publish your files to a network drive.

SharePoint: You would select this option if you use Microsoft SharePoint, a family of programs used for collaboration, file sharing, and web publishing.

❏ from the Connection Protocols area, select **File System**

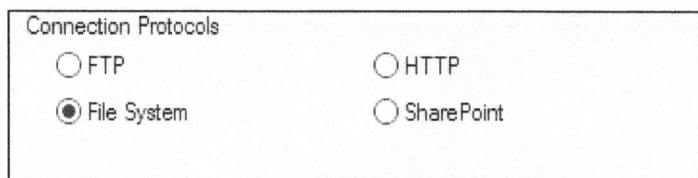

Connection Protocols
- ○ FTP
- ○ HTTP
- ● File System
- ○ SharePoint

❏ from the **Destination Path** area, click the **Browse** button (the yellow folder)

The Browse for Folder dialog box opens.

❏ navigate to the **RoboHelp2017Data** folder
❏ open the **webapp** folder
❏ select the **helpsystem** folder

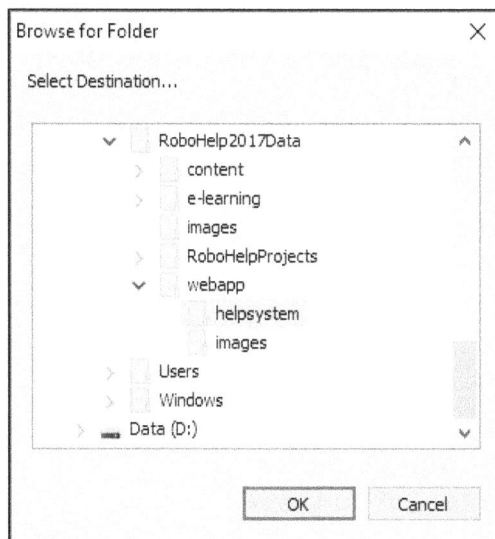

Browse for Folder ✕

Select Destination...

- ∨ RoboHelp2017Data
  - › content
  - › e-learning
  - images
  - › RoboHelpProjects
  - ∨ webapp
    - helpsystem
    - images
- › Users
- › Windows
- › Data (D:)

OK   Cancel

❏ click the **OK** button

Although you could have installed your RoboHelp2017Data files anywhere on your computer, at the very least, ensure that your Destination Path ends with **RoboHelp2017Data\webapp\helpsystem**.

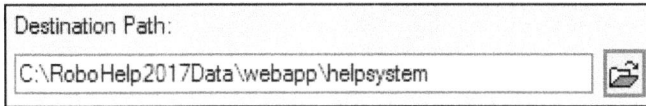

Destination Path:

```
C:\RoboHelp2017Data\webapp\helpsystem
```

❏ click the **OK** button

Your new server now appears in the list of Servers.

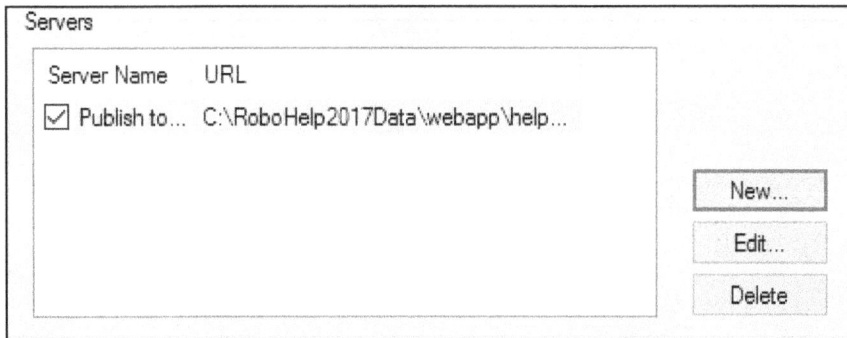

Servers

Server Name	URL
☑ Publish to...	C:\RoboHelp2017Data\webapp\help...

New...

Edit...

Delete

❏ from the **Options** area, ensure none of the options are selected

The first time you publish a project, all of the output's assets are copied and sent to the server. After that, RoboHelp sends only edited assets to the server.

4. Generate and then Publish the output files.

❏ click the **Save and Generate** button

Once the output has been generated, you are greeted with the familiar Result screen. This time, however, notice that there is a **Publish** button.

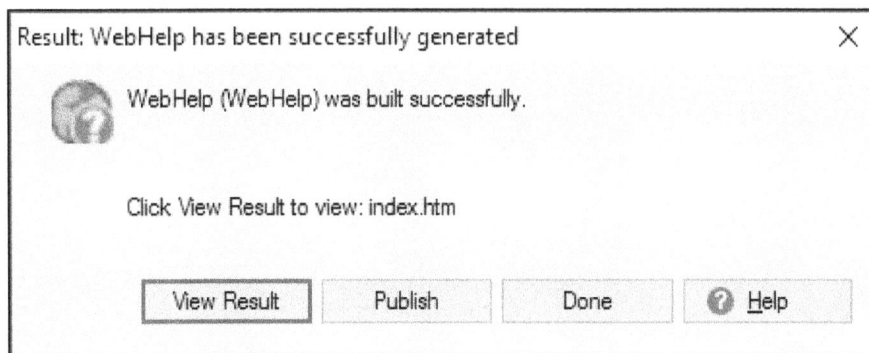

Result: WebHelp has been successfully generated   ✕

WebHelp (WebHelp) was built successfully.

Click View Result to view: index.htm

| View Result | Publish | Done | ❓ Help |

❏ click the **Publish** button

The output files are published to the **helpsystem** folder on your hard drive (not a server because this was only a test). In the following image, 485 files were published. The number of files published on your system should be similar.

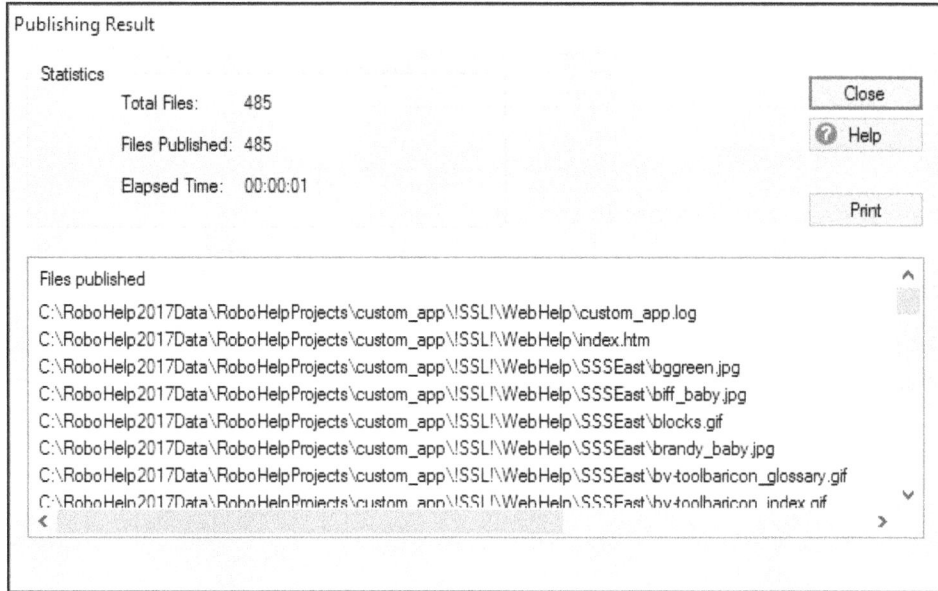

```
Publishing Result

    Statistics
                                                              ┌──────────┐
        Total Files:      485                                 │  Close   │
                                                              └──────────┘
        Files Published:  485                                 ┌──────────┐
                                                              │ ② Help   │
        Elapsed Time:   00:00:01                              └──────────┘

                                                              ┌──────────┐
                                                              │  Print   │
                                                              └──────────┘
    ┌────────────────────────────────────────────────────────────────┐
    │ Files published                                              ^  │
    │ C:\RoboHelp2017Data\RoboHelpProjects\custom_app\!SSL!\WebHelp\custom_app.log │
    │ C:\RoboHelp2017Data\RoboHelpProjects\custom_app\!SSL!\WebHelp\index.htm │
    │ C:\RoboHelp2017Data\RoboHelpProjects\custom_app\!SSL!\WebHelp\SSSEast\bggreen.jpg │
    │ C:\RoboHelp2017Data\RoboHelpProjects\custom_app\!SSL!\WebHelp\SSSEast\biff_baby.jpg │
    │ C:\RoboHelp2017Data\RoboHelpProjects\custom_app\!SSL!\WebHelp\SSSEast\blocks.gif │
    │ C:\RoboHelp2017Data\RoboHelpProjects\custom_app\!SSL!\WebHelp\SSSEast\brandy_baby.jpg │
    │ C:\RoboHelp2017Data\RoboHelpProjects\custom_app\!SSL!\WebHelp\SSSEast\bv-toolbaricon_glossary.gif │
    │ C:\RoboHelp2017Data\RoboHelpProjects\custom_app\!SSL!\WebHelp\SSSEast\bv-toolbaricon_index.gif v │
    │ <                                                            >   │
    └────────────────────────────────────────────────────────────────┘
```

❐ click the **Close** button

5. Save the project.

Publishing Confidence Check

1. Open the **Alcohol Policy** topic

2. Delete the words "of the company" from the first paragraph.

> Super·Simplistic·Solutions·does·not·permit·or·condone·intoxication·or·drinking·of·alcoholic·beverages·on·the·premises·of·the·company·or·at·an·employee's·assigned·place·of·duty·on·company·time.¶

3. Save and close the topic.

4. On the Outputs(SSL) pod, right-click **WebHelp (Primary Output)** and choose **Publish** (click **Yes** when prompted).

   The first time you published the project, around 480 files were published. Notice that far fewer files were published this time. In fact, only the updated topic and some support files should have been published.

   > Total Files: 485
   > Files Published: 12

5. Click the **Close** button.

6. Minimize RoboHelp, navigate to the **RoboHelp2017Data** folder, and open the **webapp** folder.

7. Open the **helpsystem** folder to see the published output files.

   > SSSEast
   > SSSWest
   > bsscftp.txt
   > custom_app.log
   > index.htm

8. Go back to the **webapp** folder and reopen **SimpleWebApplication**.

9. Click the link to the word "here."

   This time the Help System that you just published to the "server," opens. Congratulations! You are now a *published Help author!*

   Note: If the published Help System did not open when you clicked the word "here," the issue is likely your web browser (some browsers act cranky when you test items such as links locally). If you have an alternative web browser installed on your computer, open **SimpleWebApplication** there and retest the link. As mentioned earlier, Mozilla Firefox works best when testing Help Systems locally; Internet Explorer historically causes the most trouble.

10. Close the Help System tab (or window). Keep **SimpleWebApplication.htm** open. You will be using it again during the next activity.

Context Sensitive Help

Context Sensitive Help (CSH) allows users to get help about specific areas of a program. Users can quickly get help without having to use the Help System's TOC, Index, or Search.

Here is how context sensitive help works: To make a topic context sensitive, the topic needs a unique topic ID and a map number. This information is stored in a **map file**. The application's programmer can (and most probably will) create the map file (also known as an **H** or **HH** file). Although just about any word processor can be used to create the map file, many programmers still use NotePad.

Here's an example of a map file entry: **#define ID_AboutSSS 5001**. The text **ID_AboutSSS** is the topic ID; **5001** is the map number.

After the programmer is finished with the map file, import the map file into your project. Then match the topics in your project with the IDs from the map file. After that, generate the project and publish.

In the next few activities, you will review the areas of the Simple Web Application that are meant to be context sensitive, create a map file in RoboHelp, and assign map numbers to a few topics.

Student Activity: Review CSH Source Code

1. Attempt to get Context Sensitive Help.

   ❑ still working within the **SimpleWebApplication.htm** web application, click the link **Open just the Leave Policy topic**

   The way the programmer designed **SimpleWebApplication**, the link you just clicked is supposed to start the Help System and then open just the **Leave Policy** topic in a specific pop-up window. Instead, the entire Help System is started, and the Welcome topic opens. If you were the user looking for information on the Leave Policy, you would now have to manually search for the content.

2. Close the Help window but leave SimpleWebApplication.htm open.

3. Try to get additional Context Sensitive Help.

   ❑ click the link **Open just the Payroll Policy topic**

   The Help System starts again, but the Payroll Policy topic does not appear.

4. Close the Help window but leave SimpleWebApplication.htm open.

5. View the source code.

   ❑ using your browser, point to (but don't click) the **Open just the Leave Policy topic** link

   The code appears in the browser's status part.

   ```
   javascript:RH_ShowHelp(0,'helpsystem/index.htm>CSH', HH_HELP_CONTEXT, 45)
   ```

The text "javascript:RH_ShowHelp" causes the JavaScript file named RH_ShowHelp to activate. The next bit of text (0,'helpsystem/index.htm) is what tells the Help System to open.

The text ">CSH'" is what causes the topic to open in a custom window named "CSH." You have not yet created a custom window named "CSH"—you will do that next.

Finally, the last bit of text (HH_HELP_CONTEXT, **45**) is what tells the Help System to display the topic with map ID number **45**. Soon you will assign Map ID **45** to the **Leave Policy** topic.

6. View another source code.

   ❐ using your browser, point to (but don't click) the **Open just the Payroll Policy topic** link

   ```
   javascript:RH_ShowHelp(0,'helpsystem/index.htm>CSH', HH_HELP_CONTEXT, 46)
   ```

   The end of the text (HH_HELP_CONTEXT, **46**) is what tells the Help System to display the topic with map ID number **46**. Soon you will assign Map ID **46** to the **Payroll Policy** topic.

7. Leave SimpleWebApplication.htm open and return to the RoboHelp project.

Student Activity: Create a WebHelp Window

1. Return to RoboHelp and ensure that the **custom_app** project is still open.

2. Create a custom WebHelp window.

   ❑ on the **Output Setup** pod, right-click the **Windows** folder and choose **New Window > WebHelp**

   ❑ change the Window name to **CSH** (this is the name of the window referenced in the Source code)

   ❑ change the Window caption to **Here's the Help You Asked For**

   The caption is what the user sees in the Help window's Title bar when the Help window opens.

   ❑ from the **View** area, select **One Pane**

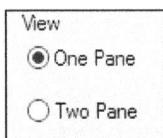

   ```
   View
   ◉ One Pane
   ○ Two Pane
   ```

   By choosing One Pane, the Help window (which is going to be smaller than the typical Help window), will not have a Navigation area.

   ❑ deselect **Use Default Browser Settings**

   By deselecting this option, you have the ability to control the location and size of the new window when it opens on your user's screen.

   ❑ change the **Placement Height** to **68**
   ❑ change the **Placement Width** to **68**

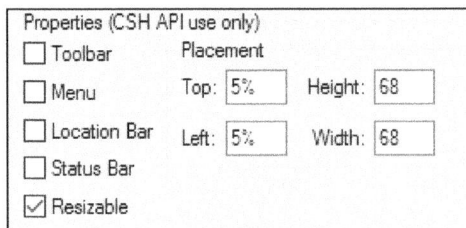

   ```
   Properties (CSH API use only)
   ☐ Toolbar          Placement
   ☐ Menu             Top: 5%      Height: 68
   ☐ Location Bar     Left: 5%     Width: 68
   ☐ Status Bar
   ☑ Resizable
   ```

   By changing the Height and Width, the CSH window will be significantly smaller than the default Help window.

   ❑ click the **OK** button

3. Save the project.

Student Activity: Assign Map IDs

1. Ensure that the **custom_app** project is still open.

2. Create a Map file.

   ☐ on the **Output Setup** pod, open the **Context-Sensitive Help** folder
   ☐ right-click the **Map Files** folder and choose **New Map File**

   The **New Map File** dialog box opens.

   ☐ type **CSHMap**

New Map File	×
Map File:	
CSHMap	
OK Cancel ❓ Help	

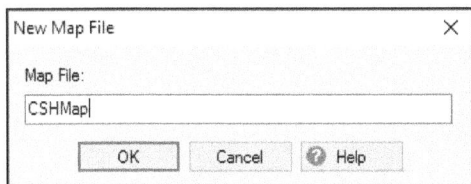

   ☐ click the **OK** button

   The new map file has been created within the Map Files folder.

   ☐ open the **Map Files** folder

   You should be able to see the CSHMap map file you just created—it's currently just an empty text file. In a moment, you'll be adding map numbers to it when you assign Map IDs to two topics.

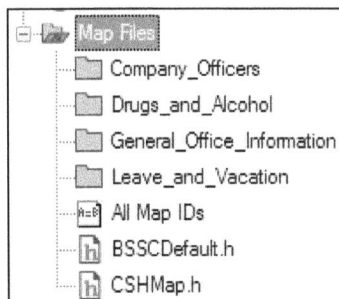

   ```
   ⊟ 🗁 Map Files
       📁 Company_Officers
       📁 Drugs_and_Alcohol
       📁 General_Office_Information
       📁 Leave_and_Vacation
       ⓝ All Map IDs
       ⓗ BSSCDefault.h
       ⓗ CSHMap.h
   ```

3. Assign Map IDs to two topics.

   ☐ in the Context-Sensitive Help, Map Files folder, double-click **CSHMap.h**

   The Edit Map IDs dialog box opens.

   ☐ from the list of topics at the right, select **Leave Policy**
   ☐ click the **Auto-map** button in the middle of the dialog box

   The **Leave Policy** topic is assigned Map ID **1**. You need to change the number to **45** so it matches the reference in the web application's source code.

Map ID	Map #	Topic
❓ⓗ Leave_Policy	1	Leave Policy

4. Edit a Map ID.

❏ select the existing Map ID (click the number **1**)
❏ click the **Edit Map ID** tool
❏ change the Map Number to **45**

Create/Edit Map ID ✕

Map ID:

Leave_Policy

Map Number:

45

OK   Cancel

❏ click the **OK** button

Map ID	Map #	Topic
?⃞ Leave_Policy	45	Leave Policy

Map Confidence Check

1. Select and **Auto-map** the **Payroll Policy** topic.
(It should receive Map ID 1, which does not match the ID used in the web application.)

2. Change the Map ID for the Payroll Policy to **46**.

Create/Edit Map ID ✕

Map ID:

Payroll_Policy

Map Number:

46

OK   Cancel

?⃞ Leave_Policy	45	Leave Policy
?⃞ Payroll_Policy	46	Payroll Policy

3. Close the Edit Map IDs dialog box.

4. On the Outputs(SSL) pod, show the Properties of **WebHelp (Primary Output)**.

5. Open the **Content Categories** group and select **SSSEast<Default>**.

6. From the Map Files area, select **CSHMap.h**. (This is the map file you created a few moments ago.)

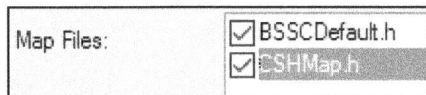

Map Files:
☑ BSSCDefault.h
☑ CSHMap.h

7. Select **SSSWest** from the Content Categories list.

8. From the Map Files area, select **CSHMap.h**.

9. From the Publish group, ensure that **Publish to WebApp** is still selected.

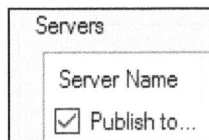

Servers

Server Name
☑ Publish to...

10. Save and Generate the output and, when prompted, **Publish**.

11. Minimize RoboHelp.

12. Return to the **SimpleWebApplication.htm** window.

13. Reload/Refresh the SimpleWebApplication web page.

14. Test the links to the Leave and Payroll policy topics.

Clicking either link should result in a topic appearing in the custom CSH window you created or in a new browser window. The behavior you see depends on your browser version.

If nothing is shown, it's possible your web browser is blocking pop-up windows. In that case, you will need to ease the restrictions on pop-ups (at least for the time being).

15. When finished, close all windows, return to RoboHelp, and close the project.

Notes

iCONLOGiC

"Skills and Drills" Learning

Module 12: Docs, eBooks, and Scripts

In This Module You Will Learn About:

And You Will Learn To:

Challenge Your New Skills:

Printed Docs

During lessons in this book, you have generated Outputs(SSL) specifically for Windows-based machines (HTML Help) and the web (WebHelp and FlashHelp). You can also generate an output as a Word document by generating printed documentation.

In the steps that follow, you will be using RoboHelp to create a Word document. If you don't enable macros in Word, the required communication between RoboHelp and Word will be blocked, and you will not end up with printed documentation output.

Student Activity: Enable Word Macros

1. Start Microsoft Word 2016 (if you are using 2013 or something older, read the **Note** below).

2. Enable Word macros.

   ❏ create a blank document or press [**esc**]
   ❏ on the **File** tab, select **Options**
   ❏ from the options at the left, select **Trust Center**
   ❏ at the right of the dialog box, click the **Trust Center Settings** button

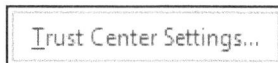

   ┌─────────────────────────┐
   │ Trust Center Settings... │
   └─────────────────────────┘

   ❏ from the **Trust Center** options at the left, ensure **Macro Settings** is selected

   Make a note of your current Macro Settings. When you are finished with this book, return to this screen and reselect your current settings. You will need to change the settings only when you want to create printed documentation out of your RoboHelp project.

   ❏ select **Enable all macros**

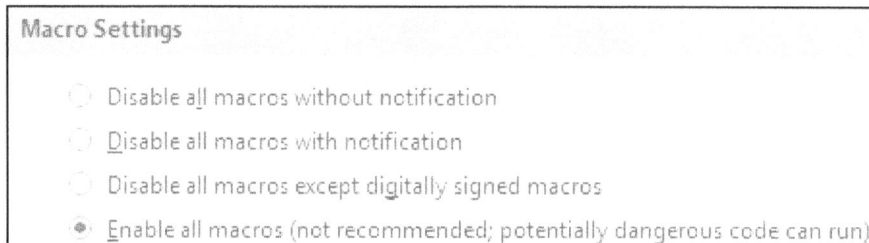

   ┌──┐
   │ Macro Settings   │
   │   │
   │   ○ Disable all macros without notification   │
   │   ○ Disable all macros with notification   │
   │   ○ Disable all macros except digitally signed macros   │
   │   ● Enable all macros (not recommended; potentially dangerous code can run) │
   └──┘

   ❏ click the **OK** button twice to close both dialog boxes

   Note: Although the process of enabling all macros in Microsoft Word 2016 is detailed above, the steps are similar in Word 2013, 2010 and 2007. If you are using Word 2010, click the **File** tab, select **Options** and then select Trust Center. If you are using Word 2007, click the **Office** button, click the **Word Options** button, and then select **Trust Center**.

3. Exit Microsoft Word.

Student Activity: Generate a Print Doc

1. Using RoboHelp, open the **Print_eBook.xpj** project file.

2. Start the Printed Document wizard.

   ❏ on the **Outputs(SSL)** pod, double-click **Printed Documentation**

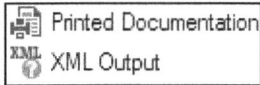

   ⊞ Printed Documentation
   ᴹᴸ XML Output

   The Print Document dialog box opens.

3. Select an Output format.

   ❏ from the Output format area, deselect **Generate Adobe PDF**

   Disabling Generate Adobe PDF should automatically enable **Generate Word DOC**.

   ❏ if you are using Word 2007 or newer, select **.docx** from the drop-down menu; if you are using an older version of Word, select **.doc**

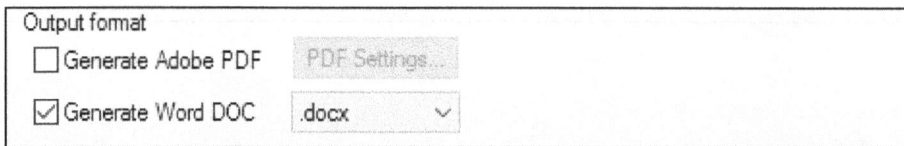

   Output format
   ☐ Generate Adobe PDF   PDF Settings...
   ☑ Generate Word DOC   .docx   ⌄

4. Specify the name of the printed document.

   ❏ in the Printed Documentation area, change the **Name** to **General Office Information**

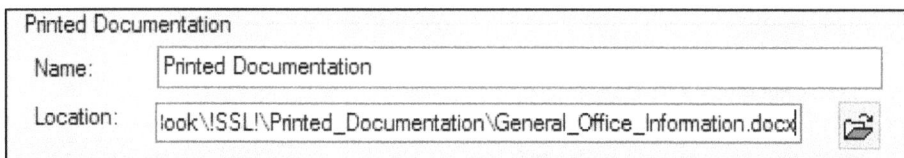

   Printed Documentation
   Name: Printed Documentation
   Location: !ook\!SSL!\Printed_Documentation\General_Office_Information.docx   📂

5. Determine what happens with the project images when the printed documentation is generated.

   ❏ from the Images area, select **Embed in documents**

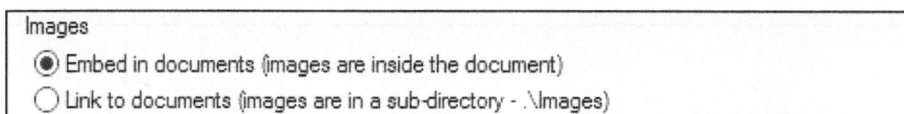

   Images
   ⦿ Embed in documents (images are inside the document)
   ○ Link to documents (images are in a sub-directory - .\Images)

6. Specify the number of output documents and the fate of the hyperlinks in the project.

❐ from the Settings area, ensure **Generate a single document** is selected

❐ ensure **Retain hyperlinks** is selected

Settings
- ○ Generate individual documents
- ● Generate a single document
- ☐ Start each topic on a new page
- ☑ Create master document
- ☑ Retain hyperlinks
- [Advanced...]

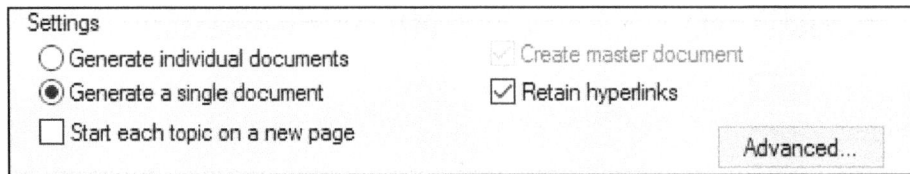

❐ click the **Next** button

Now you can control how your printed document is put together. Currently, the document is following the structure specified on the TOC.

7. Organize the topics in the chapter layout.

❐ in the **Chapter layout** area at the right, click one time on **About This Guide**

❐ click the **Remove** button [◆]

Chapter layout

[?] About This Guide
[?] Mission Statement
[📖] Drugs and Alcohol
   [?] Alcohol Policy
   [?] Drug Policy
[📖] General Office Information
   [?] Absentee Policy
   [?] Electronic Communications Policy
   [?] Nondiscrimination Policy
   [?] Overtime Policy
   [?] Payroll Policy
   [?] Special Benefits
   [?] Leave Policy
   [?] Termination Policy

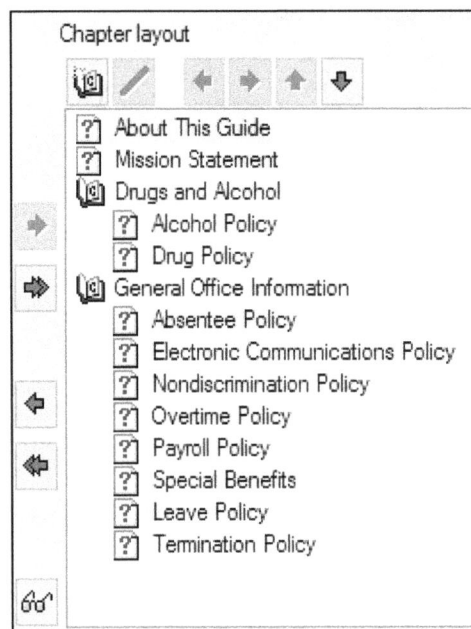

❐ in the **Chapter layout** area at the right, click one time on the **Mission Statement** topic

❐ click the **Remove** button

Printed Docs Confidence Check

1. Remove the **Drugs and Alcohol** book.

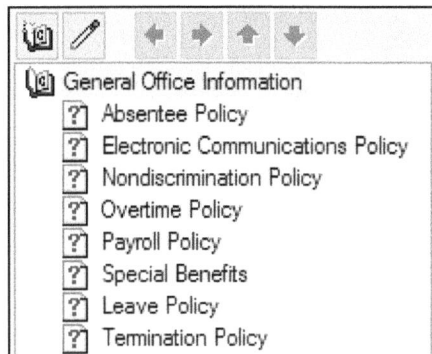

   General Office Information
   - ? Absentee Policy
   - ? Electronic Communications Policy
   - ? Nondiscrimination Policy
   - ? Overtime Policy
   - ? Payroll Policy
   - ? Special Benefits
   - ? Leave Policy
   - ? Termination Policy

2. Click the **Next** button.

   The Section Layout area allows you to add a custom Title Page (if you have created a Word document you'd like to use). You can also use this screen to control where sections appear (for instance, you can move the Glossary below the Index). However, the settings you see in the Section Layout area are fine as they are.

3. Click the **Next** button.

   This final screen is arguably the most important. Using this screen, you can control how your topic text is formatted as the project is published as a Word document. If you select Microsoft Word Template, you can map the styles used in your project with any styles in the Word Template. You can use any Word Template on your system. If you do not have a Word Template, it's best to use the one that comes with RoboHelp—Style Mapping.dot.

4. From the **Use Styles from** area, select **Microsoft Word Template**.

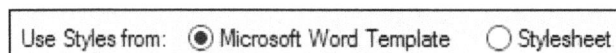

   Use Styles from: ⦿ Microsoft Word Template   ○ Stylesheet

5. From the Microsoft Word Template drop-down menu, choose **Style Mapping.dot**.

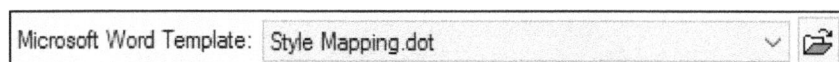

   Microsoft Word Template: Style Mapping.dot

6. From the Map Non-Heading Styles drop-down menu, choose **Project's CSS Styles (used only)**.

7. Select **Normal** in the left column and ensure **Normal** is selected in the right column.

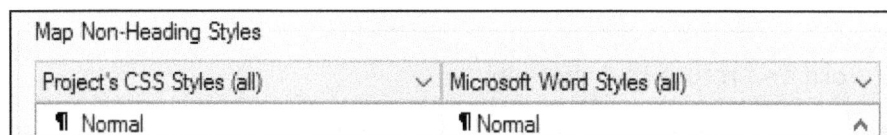

Map Non-Heading Styles	
Project's CSS Styles (all) ⌄	Microsoft Word Styles (all) ⌄
¶ Normal	¶ Normal

8. Click **Description** in the Preview area. Now you can see what your topic text will look like when the layout is generated as a Word document.

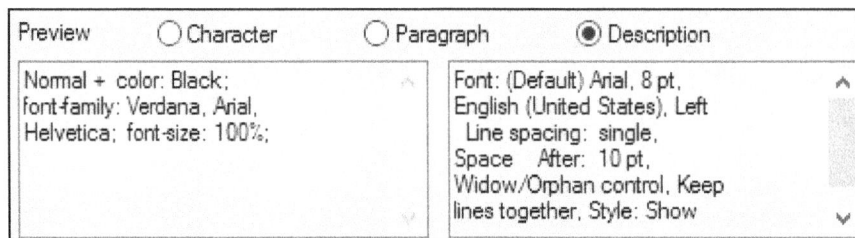

Preview	○ Character	○ Paragraph	◉ Description
Normal + color: Black; font-family: Verdana, Arial, Helvetica; font-size: 100%;		Font: (Default) Arial, 8 pt, English (United States), Left Line spacing: single, Space After: 10 pt, Widow/Orphan control, Keep lines together, Style: Show	

9. Click the **Save and Generate** button.

10. After the Word document is generated, click the **View Result** button.

11. The layout automatically opens in Microsoft Word. The document includes all of the selected RoboHelp content, a formatted Table of Contents, and an Index.

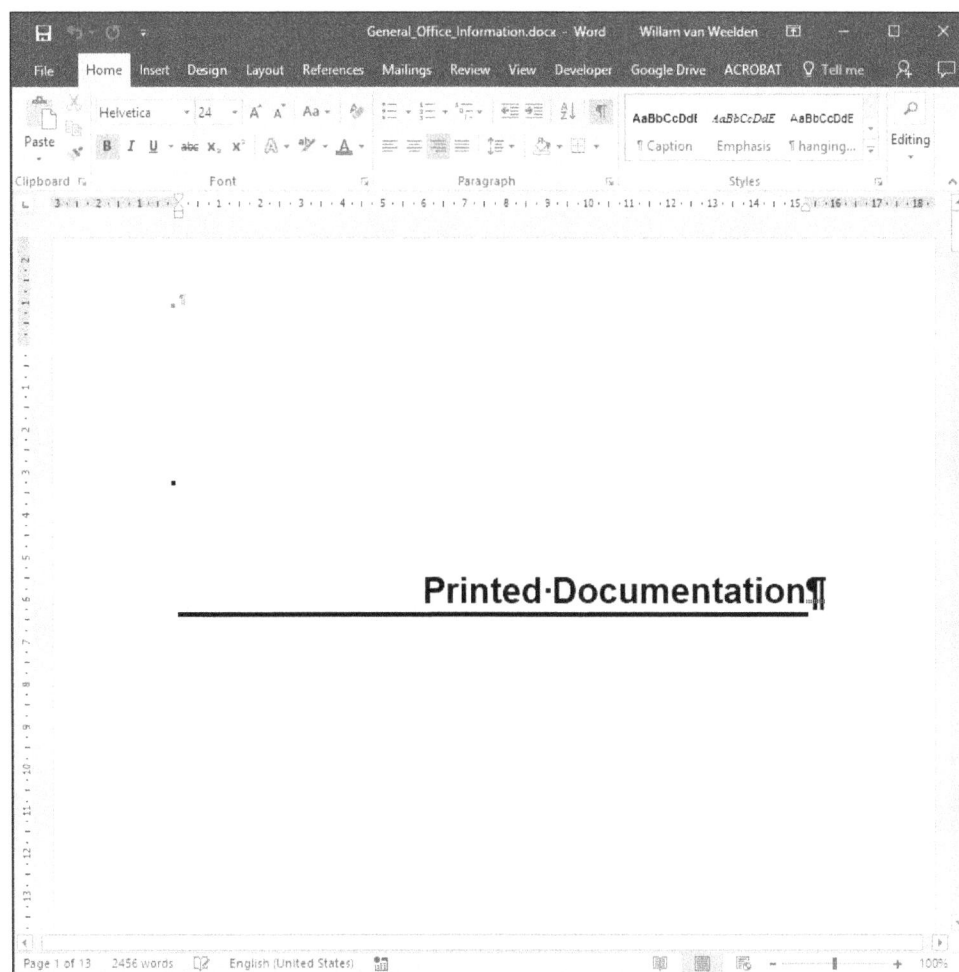

Printed·Documentation¶

12. Exit Word and return to RoboHelp.

    Note: If you are not going to be doing much RoboHelp single-sourcing to Word, you might want to return your Word Macro security to its previous settings (page 254).

eBooks

During the last series of activities you generated a print document out of a Help System. You could send the print documentation to your users, and assuming they have Microsoft Word on their computer, they could open the Word document, read it, edit it, and print it. But if your users don't have Word, they'd be out of luck. Alternatively, you could create a PDF from the Word document. Users could then use the free Adobe Reader to open and read the document. But what if you want to make your Help System available for mobile users (people using mobile devices such as the iPhone, iPod Touch, Android, Blackberry, iPad, or Kindle)? Most mobile devices can open a PDF, but the small display common on most mobile devices would make reading the PDF a challenge.

Instead of a PDF, you can use RoboHelp to generate an eBook (also known as an electronic publication) using your existing Help System. The advantage of the eBook format over PDF technology is mainly readability. When opened with an eBook reader, the text always wraps to fit the size of the user's device or display, and the user can control the font, font size, and color. Although the eBook format is flexible, it does not currently support all of the bells and whistles that you can add to a RoboHelp project. For instance, eBook readers do not support expanding hotspots, glossaries, interactive buttons (such as See Also buttons), or interactive eLearning videos.

> **Note:** In the steps that follow, you will use RoboHelp to generate an eBook file. After the eBook file has been created, you will need an eBook reader on your computer to open the eBook file. Before continuing, install an eBook Reader. Although there are many eBook readers (some free, some not), Adobe has a free eBook reader called Adobe Digital Editions (**http://www.adobe.com/products/digitaleditions**). For more information on the eBook format, visit **www.idpf.org**.

Student Activity: Create an eBook

1. Ensure that the **Print_eBook** project is still open.

2. Create a new Single Source Output to be used for the eBook output.

   ❏ on the Outputs(SSL) pod, click the **Create Output** tool 🗋
   ❏ from the **Output Type** drop-down menu, choose **eBook**

New Output	×
Output Name:	eBook
Output Type:	📖 eBook ⌄
	OK Cancel ❓ Help

   ❏ click the **OK** button

   The eBook settings dialog box opens.

3. Select an eBook Format.

❑ from the **General** group, **eBook Formats** area, select **EPUB 3**

eBook Formats:
☑ EPUB 3
☐ Kindle Book

You could select Kindle Book, but you'd first need to download an application known as KindleGen (the KindleGen Path button activates when you select Kindle Book, allowing you to download and install KindleGen). For this activity, you'll stick with EPUB 3.

From the **Options** area, notice that there is an option to Validate EPUB3 Output.

Options
☐ Validate EPUB 3 Output

If you were creating an EPUB to be imported into a resellers site (like the Apple iBookstore), you would need to ensure that the EPUB you create meets strict formatting specifications. In that case, you would select **Validate EPUB 3 Output** and install a validator (via the EpubCheck Path button). While you are creating the eBook, the EpubCheck you selected will check the EPUB file and alert you of errors you would need to correct. Because the EPUB you are about to create is just for training purposes, you do not need to validate the file.

4. Assign a TOC and Index for the eBook output.

❑ from the list at the left, select **Content**
❑ from the **Table of Contents** drop-down menu, choose **ePub**
❑ from the **Index** drop-down menu, choose **ePub**

Table of Contents:	ePub	⌄
Index:	ePub	⌄

The ePub TOC and ePub Index already exists in the project. You first learned how to create a TOC on page 44 and an Index on page 188.

5. Add Meta Information.

   ❏ select the **Meta Information** category
   ❏ change the Title to **Super Simplistic Solutions: Policies Guide**
   ❏ in the **Author(s)** field, type your full name
   ❏ in the **Publisher(s)** field, type your company name

Title:	Super Simplistic Solutions: Policies Guide
Author(s):	Bifford. P. Bifferson
Publisher(s):	Super Simplistic Solutions

   Most of the Meta Information is optional. You can continue to fill in the remaining fields as you see fit.

6. Specify a Cover Image for the ePub.

   ❏ from the **Cover Image** area, click the browse button
   ❏ navigate to the **RoboHelp2017Data** folder and open **images**
   ❏ open **ePubCover.jpg**

   Cover Image

   Path   ePubCover.jpg

   Preview

   SUPER
   SIMPLISTIC
   SOLUTIONS
   Policies &
   Procedures Guide

7. Generate the eBook.

   ❏ click the **Save and Generate** button

   The eBook is generated into the project's SSL folder, just like any other output. The final step is to view the output within an eBook reader.

   Note: As mentioned earlier, you must have an eBook reader installed on your computer to view the eBook output.

   ❏ click the **View Result** button

   The eBook opens in your computer's default ePub reader. In the image below, you can see the ePub as it appears using Adobe Digital Editions. The eBook file

can now be installed on just about any computer or mobile device that can read eBooks (which is just about every computer and mobile device).

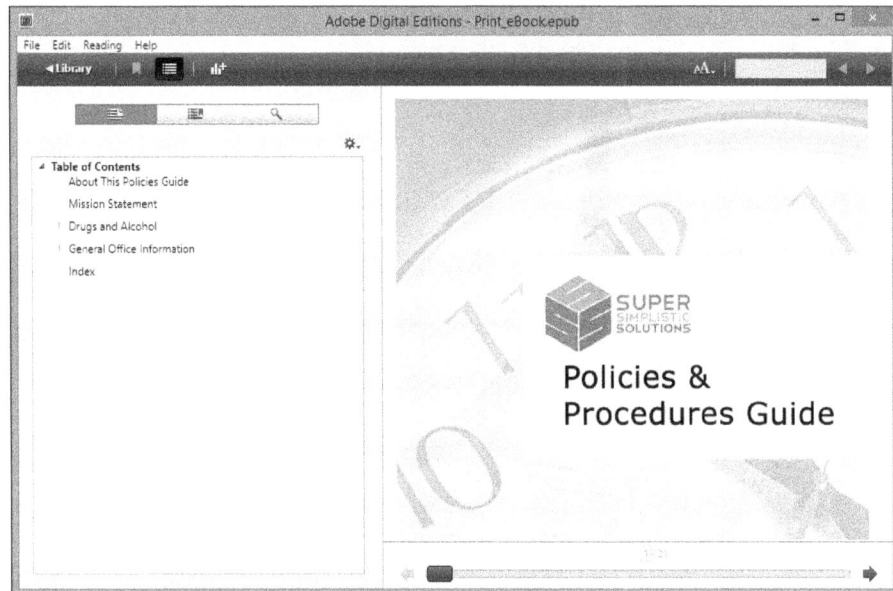

8. Close the eBook file.

9. Return to the RoboHelp project.

Reports

You can use the Reports feature to create reports about your RoboHelp project. You can create reports for the Index, See Also keywords, Glossary, Unused Index Entries, Style Sheets, Broken Links, Table of Contents, and more. You can print the reports, email them, copy them to the clipboard, and save them as RTF or TXT files.

Student Activity: Generate a Report

1. Ensure that the **Print_eBook** project is still open.

2. Change the status of some topics.

   ☐ on the **Topic List** pod, right-click the **About This Guide** topic and choose **Status > Complete** from the shortcut menu
   ☐ on the Topic List pod, right-click the **Leave Policy** topic and choose **Status > Complete**

3. Change the Topic Properties Status for a topic.

   ☐ on the Topic List pod, right-click the **Special Benefits** topic and choose **Properties**

   The Topic Properties dialog box opens.

   ☐ select the **Status** tab
   ☐ change the Status to **Ready for Review**
   ☐ change the Hours to **2**
   ☐ select the **first four options** from the To Do List area (put checks in each of the first four boxes)

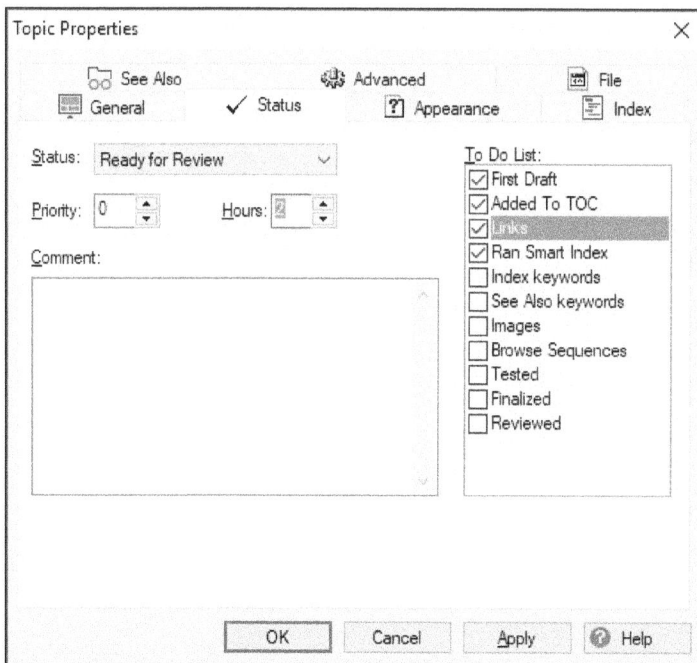

   ☐ click the **OK** button

4. Create a Project Status report.

❏ on the **Tools** tab, **Reports** group, click **Project Status**

The Project Status report appears. You can print the report and even email it to a team member by clicking the buttons at the bottom of the report.

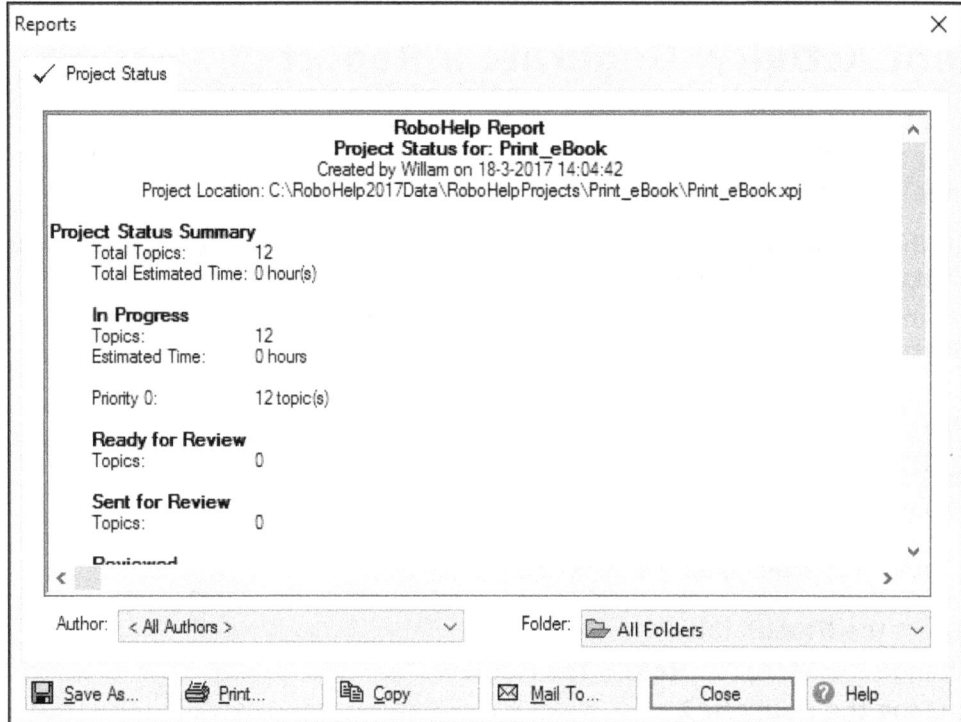

Reports	×

✓ Project Status

RoboHelp Report
Project Status for: Print_eBook
Created by Willam on 18-3-2017 14:04:42
Project Location: C:\RoboHelp2017Data\RoboHelpProjects\Print_eBook\Print_eBook.xpj

Project Status Summary
Total Topics: 12
Total Estimated Time: 0 hour(s)

In Progress
Topics: 12
Estimated Time: 0 hours

Priority 0:   12 topic(s)

Ready for Review
Topics: 0

Sent for Review
Topics: 0

Reviewed

Author: < All Authors >   Folder: All Folders

Save As...   Print...   Copy   Mail To...   Close   Help

❏ click the **Close** button

Reports Confidence Check

1. Spend the next few moments exploring the different reports (**Tools > Reports**).

2. When finished, close any reports you may have created.

3. Save the project.

Mobile Apps

You have created a Responsive Help System that catered to all kinds of devices. The only downside of responsive layouts is that users are always required to have an Internet connection and a web browser to access your content. A Mobile Application is a Responsive HTML5 output that has been packaged as an App for easier distribution. A user who installs the App can access your Help content without the need of a Web browser or Internet connection.

To create a Mobile App, you first need a **free Adobe PhoneGap Build** account. Once set up, the free account allows you to create a single App with RoboHelp. To follow along with the activities in this section, create the free account at **build.phonegap.com** now. (If you already have an account, you will need your login credentials soon.)

An Android App is easy to create because there are no additional requirements beyond setting up the free PhoneGap account. Creating an App for iOS requires **a paid Apple developer account**. Although the activity that follows covers only the process for creating an Android App, if you do have an iOS developer account, creating an iOS App works much the same way.

Student Activity: Create a Mobile App

1. Ensure that the **Print_eBook.xpj** RoboHelp project file is still open.

2. Create a Mobile App layout.

   ❑ on the **Outputs(SSL)** pod, click the **Create Output** tool 🗋

   The New Layout dialog box opens.

   ❑ from the **Output Type** drop-down menu, choose **Mobile App**

New Output	✕
Output Name:	Mobile App
Output Type:	📱 Mobile App ∨

   ❑ click the **OK** button

   The Mobile App Settings dialog box opens.

3. Set Mobile App details.

   ❑ at the top, click the **Gallery** button
   ❑ select the **Azure_Blue** layout

Select	
Azure_Blue ∨	Gallery...

   ❑ from the list at the left, select **Application Details**

❏ in the **Package** field, type **com.supersimplisticsolutions.policies**

Package*	com.supersimplisticsolutions.policies

❏ in the **Title** field, type **Policies and Procedures**

Title*	Policies and Procedures

4. Specify a Mobile App icon.

   ❏ from the **Icon** field, click the browse button
   ❏ navigate to the **RoboHelp2017Data** folder and open **images**
   ❏ open **Responsive_Logo.png**

Icon		C:\RoboHelp2017Data\images\Responsive	

5. Generate the Mobile App.

   ❏ in the **PhoneGap/Adobe Credential** area, add your PhoneGap credentials

   Adobe ID used for PhoneGap

User ID*	biffbiff@supersimplistic:	Create PhoneGap Account
Password*	••••••••••••••	Validate User ID

   ❏ in the **Platform** area, select **Android**

   Platform
☐ iOS	Signing Key Setup*...
☑ Android	Signing Key Setup...

   Note: As mentioned above, creating an Android App is free. Creating an iOS app requires you to have a paid developer account.

   ❏ click the **Save and Generate** button

   The Mobile App is prepared on your PC. RoboHelp then uploads the app to PhoneGap to create the app. (This process could take a few moments.)

❏ click the **View Result** button

6. Install the Mobile App.

❏ scan the **QR code** with your mobile device to download it

❏ once downloaded, install the Mobile App

Note: If you receive the error "Install blocked" on your mobile device, you may need to allow the installation from unknown sources. On some devices, the process to allow unknown sources to install is located via **Settings > Security** and selecting "Unknown sources." The process on your device may vary.

❏ using your device, launch the Mobile App

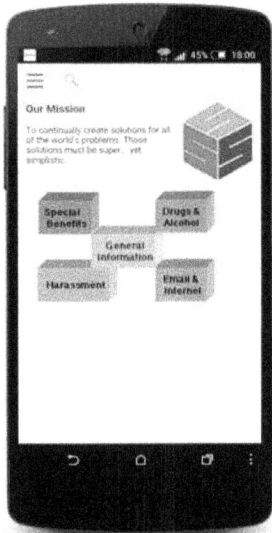

Note: Now that you've created a Mobile App, it is available in your PhoneGap Build account. If you want to create a different mobile app, go to PhoneGap Build and remove this app. In PhoneGap Build, select your app, go to Settings and scroll down. Click the **Delete this app** button at the bottom of the page.

7. Return to RoboHelp.

Scripts

If you have ever used Microsoft Word to record or write a macro, you already appreciate how much time macros can save you by automating repetitive tasks.

Although RoboHelp does not support macros, scripts (which are coded instructions) provide the same function. RoboHelp ships with a few helpful scripts, and if you are an application developer, you can create your own scripts from within RoboHelp or import them.

Student Activity: Run a Script

1. Ensure that the **Print_eBook** project is still open.

2. Open the Script Explorer.

   ❏ on the **Tools** tab, **Open** group, click **Script Explorer**

   The Script Explorer pod appears at the far right of the window.

   ❏ click the plus sign to the left of the Sample Scripts folder to expand the folder

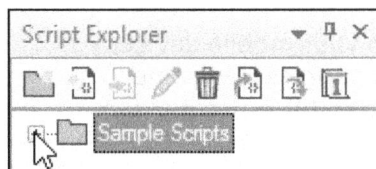

3. Use the Word Count script to get a word count for every topic in the project.

   ❏ on the **Script Explorer** pod, right-click the **Word Count Generator.jsx** script and choose **Run**

   The word count is quickly completed and the total Word Count appears at the bottom of the **Output View** pod.

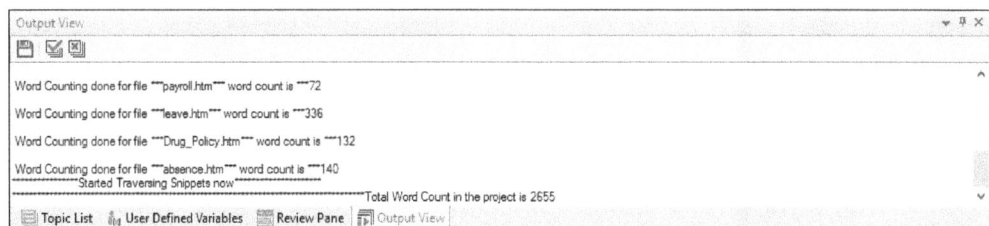

Student Activity: Edit a Script

1. Ensure that the **Print_eBook** project is still open.

2. Create a broken link.

   ❑ open the **About This Guide** topic

   There is a link to the Super Simplistic website. The link is currently correct. You'll foul up the link address intentionally to create a broken link.

   ❑ double-click the link

   The Hyperlink Properties dialog box opens.

   ❑ change the link to **http://www.ssssupersimplisticsolutions.com**

Link to:	▼	http://www.ssssupersimplisticsolutions.com

   ❑ click the **OK** button

3. Test a broken link.

   ❑ with the **About This Guide** topic still open, press [**ctrl**] [**w**] to preview the topic
   ❑ click the link

   As expected, there is no such website, and you are presented with a page similar to the image below.

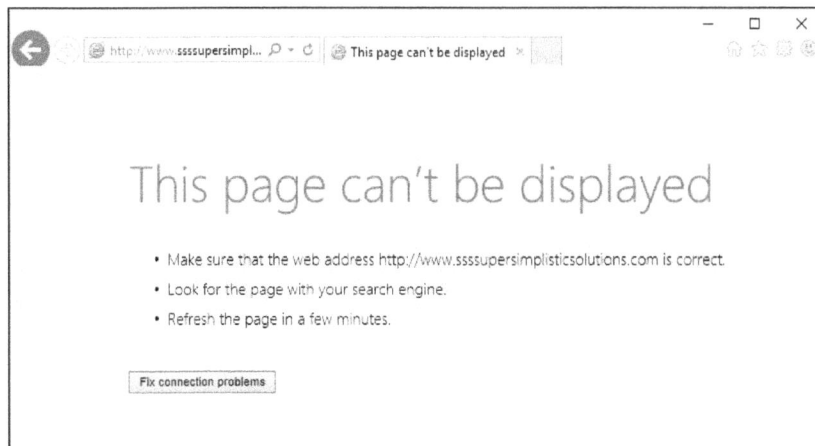

   ## This page can't be displayed

   - Make sure that the web address http://www.ssssupersimplisticsolutions.com is correct.
   - Look for the page with your search engine.
   - Refresh the page in a few minutes.

   Fix connection problems

4. Close the browser window, return to RoboHelp, and then close the topic preview window.

   You could easily correct the address right now, but the incorrect address could appear in other topics. This is a perfect job for another supplied script: **Link Converter.jsx**. However, before you can run the script, you need to make a quick edit to the script so that it knows both the incorrect address to find and the new address.

5. Save and close any open topics.

6. Edit a script.

   ❑ on the **Script Explorer** pod, right-click the **Link Converter.jsx** script and choose **Edit**

   The Extend Script Toolkit opens.

   ❑ on line 10 of the script, replace the address after **LinktoConvert** from www.oldurl.com to **http://www.ssssupersimplisticsolutions.com** (be careful not to delete the quotation marks)

   ❑ on line 11 of the script, replace the address after **newlink** from www.newurl.com to **http://www.supersimplisticsolutions.com** (be careful not to delete the single quotation marks)

```
9    //user can change this value when ever he wants to
10   var LinktoConvert = 'http://www.ssssupersimplisticsolutions.com';
11   var newlink = 'http://www.supersimplisticsolutions.com'
12   var topicmgr;
```

7. Save and close the script.

   ❑ choose **File > Save**
   ❑ choose **File > Exit**

8. Use a script to update a URL.

   ❑ on the **Script Explorer** pod, right-click the **Link Converter.jsx** script and choose **Run**

   Any files using the incorrect web address are opened and corrected. You will be notified when a file that was edited is saved (in this case, there was only one file that was edited).

   ❑ click the **OK** button

9. Confirm that the link has been updated.

   ❑ open the **About This Guide** topic
   ❑ double-click the link to open the Hyperlink Properties dialog box

   Notice that the link to the Super Simplistic Solutions website has been corrected.

10. Close the Hyperlink Properties dialog box.

11. Save and close all topics.

12. Close the project.

Student Activity: End-Course Project

If you are using this book as part of an official RoboHelp training course, your instructor may review the project that you complete following the steps below (and the steps on page 128) to determine your final grade.

❒ Open **YourFirstNameRoboHelpProject**. (This is the project you created on page 128. If you did not complete the activity, please do so now.)

❒ On the Project Manager pod, create a **New Folder** and name it **My Mid-Course Files**. *Need Help?* Refer to page 42.

❒ Move all of the existing topics into the new folder.

❒ On the Project Manager pod, create a **New Folder** and name it **My End-Course Files**.

❒ Create a new topic inside the **My End-Course Files** folder named **My Table**. *Need Help?* Refer to page 11.

❒ Insert a table into the new topic. The table must contain at least **three columns** and **three rows**. The table can be formatted to suit your taste and can contain any content you like. *Need Help?* Refer to page 164 and page 168.

❒ Apply your CSS file to the new topic. *Need Help?* Refer to page 49.

❒ Add the new topic into any of your TOC books. *Need Help?* Refer to page 46.

❒ Create a new topic inside the **My End-Course Files** folder named **My Lists**.

❒ Create a bulleted list in the topic with at least four list items that use a custom bullet. *Need Help?* Refer to page 178.

❒ Create a numbered list in the topic with at least four list items that use any numbering format you like. *Need Help?* Refer to page 178.

❒ Add an **Index** with at least 20 entries. *Need Help?* Refer to page 188.

❒ Add a **Glossary** with the following terms: **Baggage Files**, **Captivate**, **Conditional Build Tags**, and **Triggers**. (If necessary, refer to the Help System for the definition of each glossary term.) *Need Help?* Refer to page 209.

❒ Insert the **Elastic** DHTML effect into one of your topics (select **Page has been loaded** for the **When**). *Need Help?* Refer to page 122.

❒ Insert the **Spiral in** DHTML effect into one of your topics (select **Page has been loaded** for the **When**). *Need Help?* Refer to page 122.

❒ Insert additional DHTML effects to other topics. *Need Help?* Refer to page 122.

❒ Create a master page with a **footer** that contains the following text: "Created by **Your First** and **Last Name**." *Need Help?* Refer to page 225.

❒ Apply the master page to all of your topics. *Need Help?* Refer to page 225.

❒ Add a Browse Sequence to your project. *Need Help?* Refer to page 237.

❒ Open your master page and delete your first and last name.

❒ Create a **Variable** named **Developer.** The variable should have your first and last name as the Variable value. *Need help?* See page 152.

- ❒ Insert your new variable into the footer of your master page and ensure the master page has been applied to topics as appropriate.

- ❒ Spell check the entire project.

- ❒ Change the Primary Output to HTML Help and test your browse sequence.

- ❒ Create a **Custom Skin** for your project. Name the skin **YourFirstName_Skin**. *Need Help?* Refer to page 220.

- ❒ Generate a **WebHelp** Single Source Output that uses your custom skin.

- ❒ Customize a Responsive HTML5 Theme and then generate a Responsive HTML5 output.

- ❒ When finished, Batch Generate the HTML Help, WebHelp, and Responsive HTML5 Outputs(SSL).

Index

www.ingramcontent.com/pod-product-compliance
Lightning Source LLC
Chambersburg PA
CBHW080518220326
41599CB00032B/6120